The superior student in

American higher education

THE CARNEGIE SERIES IN AMERICAN EDUCATION

The books in this series have resulted from studies made under grants from the Carnegie Corporation of New York and, occasionally, from studies supported by The Carnegie Foundation for the Advancement of Teaching. These books are published by McGraw-Hill in recognition of their importance to the future of American education.

The Corporation, a philanthropic foundation established in 1911 by Andrew Carnegie for the advancement and diffusion of knowledge and understanding, has a continuing interest in the improvement of American education. It financed the studies in this series to provide facts and recommendations which would be useful to all those who make or influence the decisions which shape American educational policies and institutions.

The statements made and views expressed in these books are solely the responsibility of the authors.

Berelson GRADUATE EDUCATION IN THE UNITED STATES

Clark THE OPEN DOOR COLLEGE: A Case Study

Cleveland, Mangone, and Adams THE OVERSEAS AMERICANS

Cohen THE SUPERIOR STUDENT IN AMERICAN HIGHER EDUCATION

Conant THE AMERICAN HIGH SCHOOL TODAY

Conant THE EDUCATION OF AMERICAN TEACHERS

Conant SHAPING EDUCATIONAL POLICY

Corson GOVERNANCE OF COLLEGES AND UNIVERSITIES

Dodds THE ACADEMIC PRESIDENT—EDUCATOR OR CARETAKER?

Glenny AUTONOMY OF PUBLIC COLLEGES: The Challenge of Coordination

Henninger THE TECHNICAL INSTITUTE IN AMERICA (out of print; available from University Microfilms)

Kellogg and Knapp THE COLLEGE OF AGRICULTURE: Science in the Public Service

Kitzhaber THEMES, THEORIES, AND THERAPY: The Teaching of Writing in College

McConnell A GENERAL PATTERN FOR AMERICAN PUBLIC HIGHER EDUCATION

Medsker THE JUNIOR COLLEGE: Progress and Prospect

Perkins and Snell THE EDUCATION OF HISTORIANS IN THE UNITED STATES

Pierson THE EDUCATION OF AMERICAN BUSINESSMEN

Thomas THE SEARCH FOR A COMMON LEARNING: General Education, 1800–1960

Weidner THE WORLD ROLE OF UNIVERSITIES

The superior student in

American higher

education / edited by

Joseph W. Cohen, DEPARTMENT

OF PHILOSOPHY/UNIVERSITY

OF COLORADO

McGraw-Hill Book Company
New York   St. Louis   San Francisco
Toronto   London   Sydney

Dedicated to the emerging generations of students and particularly to Rachel, Galen, and Robbie—J. W. C.

Foreword

THIS COLLECTION of writings on honors programs in American institutions of higher education serves as the final statement of an organization that existed from 1957 to 1965—the Inter-University Committee on the Superior Student (ICSS). But the deeper sources of this volume go back nearly forty years.

My interest in honors began in 1928 when, as a young instructor recently arrived at the University of Colorado from Toronto, I was shocked to discover the small amount of knowledge and insight that students graduating with honors could command. Despite their high grades and the number of courses they had taken, these students showed little awareness of historical, theoretical, social, imaginative, or value perspectives. They lacked a sense of interconnections. In short, they didn't know what to do with the knowledge they possessed, and they had no deep sense of values.

My discovery filled me with a concern that has not left me to this day. I was angry at the fact that faculty willing and able to contribute more to teaching had no chance to do so. Whitehead's words in *The Aims of Education* sum up this feeling:

> When one considers in its length and in its breadth the importance of this question of the education of a nation's young, the broken lives, the defeated hopes, the national failures, which result from the frivolous inertia with which it is treated, it is difficult to restrain within oneself a savage rage.[1]

Whitehead, of course, was also speaking of the many excluded by the elitist English system of education; in my case the anger was prompted by the inertia I witnessed before the deep problems of quality in a state institution confronted by numbers, by routine, by the recalcitrance of legislatures. I simply felt that some of us had to begin to break through this inertia.

My rage also had a philosophical foundation, which grew out of an interest in the problem of knowledge itself. Producing intellectuals—genuine and fully functioning intellectuals—should not be thought of as a simple matter. Further, producing intellectuals in a democracy which aims at extensive education involves all sorts of questions of values, of philosophy. What I fundamentally objected to was a perversion of learning—a widespread belief that knowledge could be handed over in pieces in a joyless kind of marketlike process.

I had certain definite ideas about knowledge, about teaching, and about learning. I believed, for example, that the whole process of educating and being educated could be a joyful one, that those who felt that it is forbidden to become excited about ideas were wrong, that in fact it is the joy involved in learning that motivates

[1] Alfred North Whitehead, *The Aims of Education,* New York: The Macmillan Company, 1929, p. 22.

students to burn the midnight oil, that honors could not be properly conceived merely as harder "work." I also believed that the question of values extended beyond the boundaries of subject matter, that those concerns germane to civilized existence—broadly called the humanities—could include all areas of learning. So my professional preoccupations as a philosopher, as well as my observation of neglect of abilities and much faculty indifference, fed my desire to do something to widen the educational experience offered in our institutions of higher education. What absorbed me and kept me involved was the conviction that honors work could be richer in theory and practice; honors work to me is ideas in action.

I must add one further consideration—highly philosophical in itself but reaching beyond the province of education alone—that has kept me on the path I have followed for so many years. This is the question of institutional change. Honors programs as they are predominantly conceived in this book fall into the category of forces that make for change in an institution—in this case perhaps the most important of all institutions, the one which links the present with the past and prepares for the future. How such a change is effected has been of particular interest to me. In the educational world sudden revolutions are impossible. But this does not mean that change of any kind is also impossible, that we must be content with the *status quo*. I have viewed honors as capable of affecting the entire institution by creating a nucleus of quality, the influence of which would spread within the institution's boundaries and beyond them. The problem is not how to give something to the best students alone in an isolated and small-scale way. Instead, it is how to set in motion a force for change that will spur the institution as a whole to work to make as many students as possible into first-rate products. In the ICSS we have labored to design and listed by Aydelotte in 1925 were practically nonexistent when I made my own first survey in 1952.

My major formal effort in honors on a national level began with the formation of the Inter-University Committee on the Superior Student in 1957, the founding and work of which are described in this book. As director of this organization I traveled from Maine to San Diego, from Seattle to Coral Gables—in fact, to practically every state in the union. For the energy that I have put into the ICSS and its work I have been characterized, jocularly I hope, as many things—a St. Paul, a kind of modern John Bunyan's Christian preaching the honors gospel, a Johnny Appleseed sowing interest in honors across the nation. I have also been called an academic Pangloss.

The truth is that whatever I did accomplish I achieved by being an intellectual gadfly, a hard-boiled critic. My main task was to provoke. In essence this meant prodding the intellectually and imaginatively agonized—those, young or old, who felt that they had no recourse from the aridity of the impersonalized educational organization within whose network they were caught—into realizing the worth of what they had to offer and of what they could achieve by taking thought and inaugurating another sort of program. It meant demonstrating the importance of fighting for this program. It meant proving that quantity and quality could be reconciled.

But lest it be thought that I myself believe in the pioneer role that others have attributed to me, let me call attention to some facts. First, the efforts of the ICSS were by no means a complete innovation. As the chapter on the history of the honors movement in this volume points out, honors work in America was not a new phenomenon. Early in this century the intellectual purpose of higher education began to emerge as a crucial concern for the culture. We have to look back to Dewey as the thinker who showed us the importance of experiment in education. But there were many other pioneers. True, most of the programs existent before the founding of the ICSS were in the private colleges and many of these were very narrow in scope. But much work had been done already; not to recognize this is to shortchange our culture.

Second, I never worked alone. I may have served to arouse people to initiate or revitalize honors programs, but the interest and ability required were there to arouse. Furthermore, I was by no means the only person spreading the word, as the chapter on the ICSS in this book amply illustrates.

Third, the work I and my colleagues did through the ICSS is only a beginning. We did not try to hand out a finished formula nor did we suddenly appear on the scene with the perfect solution to a problem. We did ask questions and try to formulate some answers, but, as this book shows, many of these questions still remain unanswered. Or, to put it another way, the variety of answers to our questions is infinite.

The formal work of the ICSS seems now finished, although I am sure something equivalent to it will follow. This effort and how it began is described elsewhere in this book. Here I would like to summarize what to me are its major achievements and what still lies ahead.

The story can be told most simply with the numbers involved. The number of honors programs in American institutions of higher education has more than trebled between 1957 and 1965. I believe that the ICSS can take some credit for this proliferation.

But numbers alone indicate only programs actually in operation. They do not show where new ground has been broken. For example, although we started with the state universities, we also interested ourselves in many other kinds of institutions. The private liberal arts colleges, many of which were familiar with honors programs, make up one category. But we also reached out to teachers colleges, professional schools (for example, medical, engineering, business, and agricultural schools), junior colleges, and secondary schools. To most of these institutions honors work was a discovery.

Numbers alone give no idea of the spread of influence. The main purpose of the ICSS was to serve as an instigator of cross-fertilization. This cross-fertilization—through our direct efforts and through our mere existence as an available source of consultation—constituted the most continuously vivid and satisfying aspect of my experience in directing the ICSS. Bringing together people dedicated to ideas, seeing them set each other off on new paths—this to me has been our main accomplishment.

Cross-fertilization was achieved in many different ways. Some were more or less organized, like our regional conferences and our newsletter. Through the regional conferences we exposed to the honors idea people and institutions for whom this was a totally new concept. I am particularly proud of our first, the Southern conference, which led at once to a conference of predominantly Negro colleges and therefore opened up the whole issue of the culturally deprived and disadvantaged anywhere. Our newsletter facilitated the exchange of ideas across the country; it eventually reached about 13,000 libraries and individuals and was widely circulated by them on many campuses. Plans are now being made to continue its publication in some other form.

The influence of the ICSS spread even further through less

formal contacts—speeches, discussions, panels, visits, and correspondence. By these means we reached the major educational associations, national education agencies like the Office of Education and the National Science Foundation, the associations of teachers of various subjects—both in the liberal arts and in the professions—many of the learned societies, and a number of the honorary societies. Another area of influence is that of research. As a result of contacts with the ICSS a great deal of new work on evaluation—both of the student and the honors program—has begun or is planned. Finally, I should mention the international aspect of our work, seen in our contacts with Britain and her dominions, with the European continent, with Africa, India, and especially with Latin America. We have also been consulted by our own Peace Corps.

A great deal worth telling about the ICSS and its efforts never got into the book that follows. There is not room, nor have I had time, to capture in words more than a small part of the experiences I have had or to mention the people with whom I have worked in the course of my ICSS experience. That the work begun by the ICSS is still very much alive is proved by the fact that we have lacked the time to analyze ourselves systematically or to keep elaborate statistics. The truth is that we were never permitted to stop working. Indeed, the honors movement is still in the explosive stage, as the final director of the ICSS, Dr. Phillip I. Mitterling, avows. Some institutions are just coming to view honors programs as a possibility, others still have their doors closed to the idea. And many institutions with programs formally labeled honors have far to go before they create programs of the type discussed in this book. Meanwhile, the older programs encounter new problems calling for new solutions. There will be plenty to do in honors work for a long time to come.

In considering the work that lies ahead I should like to make two points that I believe to be of the utmost importance. Both are discussed in the pages that follow, but I think they should be mentioned here as well. The first is that a beginning must be made. An institution that waits for the perfectly designed, fully financed honors program may never have any program at all. The problem is to *start* to distinguish between the merely academic and the genuinely intellectual, to *begin* working toward the latter in attacking our culture's real problems. In this way we in fact serve even better the strictly academic purpose itself. The emphasis should be on starting some meaningful program, not on dreaming of perfection.

The second crucial point is that honors is properly, and must always be, something dynamic, something vital, something unstereotyped. An honors program can become a fixture and then cease to serve any purpose beyond filling up space in the catalogue. As some institutions discover the value of honors, others are beginning to cope with the problem of how to rejuvenate an honors program continually, how to maintain that quality of ferment and excitement which lies at the very heart of honors work, how to keep students from viewing honors as merely another part of the system that students want to beat. The honors movement has had enormous success over the last few years. Now we have to strive constantly to ensure that success does not defeat our purposes, that we do not become complacent about honors and begin to think of such a program as a settled, fixed part of the higher educational scene. To do so would be to negate all we have worked for.

Finally, I should like to say that my conviction, at the very core of my national work in the ICSS, is that the latent power in American education and culture is released by experienced affirmation, not by bleak negations. I am sure of this: Only affirmation can sup-

Preface

THIS BOOK is a collection of papers on different aspects of current work in honors. It is not meant to cover all facets of the subject. Nor are all of the papers confined to strictly separate topics; there is some repetition of themes and contradiction of ideas. But this does not seem inappropriate in a book written by several people actively engaged in a movement that is still in the formative, questing stages.

Thus, instead of presenting fixed formulas about what honors should be, the authors of this volume, the reader will find, raise some key issues and sketch out possible solutions to these issues, each on the basis of his own experience and viewpoint. A partial list of these issues might include: What is the purpose of an honors program? What should be the balance between general and departmental honors? Who makes a good honors teacher? Should honors be confined to the liberal arts, or does it have a place in professional and technical colleges and universities? Is honors equally suited to all subjects? How can we tell what a given honors program is achieving?

The volume begins with four background chapters aimed at orienting the reader to what follows. The first is broadly introductory. The second gives a brief selective history of the honors movement up to or independent of the founding of the Inter-University Committee on the Superior Student (ICSS) in 1957. The third describes the founding, work, and experiences of that organization. Most of the authors in this volume have been active in the ICSS, five (Robertson, Waggoner, Weir, Wynn, and the editor) since its origin. Thus, the outlook of this volume is largely that of the ICSS, and a review of its principles should help to illuminate the thinking presented in some of the later chapters. The fourth chapter discusses the subject of the honors effort—the superior student. It seeks to tell us who he is and something about his needs and desires.

Next come several chapters on honors programs and what they can mean in the liberal arts college, in the large university, in departments, in a particular subject (in this case, in the sciences), and in the small private college. Then, although the volume focuses on honors in higher education, a penultimate chapter discusses what is being done for the superior student in the secondary schools, since these programs have a strong influence on work in the colleges and universities. And a final chapter describes progress and still-unmet needs in evaluating the success of honors programs—an activity vital to the continuation and perfection of honors efforts.

The honors movement is for the most part a recent development, one that grew out of a realization that this country is wasting its best human resources—or worse, is failing even to recognize these resources. Those who foster honors in the colleges believe that special programs for the superior student, if properly congram there. William Cadbury is Dean and Professor of Chemistry at Haverford College; he is also Chairman of the national College Committee on Outstanding Students. Edwin Fenton is Professor of History at the Carnegie Institute of Technology; he has also worked for five years on the Pittsburgh Scholars' Program for able secondary school students. Paul Heist is Associate Research Psychologist at the Center for the Study of Higher Education at Berkeley; he directed the Psychology Honors Program at Oregon State University for three years. Lois Langland, until recently a Lecturer in the Department of Psychology of the University of California at Los Angeles and active in honors work there, is now Director of Career Counseling and Professor of Psychology at Scripps College and Pitzer College, Claremont, California. The majority of our contributors have also made frequent visits to institutions in behalf of honors. In addition, Dean Waggoner can almost be called our honors ambassador to Latin America.

I here add my appreciative acknowledgment to our contributors and to our ICSS Executive Committee and staff. I particularly wish to mention Dr. Philip I. Mitterling and Dr. Ray P. Cuzzort, Director and Research Associate, respectively, of the ICSS in its final two years. My own debt to them for their cooperation and wise suggestions on this volume's coverage and order of presentation is very great. I have incurred no less a debt to those friends who have been inveigled into reading drafts of manuscript. Professor Howard H. Quint of the University of Massachusetts, Professor Dudley Wynn, and Professor Robert B. MacLeod of Cornell, all of the ICSS Executive Committee, Professor Aaron Warner of Columbia University, and Bernard Conal of the Salk Institute of Biological Studies provided especially perceptive suggestions. I also acknowledge the extra labors imposed upon Mrs. Linnie W. Schafer and

Mrs. Mary Ann Lefler of the ICSS staff. The office of the University of Colorado Honors Program, under Dr. Weir and his secretary, Mrs. Ann Turner, yielded graciously to my frequent attacks on their files and records.

Finally, apart from the initial grant to our own program at Colorado through Dr. E. F. D'Arms, this volume could not have been written without the encouragement and help of Dr. Frederick H. Jackson and the Carnegie Corporation of New York, who have played a generous role since the inception of the ICSS.

JOSEPH W. COHEN

Contents

xxiii

The superior student in

American higher education

"HONORS" IS A GENERIC TERM for all special treatment of the superior student. This treatment has taken many forms, from a pat on the back at graduation in recognition of a high grade average to a variety of programs, some of which amount to making entirely different curricula available to these students and opening honors work to potential as well as recognized superiority.

In this book we are concerned with the second type of honors —organized attempts to provide *all* superior students with a *special* and *different* learning experience. An honors program, this book assumes, should have as its purpose to develop to the full the intellectual, expressive, and moral powers of the generation we educate within the framework of our mass, liberal, democratic society. The wide range of current attempts to reach this goal and the degree to which they are successful are the subjects of this volume.

Why honors?

A fundamental problem of our democratic society is how to produce superiority among the millions our system educates. The theme of excellence has received much attention. Books and articles on its pursuit and on the waste and recognition of talent have

1

multiplied in recent years. Despite this interest, however, the question of quality has not been met head-on by American educational institutions. Whether through anxiety to avoid any hangover from aristocratic or elitist philosophies of education, a shortage of funds, or an unwillingness on the part of faculty and administrators to put forth extra effort, this problem, taken as a whole, has been one of the most neglected in higher education.

What exactly is the problem of quality? Put most crudely, it is that many students in American institutions of learning are clearly not being, or have not until recently been, challenged to work anywhere near their capacity. As McGeorge Bundy, then dean of Harvard, noted in 1959, "The students come in all steamed up, but our traditional process of education does not keep the steam up."

But the problem is more complex than this. Beyond those students whose talents are obviously being wasted are others whose potentialities are completely unrecognized. And here it is the whole notion of "superiority" that must be explored. Is the superior student the one who consistently earns the highest grades? Or to detect the student of superior ability must we instead have some knowledge of the variety, subtlety, and creativity of growing minds? And should we perhaps be familiar with the causal factors, themselves remediable, that may have handicapped some able students? [1] The answer seems clear: The problem of quality involves detecting potential as well as preventing obvious waste; it involves learning how to fashion creative power where there was only acquiescence as well as fostering creativity that has already manifested itself.

---

[1] David McClelland has emphasized our neglect of the student in his article "Encouraging Excellence," *Daedalus,* Fall, 1961, pp. 711–724 (see especially p. 723). This issue of *Daedalus* is devoted to "Excellence and Leadership in a Democracy."

And what of the faculty? It is a commonplace now to point out that the art of teaching is becoming less and less important in higher education. The most upsetting thing about this is that it does not upset us enough. It is a tragic paradox that today many university instructors feel they will jeopardize their chances of promotion if they show too much interest in their students. Others believe that students are already ruined when they emerge from inferior secondary schools or that the young are unworthy of attention in the first place. The result is that many student minds that could have been awakened by good teaching are allowed to decay or go dead during the college years. If the superior student is to be challenged he must be offered work of high quality—and this means upgrading what has passed for acceptable teaching in many institutions.

It might well be asked how we know that students are going unchallenged. One answer is that we know by looking at the students themselves—at their reaction to the learning experience ordinarily offered them and at their excitement and joy when exposed to a good honors program.

Cases of disillusionment among bright students are not hard to find; many of the beatniks are extreme examples of just this state. A psychologist at one of our top professional institutions supplied some of the reasons when he told me:

All modern education is extremely archaic, medieval and primitive. There is much available information on how to change students' thoughts and feelings. But it is never applied ... we have a disciplinary father-son relationship. We do not capitalize on the inner drives of the student. We impose our own on them ... teaching here is by assistants, though in the "humanities" it is by mature professors. Otherwise the famous top men are busy with research and publication, with consulting for industry, government and the armed forces, or with conferencing at home or abroad. Occasionally they give a lecture; then the assistants take over.

During a meeting with a group of first-rate honors undergraduates in a large private institution in the East I asked, "When were you selected for the honors program?" One girl answered, "In the second semester of my junior year." I asked what had happened then. She promptly replied, "Nothing happened. We were told we were superior and we just sat there being superior." "Why?" I asked. "There was nothing else to do about it until I returned as a senior when I could begin work on independent study and an honors thesis." Her tone was one of resentment, and one after another the other seniors agreed with her. I then asked her, "But you have had three years of courses at an institution of high repute. Surely that meant a great deal to you?" She replied, "Right! That is quite a different matter. We knew there was a great feast of learning going on among the faculty, but always felt left out in the cold. We were never 'invited' in to the good time they seemed to be having. We watched that feast through the windows from the outside."

Although they may often be disillusioned, bright students still know what kind of educational experience they would like to have. Their aspirations are discussed in greater detail in another chapter of this book; briefly, the student who is something more than a submissive grade-getter is interested in "a dialogue, a threat, and a vision," as one such student put it—in short, an adventure in learning that calls for daring on the part of all participants and gives the student undreamed-of rewards in exchange for his daring.[2]

Superior students respond with joy when they are given the opportunity to participate in such an adventure. While visiting Louisi-

[2] See p. 54 below for a fuller quotation.

ana State University in 1958, I sat in on a freshman colloquium on *Oedipus Rex.* It was the third meeting of the group in this first, and as yet only, experiment of the newly inaugurated honors program. I asked the fourteen freshmen if they could describe how this colloquium differed from their regular freshman courses. One boy responded at once. "My main feeling, sir, is that of being free." "What do you mean by 'free'?" I asked. The answer was: "I come from a family where we read and discuss books. In high school last year I felt obliged to hide the fact or be regarded as a square. In this group I find that I am with boys and girls like myself. We all read and love to discuss what we read. Here I feel free to be myself to the utmost."

Recognition of and special treatment for the exceptional student need not await the college years. Honors work at the secondary school level can be an important part of the student's experience. The superior student in high school feels the same need for challenge and adventure that older students do, as the experience described below indicates.

In 1956 the superintendent, principal, and director of studies of a large consolidated high school in an agricultural town near Boulder, Colorado, asked me whether, if they picked twelve of their best seniors, we would give them something resembling the junior or senior honors colloquium used at the University of Colorado. The high school's initiative and the chance for an experiment outweighed the inconvenience involved, and we agreed. After initial interviews with the students, which showed them to be of impressive ability and eager to begin at once, we had the twelve come to the university for a preliminary briefing in our honors center. At the end of this session their adviser found it nearly impossible to get them into the bus waiting to take them back to their high school.

They had become absorbed by the books lining the walls of the honors library and insisted on browsing among them.

We started that colloquium with Salinger's *The Catcher in the Rye* on the almost unanimous advice of our own junior colloquium students. It shocked the high school seniors a little but challenged them no end. The second session was devoted to Arthur Miller's *Death of a Salesman*. At the end of this evening one boy, an outstanding athlete, remarked: "I never thought that you could squeeze so much out of a mere play."

What the honors approach can achieve

To say that a good honors program challenges the superior student where the regular curriculum cannot do so is another way of stating that an honors curriculum differs from a regular curriculum. This book deals in large part with the question of just how the honors curriculum might differ and what it might offer. Here I would like to confine myself to mentioning a basic, essential quality of what I consider the "honors approach" and to sketch out its implications.

The overwhelming trend in education at the moment is toward specialization. Not only the professional schools but the liberal arts colleges as well are producing technicians. In fact, today our behavioral scientists are sometimes more concerned with value issues than many a so-called humanist of the old persuasion.

If we look at the important creative work done in all fields, however, very little can be designated as "departmental" or "professional" in the usual academic sense. Creative works by definition cut across many fields; for example, we talk of the psychological, sociological, political, and philosophical insights to be found in great novels. We admire the range and penetration of these works, and we admit that they lead us to contemplate the fundamental intellectual problems of human existence.

Thus, breadth and excellence are mutually compatible goals to strive for. But this fact has been largely forgotten in the rush to develop specialists.

The trend is not entirely one-way. True, philosophy waxes more and more analytical and searches less and less for synthesis and a sense of direction, literature becomes more esoteric and alienated, and history grows more fragmented and periodized. But at the same time many engineering schools are now thinking more of the theoretical underpinnings of "engineering science" as a whole and have beome more concerned with strengthening the social and humanistic aspects of their curricula. The California Institute of Technology long ago established a powerful humanities division, and the Massachusetts Institute of Technology has long experimented with courses in the humanities, most recently with freshman seminars like those at Harvard. Schools of agriculture, architecture, and home economics are likewise moving in the direction of a more general curriculum.

The broadening of outlook in these institutions simply reflects a realization that all fields of learning, even the most technical, involve a consideration of values. In a democracy there can be no evasion, no escape from a concern with ends. This is especially true in our times, when values have been challenged, transformed, and shattered. We live in a culture which no longer gives clear and fixed answers to questions about its purposes, scale of values, or levels of expectation. The metaphors for our existence are murky ones.

The best young minds are sensitive to these conflicts and uncertainties. Their search for values can be an agonized search. But the intensity of their quest is often underestimated, and the importance of dealing with it in other than traditional ways goes unrealized. Our educational methods often seem to these students to keep their values in swaddling clothes.

The honors approach as discussed in this volume seeks to counter the trend toward overspecialization and to help students in their quest for ends. It calls for giving the student, in addition to a chance to pursue excellence in a chosen field, the opportunity to place his knowledge within a broader context. In the honors colloquium, described elsewhere in this book, the student is allowed to work toward integration of the currents of thought he is exposed to in our institutions of learning. He is permitted to ask and try to answer the important questions about what he is learning, questions that force him to probe deep into the reasons for his efforts, into the values that do or should govern our lives. In short, the good honors program works to make of the talented student specializing in any field a well-rounded, thinking person, not just a walking catalogue of information.

The superior student wants to know what he is, what we are as a culture, and what we have to offer to a world perched perilously between hitherto-undreamed-of possibilities of destruction or fulfillment. The traditional specialties, the traditional approaches to knowledge and education cannot alone give adequate answers to such questions. Only a view that is at once broader and more profound can meet the urgencies of our time. The honors approach seeks to awaken and nourish such a view.

Chapter two / Development of the

honors movement in the

United States / J. W. Cohen

THE HONORS MOVEMENT is not a mere fad created by the Sputnik scare. Nor are honors programs simply another educational method promoted by a coterie of zealots. Honors programs in American institutions of learning have a long history, beginning even before Frank Aydelotte's still-important pioneering work at Swarthmore in the twenties.

The private Eastern colleges, rather than the large universities, took the initiative in providing special treatment for talented students in the early decades of the century, and until recently their efforts have had the greatest influence. The colleges were in the more favorable position to act; at the time many of the big universities were engulfed by problems caused by their inability to select students or limit their number, the pressures of public and legislative controls, and the struggle to establish an intellectual tradition. Although several of these large institutions have had important programs of their own for some time, it is only since 1957, with the founding of the Inter-University Committee on the Superior Student (ICSS), that a systematic, coordinated effort has been made to extend honors programs to the large private and state universities.

Thus, this chapter, in describing some important contributions to the honors movement made before or independently of the ICSS, will with two exceptions be dealing with private Eastern colleges. Chapter 3 instead reviews the history, achievements, and experiences of the ICSS in its work with larger institutions.

Swarthmore: the British "pass-honors" approach transplanted

One of the earliest blueprints for a contemporary honors program is Frank Aydelotte's work at Swarthmore.[1] In 1921 President Aydelotte inaugurated a full honors program for Swarthmore's upper division. It represented most clearly the early influence of the Oxford Rhodes Scholarships, begun in 1904; Aydelotte was Oxford's first academic ambassador in this country. His basic model was the British wholly segregated "pass-honors" approach, and the program he devised was a modification of Oxford honors.

Aydelotte assumed that the experiment at Swarthmore would influence the whole range of American higher education. And indeed his innovation was loudly proclaimed and his publications on the honors approach widely read. However, because of the inescapably elitist nature of his British model, the restriction to the upper division, and the atypicality of Swarthmore itself, the public sector of American colleges and universities remained in the end

---

[1] See Frank Aydelotte, *Breaking the Academic Lockstep: The Development of Honors Work in American Colleges and Universities,* New York: Harper & Row, Publishers, Incorporated, 1944. See also Aydelotte's earlier compendium, "Honors Courses in American Colleges and Universities," *Bulletin of the National Research Council,* January, 1924, which was followed by a revised edition in 1925, and the publication by the Swarthmore College Faculty, *An Adventure in Education: Swarthmore College under Frank Aydelotte,* New York: The Macmillan Company, 1941.

largely unaffected by his program. The honors idea as developed at Swarthmore was associated with the "traditional view."

The chief weakness of Aydelotte's program as a widely usable model was its restriction to the upper division. For the lower division he relied on a revised "core" curriculum—the prevailing concept in many private colleges today. A core curriculum seemed justified by the absence in America of the European preparatory or "public" school tradition; the first two college years were seen as making up for the deficiencies of our public schools. However, as our high schools have moved encouragingly in many new directions, this argument has grown less and less valid.

From one standpoint it is perhaps unfortunate that Swarthmore's strong divisional emphasis in honors had limited impact, even in the private sector. The Columbia College Contemporary Civilization courses for freshmen and sophomores discussed below were more influential, but primarily in the sphere of general education, where they reflected and affected the emerging emphasis on a "common learning." [2] Our native progressive movement in education, growing out of John Dewey's fresh thinking on democracy and education, provided the powerful background influence. If Swarthmore's divisional approach in honors had had wider influence, there might have been a quicker liaison with the general education effort, resulting in an earlier conception of a four-year honors program and the prevention, through honors programs in general studies, of the subsequent partial deterioration of general education itself.

In 1927 W. S. Learned observed that of the ninety-three honors programs surveyed by Aydelotte in 1925 only those at Swarthmore,

[2] See Russell Thomas, *The Search for a Common Learning: General Education, 1800–1960*, New York: McGraw-Hill Book Company, 1962.

Harvard, and the University of Toronto involved enough students to be worthy of mention.[3] Nineteen years later Aydelotte listed 116 programs and referred to the existence of others. But only a score of them were in public institutions, and by his own acknowledgment many were embryonic. Some of the programs in the 1925 listing, moreover, had vanished by 1944.

Yet Aydelotte's contribution was of vast importance. He was in every way the originator of honors strategy, and we are hugely indebted to him and to his Swarthmore faculty for developing the honors concept. Here the stress on group experience in the small seminar or colloquium and the idea of divisional honors got their full real start.

Aydelotte's was also a truly national perspective. He saw the need for a variety of approaches to suit local conditions. He did not neglect high schools, state universities, research, or graduate study. Nor was he unaware of the advantages of general education and general honors; though wedded to the idea of an upper-division honors program, he somewhat timidly expressed the hope that sometime in the future institutions would not fear to extend the honors method to freshmen and sophomores. "When Mr. Aydelotte remarked that the experiment is one of more than local importance he understated a millenarian assumption which the economic depression and the extreme difficulties of rapid change in most college teaching methods was to prove over-optimistic, but which then often encouraged proponents of the system to overstate their case." [4]

The honors program at Swarthmore was so carefully worked

---

[3] William S. Learned, *The Quality of the Educational Process in the United States and Europe,* Carnegie Foundation for the Advancement of Teaching, Bulletin no. 20, New York, 1927, pp. 116–117.

[4] Swarthmore College Faculty, *op. cit.,* p. 39.

out at its inception that it still continues without modification—an experience unique in American education. J. Roland Pennock wrote in 1952: "It is a fact that for over twenty years now the honors program has been subjected to no major changes." This was further emphasized by Swarthmore Dean William C. H. Prentice: "For some reason we do not seem to need such changes, although I think that every new idea needs refurbishing after three or four years."

At times Aydelotte seemed patronizing about the mass of average students, the vocational and professional realms, the disadvantaged areas and academic "poverty pockets"—the transacademic in general. But on everything pertaining to the inside of a liberal arts and sciences college and even to engineering, for which a special division existed at Swarthmore, he had superb insight.

Harvard College: the search for "a flavor of tension upwards"

Harvard is so important an institution that the most brief history of honors must mention developments there. It was to become our first major national university. Although long in the van of formal pursuit of excellence, Harvard never attempted to incorporate honors through a major reconstruction like Swarthmore's.

There was a period when Harvard resembled the Oxford of the mid-eighteenth century in sterility—a sterility, described in his autobiography by Edward Gibbon, which had led Oxford on to the "pass-honors" reconstruction of 1804. President Charles Eliot's expansion of the elective system at Harvard from 1872 to 1897 was the first revolutionary change from the then almost universally narrow and prescribed curriculum. It was conceived as a liberating reform in keeping with nineteenth-century democracy, and it spread throughout the country. It led to endless controversy with academic conservatives, who fought its consequences of dilution and indiscriminate incorporation of courses. It was the harbinger of both good and ill. Out of the later efforts to remedy the transformation of many large institutions, private and public, into shopping centers for a huge variety of packaged courses came some of the first efforts at creative reconstruction.

The positive consequences of the elective system are our main interest here. Harvard did not waste time in applying remedies. It proceeded with piecemeal experiments from 1873 through the 1940s: the degree with distinction given on the basis of oral and written examinations, a concentration and distribution program, departmental honors, "correlation examinations" for groupings of departments, a general examination for all students and a tutorial system, reading periods before such examinations, special advising for the more able freshmen, and residential houses (only partly successful). In 1903 Lowell of Harvard even advocated an honors college, but without success. Early student complaints about the overformality of honors had led to some of these changes. Everybody is now aware of the influential Harvard publication of 1945, *General Education in a Free Society,* and its post–World War II contribution under James B. Conant.

But Harvard honors remained fundamentally confined to a strong departmental and field-of-concentration approach. Eligibility was such that one-third of its graduates took an honors degree by 1930. The number of Harvard students taking honors has now risen to over 40 percent. Yet, paradoxically, Harvard still struggles with the problem of motivation, as do other institutions of highest expertise throughout the nation.

When I visited Harvard both in 1959 and later, complaints of the concerned faculty took various forms. "Our students get brighter every year," one faculty member said. "The lower half of our student body is of such high caliber that its members would be at the top in most other institutions. The competition, honors-wise, is so severe that many, often valedictorians from their high schools, refuse to compete. 'I don't have the time to be in honors,' a student would say." Freshmen at Harvard, I was told, are "thrown into 'The Yard' to get to know each other and in the hope that they will absorb the desired climate by osmosis." As one Harvard administrative official put it, "The problem of engaging the non-honors student is the outstanding one."

Advanced placement was widely practiced first in Cambridge, and ninety-two such students were on the Harvard campus in 1959. It was seen as a great boon in high school preparation for Harvard. During a five-year period almost 10 percent of the advanced placement students were accepted as sophomores. Yet some at Harvard were genuinely worried about the advanced placement philosophy of specialization. I was told:

> It fits in with what is rampant here and it is premature. It stops the students from looking around. In many institutions of the country there is, in fact, no proper relation between advising and advanced placement. It over-encourages acceleration, although 50 percent who are through in three years will stay on here for a fourth to take powerful courses in other fields to which they aspired but had to miss. They will also do half of their work in graduate school.

At the same time I was told by Dean Bundy in 1959, "Honors here is departmental and it will always be that way." He firmly rejected the idea of honors in general studies as well. Yet in this very year the problem of motivation was already brewing the new Harvard Freshman Seminars program. When it came out, the

Byron Stookey report on these seminars corroborated in every detail the validity of beginning with freshmen and the importance of general along with departmental honors—even in the most favored of institutions. That Harvard does not call these seminars "honors" is beside the point; the pervasive concern, after all, is quality, and "honors" is but one possible designation.

Nobody at Harvard has ever said what can be heard at a number of private institutions: "We are all honors; we do not need it." Like a few other institutions Harvard says, instead: "Our students should all be honors and they are assumed to be. But they must demonstrate to us that they do not belong." Harvard cannot be charged with complacency. It keeps on innovating. It no sooner starts a new endeavor than it appoints a special committee to review and evaluate it. There is a restless search for "a flavor of tension upwards rather than of separation," as McGeorge Bundy phrased it, and Harvard is always open to change. For example, the Harvard seminars have now been extended to sophomores.

Columbia College: the citadel of general education

Honors was originally established at Columbia College in 1909 in the form of a three-year program with supplementary reading and a final oral examination.[5] Departmental cooperation was spasmodic. Three years later F. J. E. Woodbridge, John Erskine, and Cassius Keyser began another program which included a weekly conference modeled on the medieval disputations. Both programs were aimed

---

[5] See Justus Buchler's "Reconstruction in the Liberal Arts," in *A History of Columbia College on Morningside*, New York: Columbia University Press, 1954, pp. 48–136. I am much indebted in what follows to Professor Buchler's excellent chapter.

at greater intellectual maturity. Neither flourished, but the latter reappeared in John Erskine's Colloquium on Important Books plan.

The first specifically "general honors" experiment, later called the Colloquium on Important Books, began in 1919. Erskine tells of asking the faculty:

> Why not treat the Iliad and the Odyssey and other masterpieces as though they were recent publications, calling for immediate investigation and discussion? ... After two seasons of such reading the students would have an acquaintance with world literature from all countries ... Exchanging ideas for two hours they will probably teach each other more about the rich aspects of Shakespeare's genius than any lecture is likely to convey.[6]

He advocated two instructors in each class, selected for their disposition to disagree with each other.

> Lectures may be inspiring or otherwise useful but they have no place in the natural social approach to literature as I understand that approach.... The teacher ... must believe in what he is doing and he must have a personal philosophy. You do not discuss great and noble ideas at low temperature and on a low plane.[7]

Columbia's Contemporary Civilization course was established in 1919. Woodbridge, in contributing his own ideas, helped to propagate those of John Dewey and Charles Sanders Peirce, the founder of pragmatism and author of *How to Make Our Ideas Clear* (1878). The notable thing is that general honors and general education are interpreted by Justus Buchler, Columbia philosopher,

[6] John Erskine, *My Life as a Teacher,* Philadelphia: J. B. Lippincott Company, 1948, p. 166.
[7] *Ibid.,* p. 170.

as the core of the change—the first real break from the old order in Columbia's development.

> ...the force of the German academic tradition had nearly resulted in Columbia's graduate and professional schools devouring the college that had mothered them. That crisis had come at the end of the century. Once the threat had passed, there rapidly developed a cosmopolitan union: the College and the University schools acquired new meaning while keeping their integrity within the orbit of a larger academic community. In such a community, the academic imagination could breed and nurture a distinctive conception of the liberal college.[8]

He regards this change and what followed as correcting the trouble with the courses in the old curriculum, which was:

> ...that the rationale of their interconnection was ill-defined, and the whole mode of study too tight and departmentalized. The widely differing (as well as the truly common) needs of students were largely ignored, and the conception of basic preparation was dubious and unimaginative. It was against such a curricular psychology that the founders of Contemporary Civilization and of Honors reading struck hard.... Never mind the conventional mechanics of study, they urged. Vitalize and dramatize the values inherent in it, and the tools will take care of themselves. Make the student conscious of ideas; the traditional disciplines and techniques will be embraced by him as means to that larger end.[9]

We are told that many of Dewey's former students played a role in the post-war Columbia pioneering, with its threefold stress on inter-departmentalism, classroom discussion with freshmen, and direct study of original works.

[8] Buchler. *op. cit.*, p. 49.
[9] *Ibid.*, p. 68.

What I have already described of its beginnings and rationale made Columbia College a citadel of general education. To the Contemporary Civilization course was added in 1928 a sequence of two Humanities courses for freshmen and sophomores. The general honors program became in 1932 the Colloquium on Important Books, restricted to seniors (now a two-year program including juniors).

"Important Books" at Columbia was not the same as the "Great Books" we are now familiar with (particularly as studied at St. John's). "Important" was usually conceived at Columbia in a Deweyan manner, as indicating works that could emancipate from the trivial, liberate the mind, open doors closed by disciplinarian pedantry. Woodbridge described Columbia's program as "a discipline of present excellence."

An attempt to inaugurate a general sequence in the physical sciences like those in the humanities and social sciences, significantly enough, did not succeed. The influence of the professional approach in this field was apparently too strong.

The seminar method spread as a technique in departments, between groups of departments, and in the general education courses. In both the Contemporary Civilization and Humanities courses the stress was on direct study of original works—in the social sciences for the former, in literature and the arts for the latter. Columbia tied the upper-division departmental honors into these lower-division courses.

After Columbia inaugurated it, lower-division general education spread to 200 colleges, according to Buchler. Columbia, rather than Chicago, Yale, or Harvard, was the true point of departure.

Wisconsin: a brief, isolated experiment

One other notable experiment, in this case at a state university, deserves mention—Alexander Meiklejohn's synthesis of idealism and American pragmatism and progressivism at their best which led to his Experimental College at Wisconsin. Unfortunately, the Experimental College lasted only five years (1928–1932); it was unable to survive in the face of powerful opposition in this advanced state university.

The Experimental College was a lower-division branch only. While not an honors program as such, it was by its very nature self-selective—something like Reed College. The freshmen studied fifth-century Athens; the sophomores, Henry Adams and modern America.

Meiklejohn's idea of a laboratory college of this sort parallels in its experimentalism the ICSS conception of honors programs as pilot projects calculated to have their ultimate impact in each college and university upon the quality of the whole institution. But the ICSS conception is primarily one of an experiment within, not apart from, established curricula.

The University of Colorado: experience of a large state university

The idea of honors grew slowly at Colorado. There was no preconception that what happened there might be influential elsewhere. Honors was a program in the College of Arts and Sciences only. Having been personally involved from its beginnings, I can here present from experience a brief vignette of its development.

In 1928 I was a member of a small committee to consider a better way to award the degree with honors than the prevailing method of averaging grades in separate courses. It was then that my own battle began for a preparatory program that would make mandatory *general* as well as *departmental* honors and generate an honors outlook, rather than a grade approach, in both. This committee succeeded in arriving at agreement and achieving faculty approval by 1930. The award of honors on grades alone was formally abandoned. An Honors Council was established to work out the general program, which began with extra reading under guidance, and to help inaugurate and equalize departmental programs. From the beginning some budgetary provision was made for an honors library and a bulletin on honors which also listed the important books to be read.

Administrative goodwill developed in its most cogent form—an increasing annual budget—though it took years for even partial official acknowledgment that the teaching load should be reduced for honors participation. The Council made strategic compromises of many kinds in order to retain the support of some departments hostile to the whole new concept of honors and to the mandatory general honors approach. Student support, both grateful and constructively critical, grew steadily, and devices were developed to elicit further criticisms and suggestions, notably through the students' own Honors Union Council. Pressure from students and the Council itself led in 1940 to the first appointment of a permanent half-time director—E. F. D'Arms, a Princeton-trained classicist.

Professor D'Arms made a valiant effort at critical analysis of our first ten years. He pointed up the shortcomings of our awkward program, its promise, and its dilemmas. He laid a firmer foundation for a series of honors offerings. Consultations with honors students became far more systematic. When he left during World War

II for a government military post, I was appointed to take over the directing task, which D'Arms described then to me as a thankless struggle with widespread noncompliance and consequent frustration. But there were already a large number of dedicated faculty people who knew what they were about and had the will and wit to outflank opposition, and support kept growing.

In 1943 our primary concern was how to preserve the general effort in the face of the war, which was disastrous to many an honors program elsewhere. Our major solution turned out to be a series of "World Crisis Courses."[10] After 1946 our Division of General Education was established with four courses, each worked out under the leadership of outstanding members of the Honors Council, but with an eye to the needs of general honors as well as of the total student body. Upper-division department honors programs kept going, with varying success.

One of our greatest compromises, which the war crisis made necessary, was to abandon the absolute requirement that a student take general as well as departmental honors and to permit one or the other or both; as it turned out, approximately half the honors students chose both. Compromises like these kept the honors idea alive. Our strongest students were the greatest supporters of the combination of general and departmental honors. New additions to the faculty, the growth in general honors groups and colloquia, expansion of the honors center, and the annual honors

[10] President Aydelotte is in error when he asserts in *Breaking the Academic Lockstep,* p. 95, that general honors was abandoned at Colorado during the war. A total of forty-five students graduated with *general honors* between 1943 and 1945, in addition to those who graduated with departmental honors only.

convocation under the program's auspices kept the honors idea alive and growing.

In 1947 I was invited to attend Columbia College's Colloquium on Important Books. I noted at once how similar in spirit and competence this program was to the Essay Club established at Colorado in the early thirties by Charles D. Abbott, which he had modeled on New College, Oxford. This club—by then there was one for men and one for women—was not formally part of honors, though most participants were honors students. I determined to try out the colloquium principle within our honors program. One trial run in 1947 led to the formal inclusion of an honors senior colloquium. It was immediately successful. Working toward improved techniques, we began tape-recording the fruitful discussions in this colloquium. The following year the junior colloquium was established: Both gave credit but no grade. The students of both colloquia repeatedly insisted that the colloquium discussion technique be extended to the many honors theme groups that were the basic offerings of our general honors program. From the very beginning they had criticized the resemblance of many of the theme groups, limited to ten students each, to regular classes. We found ourselves doing all we could by exhortation and pleading with the honors faculty to follow the conference method. It was no easy task.

Few of our ideas and practices, of course, were brand new; cues were taken from every source. If we made what turned out to be a general contribution, it lay in working out some of the main lines of a relatively unified and institutionalized program for the furtherance of quality and in dealing with (but not always solving) many of the problems inherent in the honors effort. We had, moreover, kept this program going through many crises.

The examples given above do not cover all significant landmarks in the evolution of the honors movement in this country. Important too were the experiences with honors of Princeton, Reed, Chicago, Yale, and Kansas (a detailed history of honors programs at Kansas is given in another chapter of this volume).

However, it is hoped that these sketches of the varied efforts at Swarthmore, Harvard, Columbia, Wisconsin, and Colorado give a fairly comprehensive picture of how far honors programs and special efforts had progressed and some of their salient strengths and weaknesses by the time the ICSS was founded in 1957.

UNTIL RECENT YEARS organized attempts to set up special programs for abler students, for the most part confined to private Eastern colleges, have been largely isolated. But since 1957 students, faculty members, and administrators all over the country have been able to pool their experiences in working to meet the needs of talent, overt or latent. This coordination has been made possible through the work of the Inter-University Committee on the Superior Student.

History of the ICSS

The ICSS began to take form when the Rockefeller Foundation awarded a grant to the University of Colorado to expand its honors program. This grant also provided funds for the director of honors at Colorado to visit various schools and organizations in preparation for a national conference on honors, which was held in Boulder in June, 1957.

The Boulder conference was the first step toward a systematic analysis of the need for new approaches to challenging the superior student. Twenty-seven large institutions, both public and private, sent forty-three conferees; participants were balanced between faculty and administrative personnel directly involved in whatever honors efforts their institutions were already making or were interested in making.

The steering committee of the conference[1] was a group of dedicated men thoroughly aware of the magnitude of the problem. Their richness of experience and vision and their aptness in expression enabled them to make vital contributions to the search for methods of dealing with talent other than through the customary curricular tinkering.

There was little at the Boulder conference resembling the formal and multiple routines of the typical national annual conference on higher education. The sessions were all plenary. The inclusion of a panel of nine honors students from Colorado's honors program made a telling difference. Here were the direct objects of the conference's concern, and they gave freshness and vivid embodiment to the themes discussed. Their performance was so impressive that such panels were included at the subsequent major regional conferences—Southern, Eastern, and Western.

The main sessions in Boulder covered present and proposed plans, general and departmental honors, honors techniques, honors and the high school, honors and the university, and budgetary and administrative problems. The sense of adventure with ideas hitherto only half explored and a feeling of camaraderie and mutual stimulation were pervasive. The conclusions of the conference, first drafted by Prof. Edward W. Strong, closely followed the course of the

---

[1] The members of the steering committee of the Boulder conference were Joseph W. Cohen, Edwin Garlan, H. F. Harding, Robert B. MacLeod, James H. Robertson, Edward W. Strong, George R. Waggoner, Walter D. Weir, and Dudley Wynn.

deliberations. They constitute the core of the current version of the "Sixteen Major Features of a Full Honors Program," [2] which reflect both theory and a set of practices.

Encouraged by the Carnegie Corporation, the steering committee met again in Boulder in October, 1957, and defined the steps to be taken as a result of the conference findings. These were:

1. The formation of a central agency, to be called the Inter-University Committee on the Superior Student, which was to operate independently and act as a clearinghouse for information on honors activities across the nation and an information service on honors programs of the sort advocated by the conference.

2. The periodic publication of a newsletter, *The Superior Student,* devoted to honors programs, to be mailed upon request to key faculty members and administrators.

3. The immediate launching of a program of visits to selected institutions to disseminate ideas growing out of the work of the ICSS and to prepare for two proposed regional conferences—one in the South in 1958 and another in the Northeast in 1959—primarily aimed at large public institutions. (Self-generated all-state conferences for all colleges, private as well as public, were also envisaged.) [3]

4. The initiation and development of liaisons with high schools, higher educational associations, and educational publications on matters pertaining to honors programs.

Shortly after this meeting a proposal to the Carnegie Corporation for aid resulted in a grant of $125,000 for a 2½-year period to

[2] These sixteen points, which are discussed below, appear in the Appendix to this chapter.

[3] A list of conferences playing a major role in stimulating interest in honors programs appears in the Appendix to this chapter.

begin in February, 1958. The University of Colorado was chosen as the location of the ICSS office. The Carnegie grant was renewed in June, 1960, and this aid supported the work of the ICSS for two more years. In the last few years of its operations the Committee received aid from many other foundations, private and public, and from the supporting memberships of colleges and universities.[4]

The ICSS ended its operations in the summer of 1965; it was felt that by this time the honors movement had reached the point where the colleges and universities could themselves carry forward its development.

Committee membership

A core of seven of the original steering committee of June, 1957, continued throughout to serve on the ICSS Executive Committee. They were Joseph W. Cohen, Robert B. Macleod, James H. Robertson, Edward W. Strong, George R. Waggoner, Walter D. Weir, and Dudley Wynn. This group was later enlarged when the Executive Committee itself was created to include Edward A. Cameron, North Carolina; Robert D. Clark, Oregon; John H. Franklin, Brooklyn College; Samuel P. Hays, Iowa; Robert E. Johnson, Illinois; Margaret Mead, American Museum of Natural History; Howard H. Quint, Massachusetts; Cecil G. Taylor, Louisiana State; and Sterling M. McMurrin, Utah. Three shorter-span members were: Harold F. Harding, Ohio; Roger G. Page, Minnesota; and Harry H. Ransom, Texas. The latter served also on the planning committee for the ICSS in October, 1957.

[4] The Edgar Stern Family Fund, United States Steel Foundation, Ford Foundation Fund for the Advancement of Education, National Science Foundation, Laurel Foundation, Pittsburgh Forgings Company Foundation, U.S. Office of Education, and 338 institutions and educational organizations provided funds.

The Sixteen Major Features

If a national committee had been set up in the thirties or forties to distill a set of principles to guide programs for superior students, and if it had based these principles on a survey of prevailing views and practices, something like the following would probably have emerged:

1. An honors program should recognize and train future scholars, i.e., future graduate students. Honors should be reserved for the departmental major or field of concentration, since the goal is to create top specialists. Further, it should be available only in the upper division; the lower division is a formative period only and does not merit the concern of the productive members of the faculty.

2. The standards of selection for admission to honors should be rigorous. Students should be chosen by the department head or his committee at the end of the first or second semester of the junior year. The best students will reveal themselves through the competition for grades, and grades are thus an acceptable measure of both ability and motivation.

3. Honors requires no changes in the existing curriculum. Since high academic achievement is always a lonely striving and results from a willingness to do extra work, honors can consist of independent study and research. When a student qualifies and can fulfill his requirements for the degree, he may take a beginning graduate course in his major to accelerate his progress.

4. The main emphasis should be on the student's intellective, analytical, critical, and research prowess, not on his creative, intuitive, or symbolic powers.

This is an imaginary but nevertheless quite authentic version of what has for the most part been meant by "honors" since the twenties. How do the principles of the ICSS differ from this traditional view?

The Sixteen Major Features of a Full Honors Program are given in full in the appendix to this chapter. They incorporate whatever the Committee felt was valuable from the prevalent view of honors summarized above. But they also called for some important innovations.

For example, the ICSS proposed less emphasis on specialization than had been common. It stressed the importance of a four-year program, one that would include both general and departmental honors. Talented and otherwise promising students, it suggested, should be identified and made to participate in honors as early as possible—ideally at the time of college entrance. Honors belongs in professional schools as well as in the liberal arts colleges. Increasing the work load is not enough to qualify as real honors; talented students, the ICSS insisted, require a different curriculum and different teaching methods and materials. The stress should be on excellence rather than grades, and this stress on excellence should help to raise the level of the entire institution. And finally, students themselves should help to formulate the honors program through suggestions and evaluations. In brief, honors is not simply a device to produce good specialists faster, but a means of enriching the intellectual life of the student along lines that he, with expert and sympathetic faculty guidance, could learn to choose for himself.

These Sixteen Major Features suggested what *might* be achieved; they provided a sort of check list that any institution could use in taking inventory of its honors efforts. They were not dogmatic, but instead offered many alternatives to be considered according to the institution's available resources. No one professes that they are the last word about all that can be done, since the last word is never said. How they will be implemented and amplified in the future, as more and more institutions grope with the problems of providing honors, remains to be seen.

Work of the ICSS

In addition to arranging conferences, the ICSS's work consisted of visits to institutions to stir up interest in honors programs and to gather information on programs already in progress, and publication of the newsletter.

Direct confrontations with faculties, administrators, and students provided the sinews of the Committee's program. During these visits professed intentions and the siren promises of catalogues or brochures were compared with actualities. Also, a generalized exposition of what might be done in honors was transformed into a detailed and lively debate on what might be most important for the institution in question, and mistaken conceptions were corrected. Above all, these visits provided an ever-growing file of examples that proved extremely helpful for clarifying issues and pointing up existing possibilities.

A visit could involve seeing such diverse groups as a committee on honors or on curriculum revision, admissions officers and counselors, committees from various professional schools, a special section of freshmen, a selected group of honors students, and a seminar or colloquium. It could also involve interviews with individuals and meetings with all deans or all department heads, with the president or provost, or with the faculty as a whole. The scene could change rapidly from institution to institution. At one there might be harmony and coherence of intent. At another "balkanization" might be the rule: Each dean or department head would be impervious to all the others. At times a perceptive new director superbly adequate to the task of diagnosis and prognosis could explain a complex situation clearly. At others a poorly chosen director could leave everything in a sea of opacity.

Organizing visits to institutions with a background of established honors programs was relatively easy. But at some schools it was difficult to know whom to see next or what to stress at a coming meeting. Thus, many visits necessarily entailed constant improvisation. Nearly every member of the ICSS, whether an associate or a member of the Executive Committee, traveled to institutions and participated in conferences both in his own vicinity and far afield. As director up to 1963, I took on a good share of these visits. During this period I made roughly 300 visits and participated in 100 conferences.

From the very beginning of these travels ICSS members intended to achieve more than the direct communication of the honors ideal. We were also preparing for coming regional conferences, choosing the most likely representatives and speakers from selected institutions, or seeking out contributions to the newsletter describing the import of some old or emerging development important for honors. We were also trying to convey to appropriate institutions the need for state or area conferences developed on local initiative. Finally, as the second Carnegie grant approached its termination, we were trying to interest appropriate foundations in supporting our national work. On numerous occasions we asked that an institution invite representatives of interested neighboring colleges or universities to participate in some appropriate portion of a visit. Many graciously cooperated. We were also invited to participate in meetings of national, state, and regional associations.

In short, through visits the ICSS tried to interest everyone it could reach in honors, set in motion plans to reach even more people through conferences, and learn everything that could be learned about the current status of existing honors programs.

A second important part of the Committee's work was the newsletter, *The Superior Student*. It began in April, 1958, with an issue of 2,000 copies. By 1964 circulation had risen to over 12,000. Out of a total of forty-eight issues eleven had to be reprinted.

Like the rest of the Committee's work, the newsletter was an improvisation. What to include or omit, what articles to solicit, and what to excerpt from various reports and programs was decided on the basis of the needs of the moment. The ICSS was primarily an information service. Its task was to keep an ever-widening audience informed about every higher educational activity relevant to honors. The newsletter had to be affirmative yet critical, current yet historical. It had to discriminate enough to eliminate lofty rhetoric and wishful thinking that ignored constraining actualities.

Thus, the newsletter aimed at being concretely informative, but also at supplying occasional deeper analysis of main issues of theory and practice if some disturbing misinterpretation, patent overstress on subordinate facets of honors practice, or neglected area of effort came to its attention. Among many others it elaborated upon the themes of high schools–college liaison; honors in culturally disadvantaged institutions; honors in the professions and all-university programs; acceleration, independent study, and dialogue; honors and the preparation of teachers; women in honors; honors in the creative and performing arts; and research and evaluation.

The newsletter also tried to keep abreast of everything fruitful that was being done in any field of study in the name of honors. It did not cater to any single category of institution; although the conception of quality and the resources of the various schools throughout the country differed enormously, it was felt that each should receive any information that would allow it to make what it could of its potential for upgrading its efforts. The value of such an inclusive approach was proven over and over again.

The ICSS was often informed of the newsletter's helpfulness. When a survey made in 1962 asked those on the mailing list if they would be willing to pay a modest subscription fee for the newsletter if it were no longer distributed free, more than 2,000 subscribers answered yes.

There were dissident voices: Some felt that the newsletter did not contain enough direct criticism and others argued that it was prone to oversophisticated editing and promotional afflatus.

But the give-and-take review of expanding practice and the divergent, often contradictory criticism possible in a newsletter seemed more appropriate to the situation than a one-shot report on all programs, like Aydelotte's single publication in 1944. This approach, it was felt, was more in keeping with the endless variety and mobility of the educational scene—particularly throughout these years when so many institutions were making a first start or a new beginning.[5]

Some observations from the ICSS experience

The work of ICSS members—visiting institutions, editing the newsletter, participating in conferences, and in general striving to learn about and foster honors programs across the country—built up a wealth of observations about the current situation of honors. Some of these are presented below.

[5] The newsletter is available from University Microfilms, Inc., Ann Arbor, Mich. The files and documents of the ICSS are with the Western Historical Collection, Norlin Library, Univ. of Colo., care of Mr. John Brennan and are available within discretionary limits.

There have been eight deans or ex-deans on the Executive Committee of the ICSS since its origination. One of them, George Waggoner, has always been somewhat skeptical of the belief that honors must "well up from the faculty." He feels that honors should "well up" from all sources of responsibility, administrative or faculty. And certainly honors programs have resulted from the imagination and drive of thoughtful people regardless of their position.

Although top administrative officials in a public institution often raised such obstacles to honors as the problems of financing and legislative opposition, they could also be the most ardent advocates of honors. True, at one A. & M. school the president had to intervene before the liberal arts faculty could be invited to a meeting on honors; an influential dean had seen fit to exclude that faculty, in the belief that liberal arts was but a minor appendage of the science and engineering program. And in other cases influential deans, near retirement and weary of controversy, have been hostile or indifferent to an innovation that might have added tension to their final years.

But on the whole administrators have often stood at the forefront of the development of a modern honors program. The president of the University of New Mexico, on his own initiative, found the money to give every needy freshman honors selectee a special scholarship. At the University of Virginia it was a group of top deans who gave most serious thought to the problem of honors; just as, to name some at random, it was a dean who took the initiative at Vanderbilt, the University of Houston, Georgetown, Roosevelt, San Diego State, Southern California, Colorado College, Columbia's School of General Studies, and Wisconsin's School of Education. Sometimes the leading figure was another administrator; for example, at Illinois a provost provided the necessary impetus and, curiously enough, at Hamline, a regent.

Certainly, recognition of the value of honors by top administrators has played a crucial role in the spread of programs throughout the country. Yet it was, of course, the usual thing for initiatives of every sort to come from faculty: from committees of review, of curricular study, of academic standards and the like; from a single department or division; even from the imaginative improvisation and persuasive power of a single faculty member. The examples are legion; "welling up from the faculty" is no empty phrase.

Whether the initiative to institute an honors program comes from the administration or the faculty, certainly one point is clear: Both must cooperate if the program is to succeed. The responsibility for ensuring that this is the case belongs to honors directors, councils, and committees. It is their job to gain broad cooperation from the faculties and from all other echelons of campus officialdom: the dean of students, dean of men, and dean of women and their staffs; admissions and counseling personnel; student health and recreation personnel; and dormitory directors. Often this effort should include the official advisers of preprofessional students in liberal arts and the other schools in multipurpose universities.

THE HONORS FACULTY

As important as institutionwide cooperation to the success of an honors program is the faculty's ability and desire to teach in honors. Thus, wise selection of the honors faculty is all-important. Good directive rules to follow are these: Criteria for faculty selection should be flexible; as many competent faculty members as possible should participate (alternating if necessary); and honors students should be consulted for new cues in selection.

But who is the faculty member suited to honors teaching? Generalization can be dangerous; the teacher competent to teach honors can be found in all faculty ranks. I venture to suggest, however, that the younger and mid-rank faculty members are likely to be the source of the best honors teaching. These will now include some people with experience in the extensive undergraduate honors programs of the past decade, and this experience can be very valuable; after all, honors products of the noted older programs were most effective in founding and energizing the programs existing today. In addition, the younger good faculty person is closer to the students. He is less likely to have yielded as yet to the motives of the academic marketplace. Moreover, if a younger instructor of parts is selected early to take an honors group, his will to teach at his best will be fortified and his respect for the institution as a community of learning strengthened. Nor will his career be harmed: Honors teaching and productive scholarship do not necessarily conflict with each other.

A faculty member *professionally* competent to teach honors is not always suited to the task in other ways. Teaching habits that grow out of a long tradition in which honors teaching played no part can be difficult to break and can cause serious problems. For example, teachers trained in more formal ways can suffer from timidity with newer methods that involve greater freedom on the part of both teacher and student; reactions to this discomfort can be cynicism, pseudo-objectivity, or an attempt at evasion that hides under the guise of sophistication. Some examples from my own experience will illustrate.

At a seminar on the *Theaetetus* of Plato in one institution, the only thing that happened was that the single professor in charge gave a subtle and expert analysis of the dialogue. He left no opportunity for discussion. The students took notes and asked an occasional question. This seminar differed in no way from a regular course in philosophy.

At another institution I sat in on a discussion of a penetrating essay in *Daedalus* entitled "The Nth Country." The students were to consider the balance between its dreadful and hopeful aspect for the future. With one exception, a reasoned and buoyant report by a Negro student, the consensus about the future was "dreadful." But the discussion among the students included wholly unbalanced and historically false interpretations of racial conflicts in the past. Not once were these clearly challengeable views criticized by the instructor. I was moved eventually to point out the errors that had been made and evince surprise that no one had taken issue with these statements. When the session was over the instructor privately expressed his appreciation for my interruption. "I could not have done so myself," he added, though he never explained why not.

The honors students in a third institution had so enjoyed the experience of colloquia in the first semester that they wanted this method used in a regular course in the spring, one that included nonhonors students as well. The professor agreed. The assignment for the class I attended was Arthur Miller's *Death of a Salesman*. The professor was late, and the class sat waiting in silence. I suggested that they begin a discussion, a student responded, and a good dialogue began to develop at once.

Minutes later the professor arrived. He seemed unimpressed by the lively exchange already going on, and insisted immediately: "Stop! Stop! Stop! I must first read you a review of this play from the periodical *Commentary*." He proceeded to present verbatim a long and partisan attack on the play. And throughout the session he argued vehemently for the one-dimensional interpretation he had presented and beat down every student objection. He had thus begun with his own answer.

The explanation for his conduct may be very simple. Confronted by his own class—honors students or not—the professor may have automatically returned to his habits of teaching in regular classes; the colloquium technique may have been for him something to use in a designated honors offering only, in which, at this university, he cooperated with another instructor from a different field and thus could not rely on the individual authority of the single lecturer.

In many institutions it will take years to resolve problems like these—to produce a faculty able to guide students as they grope toward intellectual development. Certainly teaching within an honors program must be vigilantly appraised. In addition, faculty perspectives can be pooled; it is important to approach these problems openly and make the experience of others in solving them available to all.

Finally, the graduate schools in preparing specialists might exercise in the future a more conscious concern for producing the honors type of teacher, i.e., one not only knowledgeable about a particular field but also able to deal with its interconnections with other fields. In this way they could help to "restore the dialogue" between the disciplines that Robert Maynard Hutchins and so many others have called for. Of course the graduate school's indispensable function is to produce high expertise in different fields. However, it now faces—even from within—the extraordinary interinvolvement of types of expertise and the early obsolescence of research enterprise. Incoming students from some honors programs are going to want to explore the interconnections between fields of specialization; they will not be content with becoming specialists only. Our graduate schools have been attacked and defended; the defense and the attack can be reconciled once there is a will to do so. The graduate schools can certainly be made to contribute deeply to the problems of quality in higher education.

THE COLLOQUIUM

Use of the colloquium—or the "seminar," "theme group," "conference method," or "symposium," as it is variously called—is at the heart of the honors method. For freshmen the colloquium is a training ground in the honors outlook; for seniors it is often that outlook's fullest embodiment and realization—a framework for the infighting and cross-fertilization of young minds in quest.

No single feature of an honors program is less well understood. Discussion of the colloquium method has been rare in the flood of contemporary writing on the processes of education. This is not surprising; only a handful of colleges and universities have built up experience with it, and until very recently most public institutions of higher learning have been ignorant of it.

What is at the heart of the colloquium? The generation of living dialogue, the confrontation of ideas and values with all the vigor, sincerity, and aplomb of which superior students are, or can become, capable. The colloquium is the realization of the sense of style, both in discussion and in writing; of the interplay of poise, gravity, humor, passion, controversy; of the effective use of what is known and the expression of what is valued—all within a freedom that allows the full swing of divergent viewpoints. For some it is a first chance to discourse, and this ability, once found, becomes a permanent acquisition. For some it allows the fullest involvement of the psyche. Ideally, for all it will be accompanied by that emotive ingredient, that camaraderie which in Plato's language is "love" and in Aristotle's the "friendship" of good minds.

As a method, does the colloquium make for mere freewheeling dilettantism, or is it a form of discipline? The answer is that in a colloquium the primary discipline is that imposed by the work being read and explored, of the art, poetry, or music being appreciated, appraised, and criticized. The faculty and the student's peers are there to insist on keeping to the supporting passage and to detect and puncture the glib, discount the slovenly, refuse to accept the irresponsible or irrelevant. Students speak of their reading for a colloquium as being different from any other, for while reading they know that they will be confronting the challenge of other students as well as that of the book.

For the faculty, as for the students, the colloquium is an experience wholly different from the lecture, however richly informed or stylistically polished; and also wholly different from a "lone wolf" independent study project or an individual student-teacher tutorial. In the colloquium the teacher must learn when to wait and when effectively to interrupt, to erupt, to explode; how and when to exemplify for the students the relevance of his own maturer mind amid the clutter of student opinions and gropings; how to avoid providing them with the answers and let them work up to the significant questions.

By fostering these skills in both student and teacher the colloquium can contribute to every other mode of honors learning and teaching—the traditional course, the lecture, the laboratory, the departmental special section, the honors theme group, the interdepartmental course, the tutorial, and the independent study project.

Does the college change students' values? Despite the pessimistic reports to the contrary, experience indicates that the colloquium at least does, and powerfully so. To establish and perfect the colloquium is indispensable for every honors program. It is the good undergraduate's finest adventure of ideas, the professor's most stirring challenge.

FINANCING THE HONORS PROGRAM

The creation of quality through institutional commitment and the involvement of faculty is not without its costs. But when it comes to financing programs, a characteristic reaction of some administrations is to say, "Very well, you have thought of a better way of doing your job. Do it! But we have no way of funding the enterprise." A full and openly acknowledged budget for an honors program has been a rare thing except in some of the most affluent private institutions.

Many early programs were left entirely to the dedicated faculty who devised them; they took on the added load with no extra pay. More recently, however, faculty members have been less willing to commit themselves so generously. When a committee at a large Western university recommended an ambitious program, it was told that it could go ahead but that no financial support was forthcoming. The committee withdrew its recommendations. A program did get started two years later, but only after a budget had been approved. At some major state universities I was told privately by leading members of the faculty, the very ones most qualified for participation, "Yes, I am all for it, but if this means something *in addition to* my present load—if it is going to interfere with my research—then I want nothing to do with it." Thus, an honors program today needs funds if it is ever to get off the ground.

Even when funds are available, they are sometimes misused. A private and distinguished university, stimulated by a grant, committed itself to a vast expenditure in a senior general education experiment. The grant only fractionally covered the actual cost of the many required offerings for *all* senior students. At this same school top faculty men complained to me that they wanted honors "across the board," but that the undifferentiated undertaking—costing seven times the amount of the grant itself—was exhausting the funds needed for a four-year honors program.

Why is gaining budgetary support for honors so difficult? One reason may be that budgets are more influenced by encrusted habits than current needs. Introducing a new budgetary element like honors thus involves fighting some strong prejudices.

Also, the actual worth of an honors program is evidently not understood by everyone. For example, educational institutions are not always sure which is more important—providing opportunities for the upper end of the spectrum of ability, or raising the level of the failing or conditional student through remedial work. Perhaps owing to some false conception of what a democratic system entails, institutions have been willing to give much more support to the latter effort. Many of our institutions, particularly the public ones, have made extravagant expenditures on remedial work while ignoring the importance of honors. For example, while many honors programs have failed to get started or were limping along for lack of funds, a single department of mathematics in a large California state college was spending $25,000 a year for a remedial course calculated to help students pass *another* remedial course. And a single English department at another large state college offered a remedial composition course that involved a $75,000 annual expenditure.

Estimates of the ratio of special expenditures on the retarded to those on the student of high ability range from 10 to 1 to 100 to 1 (the latter was made by a statistician in the Office of Education four years ago). A ratio as huge as 100 dollars spent on educating the retarded for every dollar spent on ability, actual or potential, indicates an educational philosophy no more democratic than if the ratio were reversed.

Finally, sometimes the actual costs of honors are overestimated. The dean of arts and sciences at a large state university pointed out that ability sections of twenty or twenty-five students, honors colloquia of twelve or fifteen students, or honors theme groups of ten were not serious budgetary problems for large institutions. Unlike individual independent study projects or tutorials, he added, these are all groupings of students in classes. Far more important, he went on, were the benefits accruing to the institution as a whole—consequences which more than justified the budget allotted them. I heard a dean at Michigan sharply take issue with an advocate of large classes through the use of television and other media. He pointed out that it has been commonplace for years for every self-respecting institution to permit and budget for small classes in departments like classics or Oriental languages, and that there was no reason why this practice should not continue.

Summary

The ICSS served from 1957 to 1965 as a clearinghouse for information and as a source of theory on the purposes and methods of an honors program suitable to present educational needs. It worked to bring to the larger universities and public institutions the benefits of the honors programs that some Eastern colleges and a few larger institutions had offered for some years, while at the same time helping to adapt these programs to the special situation at each institution.

The concept of honors that the ICSS sought to disseminate is not, as some would believe, a mere preaching. Experience has clarified and confirmed its value in a wide variety of actual situations. Experience has also strengthened theory through accompanying evaluation, both subjective and objective, at every stage of the program. (And, it is hoped, evaluation will be extended in the future to the student's development beyond the academic world.)

The greatest benefit of the ICSS-sponsored type of honors is that it can stimulate toward quality every type of institution of higher learning. It is not an elitist system, but one that aims at raising the standards of students and teachers—in professional as well as liberal arts institutions—by providing models to emulate and by increasing motivation. It has been very rare for an honors program designed along these lines to die out, as many of the older types of programs of two or three semesters' duration were wont to do.

This type of honors program produces a faculty member who, in addition to handling general and departmental honors, is also available for the growing number of large general courses, divisional or interarea. Through his honors experience he becomes more interested in improving these courses. His skills are sharpened by the experience of teaching jointly with faculty men from other fields and by the challenge of superior students. He becomes a greater force for improvement of quality in the institution as a whole.

The ICSS honors program also moves the educational institution toward a confrontation with the problem of overspecialization described in the first chapter of this volume. It may prove to be one important answer—perhaps *the* answer—to the question of how to introduce and propagate the interdisciplinary approach that American education needs so much in our times. If so, the ICSS, through its work and its influence, will have made an invaluable contribution to American life.

Appendix to Chapter three

THE SIXTEEN MAJOR FEATURES OF A FULL HONORS PROGRAM

1. Identify and select students of higher ability as early as possible. This involves far closer cooperation than has hitherto been the case with high schools and preparatory schools. It also involves making full use of the new experience that has accumulated on the proper uses of predictive techniques, past records, entrance tests and interviews, as well as of studies of aptitude, motivation, readiness, and achievement.

2. Start programs for these students immediately upon admission to the college or university, and admit other superior students into these programs whenever they are later identified by their teachers.

3. Make such programs continuous and cumulative through all four years, with honors counseling especially organized and equally continuous.

4. Formulate such programs so that they will relate effectively both to all the college work for the degree and to the area of concentration, departmental specialization, or preprofessional or professional training.

5. Make the programs varied and flexible by establishing special courses, ability sections, honors seminars, colloquia, and independent study, all with course credit. Advanced placement and acceleration will serve in a contributory role.

6. Make the honors program increasingly *visible* throughout the institution so that it will provide standards and models of excellence for all students and faculty, and contribute to the substitution of an "honors outlook" for the "grade outlook." For the latter purpose, gradelessness in some honors offerings—i.e., a "pass-fail" approach— is a frequent advantage.

7. Employ methods and materials appropriate to superior students. Experience has shown that this involves:

   a. Bringing the abler students together in small groups or classes of from five to twenty

   b. Using primary sources and original documents rather than textbooks where possible

   c. Eliminating lecturing and predigesting by the faculty of content to be covered; approaching the subject matter to be covered selectively; discouraging passive note-taking; encouraging student adventure with ideas in open discussion—the colloquium method with appropriate modification of this method in science and professional schools

   d. Supplementing the above with increased independent study, research and summer projects, honors study abroad, and imaginatively conceived summer institutes

   e. Providing for continuous counseling in the light of the individual student's development by teaching personnel rather than by full-time nonteaching counselors; but the professional counseling staff should include specialists in honors

   f. Differentiating between the needs of men and women in counseling in the light of the steeper erosion of talents after graduation among the latter

   g. Embodying in the program the required differentia between the creative and the formally cognitive approach

   h. Giving terminal examinations to test the honors results

8. Select faculty qualified to give the best intellectual leadership to able students and fully identified with the aims of the program.

9. Set aside, where possible, any requirements that restrict a good student's progress, thus increasing his freedom among the alternative facets of the honors and regular curriculum.

10. Build in devices of evaluation to test both the means used and the ends sought by an honors program.

11. Establish a committee of honors students to serve as liaison with the honors committee or council. Keep them fully informed on the program and elicit their cooperation in evaluation and development.

12. Use good students wherever feasible as apprentices in teaching and as assistants to the best men on the faculty. Even freshmen can sometimes serve in this capacity. There is increasing use both of available research institutes and laboratories in the area for a semester or a summer. Foundation funds in support of such undergraduate research and independent study projects are increasingly available.

13. Employ honors students for counseling, orientation, and other appropriate honors purposes within the general student body.

14. Establish, where possible, an honors center with honors library, lounge, reading rooms, and other appropriate décor.

15. Work toward closer liaison between the undergraduate honors program and the graduate school.

16. Ensure that such programs will be permanent features of the curriculum and not dependent on temporary or spasmodic dedication of particular faculty members or administrators—in other words, institutionalize such programs, budget for them, and build thereby a tradition of excellence.

IMPORTANT CONFERENCES ON HONORS, 1958–1964

Southern Invitational Conference, University of Louisville, November, 1958

Eastern Invitational Conference, University of Michigan, June, 1959

Southern University Invitational Conference (for institutions predominantly Negro), Southern University and A. & M. College, February, 1960

Western Invitational Conference, University of California, Berkeley, April, 1960

ICSS Honors Directors Conference, "The Problems of Developed Honors

Programs and the Problems of Research and Evaluation," University of Colorado, June, 1961

Conference on Honors and the Preparation of Teachers, University of Wisconsin, April, 1962

Conference on Talented Women and the American College, "Needed Research on Able Women in Honors Programs, College and Society," Columbia University, May, 1964, in cooperation with the U.S. Office of Education.

ICSS Honors Conference, Denver, April, 1965.

Chapter four / The superior
student: characteristics, aspirations,
and needs / James H. Robertson,
University of Michigan

THE MOST HEARTENING, hopeful, and constructive recent development in American education has been the increasing attention given by educators on all levels to the intellectual needs of bright students. The steadily accelerating growth of honors programs across the country, especially during the last seven years, is tangible evidence of this awakened concern for quality. In elementary schools, in high schools, in junior colleges, in liberal arts colleges, in private and public universities, in graduate and professional schools, responsible teachers and administrators are providing a wide range of opportunities designed to engage the full interest, talent, and intellectual power of their bright and ambitious students. As a consequence, American education in general is now moving toward democratic maturity by giving the most promising young men and women a fair share of the special attention that had been reserved for remedial students and problem children. The "egghead" may not yet be a national hero, but he is now being sought after, respected, and encouraged.

Who are these students now described by such awesome adjectives as "intellectually talented," "able and ambitious," "superior," "honors"? What are their qualities, aspirations, personal characteristics, values? What do they expect of themselves, of their teachers, of their education in general? What frustrates them and what stimulates and challenges them? How adequate and equitable are the present criteria for identifying them? Do these students merit the special courses, special privileges, special advising, and other perquisites they are now receiving?

The evidence needed to answer these questions is still fragmentary and inconclusive. But experience with and testimony of able students are beginning to provide tentative answers; at least, some long-enduring misconceptions about these students are fading.

Changing view of the young intellectual

There still persists an uneasy feeling that the young intellectual is standoffish, unrealistic, noisy, nonconformist—in short, that he may not know enough to come in out of the rain. There also persists an opposite view—one endowing him with virtues the total of which no human being has ever possessed, with the possible exception of the modest Benvenuto Cellini. Intelligent, talented, creative, self-confident, poised, articulate, brilliant—the list goes on like a catalogue of merit badges reverently pinned on a kind of academic Eagle Scout. Both conceptions do violence to the essential humanity of the young man or woman who happens to be blessed with superior intelligence and is not afraid to develop and use it.

Although unquestionably there are as many oddballs among nonhonors as among honors students, these widely held fallacies cannot be dispelled easily by argument. They do yield, however, to fact and experience. The existence on a campus of an honors program catering to honors students who live and breathe among their fellow mortals can serve to show the community that intelligence of a high order and the ability to come in out of the rain are not mutually exclusive qualities.

An increasing number of surveys and studies support this conclusion. One such study, completed in October, 1962, at the University of Illinois, was designed "to discover how the undergraduate student body at Illinois viewed this newly created group of 'scholars' and through this to infer something about the general academic climate of the campus." This study was conducted by Miss Dora E. Damrin, assistant director of the University of Illinois Honors Programs. One of her findings was that "intellectually, personally, morally, the typical scholar is not only accepted by his peers but also is held in rather high regard by them." Having had the experience of knowing honors students as people, the overwhelming majority of students who responded to the questionnaire rejected the notion of the honors students as a "type." In addition, Miss Damrin found very little evidence of envy. The nonhonors students endorsed the concept that better students were entitled to an education worthy of them and saw quite clearly that equality of opportunity requires that educational opportunities be pitched at varying levels.

The honors student speaks

Bright and able young men and women experience the same self-questioning, the same anxieties, the same social triumphs and failures, the same problems of choice, the same difficulty meeting deadlines as do all other young men and women in search of personal identity and a useful place in the sun. If anything, the superior student suffers more because of his talents. He is quicker and more severe in his self-analysis, he demands more of himself, he has a more difficult time settling on his educational and professional goals, and he is indifferently successful in his efforts to channel constructively his strong urge to rebel. In addition, he has high hopes that his college experience will be stimulating and adventurous. When it is, he responds gratefully and enthusiastically; when it is not, he turns away with sharp regret and, occasionally, with cynicism.

These traits and aspirations are admirably revealed by the honors students themselves in their conversations, in their panel discussions, in their published statements, and in their intellectual autobiographies. At major regional conferences on honors sponsored during the past seven years by the Inter-University Committee on the Superior Student at Boulder, Colorado; Louisville, Kentucky; Ann Arbor, Michigan; Berkeley, California; and Madison, Wisconsin, the honors students on the program invariably stole the show. Their searching, forthright, perceptive comments and their refreshingly frank speech were like a sea breeze in a faculty committee room. Students from Colorado, Michigan, North Carolina, Kansas, California, Oregon, New Mexico, South Dakota, Texas, Wisconsin, Kentucky, Massachusetts, New York, and elsewhere engagingly personified the values and outcomes of the honors opportunities accorded them on their home campuses. There was little need for reassuring speeches or speculative statements from the assembled deans, directors, and faculty after the honors students had spoken.

ASPIRATIONS . . . AND REALITIES

What is it these bright students want from their educational experience? What they want coincides closely with the aims that most colleges and universities bravely state in their bulletins and announcements. The honors students simply ask that the promises be fulfilled, that the statements truly guide the educational program. Specifically, the abler students want to be involved in a meaningful dialogue with their instructor, their peers, and with themselves; they want to be "threatened," i.e., compelled to question and to reexamine; they want to get "a vision," to reach beyond knowledge into wisdom and discovery.

These aspirations were succinctly and effectively summarized by Norton F. Tennille, an honors student at the University of North Carolina, who wrote:

> First there must begin in the classroom a dialogue—a dialogue between professor and student, between student and student, but most importantly, between the student and himself. The dialogue must be open and frank.... [It] must begin in the classroom, but it must extend into the entire life of the student.... Secondly, the classroom experience must pose a threat. The student must be threatened; he must be driven outside himself; he must be compelled to question himself and his values and the values of those among whom he lives.... This is not to say the classroom should breed insecurity; it means the student should be thrown into a state of creative tension in which the foundations for the only valid security can be laid, that security which rests on individual thought. Finally, the student must be shown in the classroom a vision. So often in a college course the individual sees only a textbook, a syllabus, a lecture, an hour quiz, the final exam and a passing grade. He must be led to see that ... beyond the course and the daily preparation lies a discovery, the reward of which is far greater than a diploma or a Phi Beta Kappa key.

What happens to these expectations? Three years ago, Professor Robert C. Angell, then director of the college honors program at the

University of Michigan, asked a number of seniors to write a critical, autobiographical account of their experiences in the honors program in particular and in the college in general. Eighteen seniors responded, most of whom had entered the honors program as freshmen. Their lively, readable, personal essays reveal a great deal about the student and the educational experiences and instructors that "made a difference." They also indicate a wide diversity of talents, interests, backgrounds, and temperaments, and point up the foolhardiness of attempting to stereotype honors students. Although the group is from a single campus, corroborating evidence from honors students enrolled at other colleges and universities supports the view that these statements constitute a reasonably good basis for drawing general conclusions about the best students on most campuses.

The main common denominators apparent from these autobiographies were superlatively good high school records, high scores on aptitude and achievement tests, and an eager recognition of the need and desirability for entering college. In addition, practically all of these students had been active in extracurricular activities in high school. The records of many showed leadership in elective student government positions; experience editing the school paper or yearbook; active participation in such sports as track, swimming, basketball, and football; leading contributions to dramatic productions; membership in the school orchestra or band or chorus. Their cultural and economic backgrounds were varied. They came from small high schools in rural areas, large metropolitan high schools, and suburban high schools; a few were from private preparatory schools. They included sons and daughters of farmers and white-collar workers who had not attended college as well as children of doctors, lawyers, and teachers. Although some of the students had not traveled outside the state, the majority had made extensive trips around the country and a few had lived abroad for a year or more. Many of them were contributing to the cost of their education.

Despite different cultural and economic backgrounds, these autobiographies reveal a marked similarity in the misgivings, self-questionings, frustrations, triumphs, and discoveries that chart the way toward personal and intellectual maturity. These able students confessed that they felt uncertainty about their intellectual abilities early in their college careers. Very few of them considered high school achievement a very reliable indicator of excellence. As one girl, an honors student in zoology, wrote, "I never had any need to prove myself previously. My first impression of my [college] classmates was they were brilliant, sophisticated, male. I could see no similarity between them and me, a rather backward one-down type girl." Another young lady, in English honors, confessed: "In high school I had the highest grades by far of anyone in my small class of thirty. At the time I was pretty sure I was smarter than anyone else in the class.... Well, college soon corrected that notion. And incidentally it took only about three months for me to accept finally that [high school] grades and intelligence are more frequently unrelated than they are related." Even good grades in college did little to bring reassurance. A senior, reviewing her freshman experiences, wrote that she "studied all the time except when she was eating or sleeping." Although her diligence was well rewarded because she "had very good marks for both semesters, nevertheless, I continued to feel inferior both academically and socially."

During their freshman year many felt the need for intensive study—for both reassurance and escape. They devoted long hours to their books and assignments chiefly because of self-doubt, fear of competition, or fear of faculty or parental disapproval. There was little evidence of delight in their courses, of love of ideas. "In high school," wrote one young man, "my whole scholastic life was centered around competition. We had a very intelligent class, and from the ninth to twelfth grades it was a constant, below-the-surface struggle to see who could outdo the other students for the best grades. I had this attitude when I came to the University, although I was unaware of it.... I studied hard, went to three meals a day, made friends with other guys on the floor." But he felt dissatisfied with his good grades. Something was missing. "I can see upon looking back over my college career," a senior confessed, "that I studied most when I was most unhappy. It was a way of getting away from my troubles and securing esteem for myself in my own estimation." Some students hid the fact that they were studying excessively from their classmates in order to preserve the illusion of effortless brilliance. In a freshman honors mathematics course, for example, the students impressed each other by their evident ability to solve long and hard homework assignments easily and correctly. Later, from the safe vantage point of the sophomore year, the members of the class "confesed to each other that we had spent most of the weekends solving these problems but thought that the 'others' in the class had no difficulty with them."

Most of these students declined to accept the grade point average as an adequate measure of educational growth, usually before the freshman year was over. "I learned," said one young man, "that the system of grades is a very unimportant thing. It doesn't really matter so much what grade the teacher gives you and what kind of a person he thinks you are; it's more a matter of deciding for yourself what you want out of a course, what you yourself feel you have gained from it regardless of the grade, and how you, as a student, judge the teacher's merits and faults." A diplomatic, perceptive young lady stated: "A good share of the pressure to study for exams and 'get grades' comes from the other students. Anxiety is contagious. After exams neighbors would turn to neighbors and see how they had done. I endeared myself to many by always stating a mark lower than theirs."

Along with this early skepticism about grades went an impatience, almost indignation, with imposed requirements. Without exception, the honors students rebelled at having to take certain courses simply to fulfill degree requirements. A characteristic response came from one girl who wrote feelingly: "[I have] a rebellious attitude toward learning and studying for any other reasons than to have fun and to help myself and others grow. Specifically, plunging into books and classes for four years to get a degree is one of modern society's most revolting activities. It makes me angry that I'm a part of it. When I first came here, I was extremely irritated to have to take this or that course because it fulfilled some distribution requirement.... I prefer to start a new course with a spirit of curiosity, not resentment." Although she admitted that most of these required courses turned out to be interesting and profitable, she observed that "there must be a more intelligent way of persuading students to explore new fields than by wiring degree requirements around them."

Another dissatisfaction felt by the honors students resulted from their critical awareness that many of their nonhonors courses were undemanding and ritualistic. As one girl stated, "I had a difficult time becoming truly involved in what I was doing. I attended class regularly and took careful notes, but I found that it required largely memorization. There was little opportunity for creative, intellectual effort." Another young lady made the same observation with the added generalization that academic docility is more prevalent among women: "I think most boys get a lot more out of college than do most girls. I found this particularly true in honors classes. The girls did homework carefully and always answered the professors' questions. The boys read outside books and asked the questions."

CRITICISM OF THE FACULTY

The judgment on instructors who appeared incompetent, casual, dogmatic, or unperceptive was swift and merciless. Although most of the arrows were shot at teachers in nonhonors courses, some honors faculty were targets as well. An English teacher who "didn't try to see beyond a misplaced comma" was indignantly labeled "an amorphous mass who understood nothing." A comparative anatomy laboratory course "was conducted so as to make rote memory necessary and understanding superfluous." One honors student, qualifying for a teaching certificate, took the required education courses with unhappy results: "They were every bit as mediocre as I had anticipated; in fact, they were even more so.... It is a shame that time should be wasted in such a way. I soon found, however, that I could get good grades in education with almost no work and effort and so I simply added them, a few at a time, to my regular load of classes." In a mathematics honors course taught by a dull, uninterested instructor the class engaged in a mild form of sabotage: "A sort of collective laziness set in and we told jokes and anecdotes at the expense of the instructor." An introductory psychology course was "boring and insipid"; a Russian class was "nothing but drudgery. The teacher was sarcastic, and I began to slink into classes late and unprepared;... I cut German half the time because of a revulsion I felt for the teacher." An eminent research chemist with a dazzling publication record proved something less than satisfactory as an instructor, according to an honors major deeply resentful of his pedantic bombast:

> We laughed wildly about him when we believed he was not in the vicinity. Since he never supervised our lab, we got away with doing only half as many experiments as the nonhonors students did, and our four-hour laboratory periods degenerated into good-natured T.G.I.F. parties and often adjourned to the Union Snack Bar.... It is because of this man that I began to ask myself why I had ever wanted to major in chemistry. Only when I cut class and read the various good textbooks that were available in the library did I appreciate the impersonal beauty and the careful logic of physical chemistry and the nature of the dilemma that exists in the painful attempt to fit mathematical theory to the real physical world.

PRAISE OF THE FACULTY

On the other hand, the honors students were unstinting in their praise and gratitude for the instructors who made them see the possibilities open to them. In every case, it was the personal impact of a dedicated, able teacher who "made the difference." The transformation from unhappy, two-dimensional students to excited, purposeful, motivated young men and women with a hunger and a love for learning is the justification and reward for all who teach. Although other influences undoubtedly play a part in this transformation, the students paid special tribute to individual faculty members who caused "the spark from Heaven to fall." Here are some of the bouquets laid at the feet of these teachers. To a professor of English: "He communicated to me through the classroom procedures his own love for literature and his own scholarly attitude toward it. I began to develop a small love and appreciation of my own.... I found I was doing the work of this particular course not so much because I wanted a good mark but because I loved the work itself. I found in this activity just what I had been needing, some real, original, creative effort of my own. Consequently, it was not surprising that I chose English as my major." To a professor of mathematics: "His sincere interest in the material and in all the students made me feel particularly responsible for my work for him. He took a personal interest in me, gave me special little proofs to work out.... He was the first to make me think that there is perhaps more than mechanical work involved in study...." To an honors counselor: "He has remained as my most stimulating faculty friend. He was the first to help me understand that a great work of art is more a thing of beauty, closed and formed in itself, than an expression of experience or philosphy." To a zoology professor who, recognizing a student's interest and potential, arranged for an assistantship at the Bermuda Biological Station: "The Bermuda trip was my first professional adventure.... There I learned to be completely aware of my surroundings. The most dignified and important of scientists would show just as much curiosity and excitement over the octopi's color changes as a little child. More than ever I felt how impossibly large and undeserved the gift of life is." To a number of teachers, not so much for what they taught, but for sharing their enthusiasms and their views of the world with their students: "Professor B.'s course in zoology was probably the most unsettling experience I ever had. Material presented, mostly through side statements, just an aside here, an off-the-cuff assertion there, occupied my thinking for many months after the formal course was terminated." "I was not alone," wrote a senior in English, "in feeling a great admiration and respect for Dr. B. The class sessions which he held were so enjoyable and worthwhile that it was a real joy to attend them. I can even say that I went with a great deal of antici-

be a repetition of high school experiences, or if it involved much busy work, it was jettisoned with no compunction.

Rather than fill up their days and nights with socializing, partying, committee work, and student politicking (although these activities were not neglected), the honors students all yearned for more free time to browse, to reflect, to explore inviting byways, to be alone. "One thing I've found rather annoying," wrote an honors student in zoology, "although I probably would not have it any other way, is the multitude of desires and opportunities which are always present and pulling at odds. There is such a choice of lectures, concerts, and plays, many of which I've taken advantage of, that one always feels he is missing something (and he is, obviously). Every time I go into the stacks at the general library, I feel this immense frustration at being so near to the books I want to read and yet having just two eyes and twenty-four hours in a day." "In every class," wrote a journalism honors student, "so many interesting side-lights have flickered but there's never enough time to pursue but a few of them."

Another, more significant need for time is felt by many students, but especially by those in honors. It is the need for time to sort out experience, to review career plans, to gain perspective so there is relevance and coherence in the educational process. Several honors students spent a very profitable year abroad in travel, study, and maturation. Another took time off to work for a semester. The majority who remained in residence, however, admitted that during at least one semester they had worked far below their potential chiefly because they were unsure of their goals—and sometimes because they were just plain tired.

The special privileges accorded honors students for independent work, for research and laboratory assistantships, for courses and seminars with stimulating teachers and all modifications of rules and requirements were gratefully acknowledged as valuable in providing encouragement and a welcome break from routine. There is a heartening response to any move to grant freedom, responsibility, and personal dignity to these interested, able students. "I am now more directed, independent, and aware," summarized one senior. "I have gained a confidence, a purpose, and a curiosity which portends a full and happy life."

THE HONORS EXPERIENCE

The common theme of these testimonials is a deep gratitude to those teachers who helped bring about a love affair with learning. Most of the autobiographies relate a gradual discovery of interest, excitement, devotion, and sheer delight in ideas—a discovery immeasurably assisted by those teachers who shared their love with their students. To become aware that learning is discovery, not absorption of facts, and to find the courage to eschew flirtation for full engagement—these are the two major factors that lead from intellectual timidity and uncertainty to a full and purposeful intellectual life.

This happy conversion comes as a result of a revelation, not from any formula. Students, especially the bright and sensitive ones, need to go through a necessarily painful period of self-analysing, of reexamining values, of questioning the safe and easy, of discovering the emptiness in docility, mediocrity, and cynicism. The despair of bright young men and women in their lonely struggles for a satisfying maturity is both deep and dark. They expect so much more of themselves and are acutely conscious of how little they know and how bewilderingly varied is the world of knowledge whose horizons keep retreating. The frightening, urgent need to make informed choices keeps pressing in on them. When, however, they do settle on a fixed course and begin moving steadily and confidently toward a self-determined destination, the uncertainty and despair drop away and are replaced by joy and excitement.

Not all students in the honors program achieved this awakening. Sadly, there were two whose autobiographies revealed they had chosen to stay wrapped snugly in a cocoon of acceptable grades. With little insight, courage, or self-confidence, they chose to make their college experience scarcely more than a superficial encounter with courses and examinations dutifully and successfully passed.

Apart from these two, all of the honors students underwent the liberating transformation from docile, conforming, rigid freshmen to questioning, discriminating, flexible seniors. As one girl wrote, "I don't think any experiences in the last few years have put brand new traits in me. Rather, I think I've been rearranged.... I think this sort of process of selection and nourishment is inevitable; it would have gone on no matter what I'd been doing these past four years. But I do believe the specific selections were determined by college experiences.... It should be apparent that I'm not quite sure about several things. In fact, I'm very unsure about many things. This is a major effect of my college experience. I do not mean that I am a lost, floundering soul who has been completely disorganized by higher learning. I prefer to think of my state as one of reasonably organized suspicion."

It is clear that honors students differ in degree, not in kind, from their fellows. The able students are more articulate, more quickly impatient with mediocrity and conformity, more courageous, and more questioning, but these are quantitative differences only. Consequently, the concern shown by any college or university for improving the climate of excellence by creating or strengthening educational opportunities for its honors students can very well result in raising the sights of all who learn and all who teach.

Selecting students for honors

Not only are honors students a delight to have on campus, they have also become institutional status symbols. During the past few years a lively competition has developed among colleges and universities to attract as many bright students to their campuses as possible. A National Merit Scholarship winner is wooed almost as ardently as the literate all-state fullback.

Once the able students have been recruited, the questions of selection and accommodation become important. How many are interested in and qualified for the special educational challenges afforded by an honors program? What resources can be devoted to support such a program? The number of students designated as "honors" will depend on local answers to these two questions.

Another way to face the issue is for each institution—whether major university, small college, junior college, or professional school—to ask itself, "How many of our best students are not now being sufficiently challenged and what are we prepared to do about it?" This relative approach keeps the question in a realistic, local context, where it belongs. Since the basic purpose of an honors program on any campus is to identify and stimulate the students with the best potential and thereby invigorate the entire educational enterprise, the fact that definitions of the honors student may differ is not material. Used with discretion, this flexible approach to choosing honors students allows unselective state universities and community colleges, as well as the selective colleges and universities, to provide programs designed to identify and to stimulate their best students.

Whatever approach is used, however, it should ensure that the number of honors students chosen is neither very small nor very large. Selecting only a few students for honors will not make for a program that is workable and that affects the rest of the institution; including a great number of students in an honors program falsely implies that the academic millennium has arrived.

How are the students with the best potential identified? The process requires wisdom, experience, and humility. High school records, aptitude and achievement test scores, and honors, scholarships, and prizes won are important and useful data and provide a valuable common denominator for selection. It is a mistake to make them the sole consideration, however, or to succumb to the temptation to convert them into convenient, quantitative measuring rods. For example, one serious limitation of the tests currently used is that the scores of students of good native ability but poor cultural background are not a fair index to their intellectual potential. Further, these data do not indicate such subjective, personal qualities as values, motivation, aesthetic sensitivity, and creative potential. Although tests are currently being devised in the hope of shedding some light on these elusive qualities, observation, evaluation, and informed personal estimates are still our main bases for judgment. The thoughtful impressions of high school teachers and counselors and the results of personal interviews on campus can contribute to a reasonably fair estimate of a student's willingness and readiness to grow.

Although some feel that selection can be deferred until after a student has proved himself on campus, the additional evidence of good grades in regular freshman courses is not worth the grave risk such delay entails. Eager, enthusiastic, and poised for flight, the bright freshman has high hopes that his initial experiences in the college will be an exciting new intellectual adventure. He needs to be given the special attention and challenging educational opportunities he merits and yearns for at the very beginning; if he finds his expectations thwarted he may become disillusioned and search for satisfactions outside the classroom.

To allow for any misjudgments in the initial selection, freshmen admitted to an honors program should be expected to prove themselves in their course work, especially in any honors courses they undertake. If their ability or readiness has been overestimated, it is no kindness to carry them along. Conversely, if students previously overlooked, or promising transfer students, demonstrate a capacity for and interest in profiting from honors opportunities, they should be invited to join.

In brief, admission to and retention in honors should rest on periodic reviews of each student's achievements. Selecting participants should be a continuing, dynamic process, not an isolated, static one.

Guiding the honors student

If the honors student is to get the attention he merits, the student-teacher relationship, as fruitful and essential as it is, must be supplemented by the availability of informed, interested faculty advisers. As we have seen from the autobiographies of the graduating honors seniors, their first exposure to the complex, rigid, confusing regulations and requirements of the college can result in dismay, rebellion, and frustration. Informed advisers would be necessary if they served no other function than to guide students through this labyrinth.

But the justification is far greater than this. If they are to help able students custom-build academic programs appropriate to their interests and ambitions, faculty advisers must talk with each student to gather information about his interests, background, reading, goals, and talents. They can also take the sting out of "requirement" by explaining the rationale for and the educational relevance of courses in fields that may seem alien to the student's present purposes. More important, an interested, informed, available adviser can become visible, tangible evidence that the student "matters," evidence to counteract the dehumanizing effects of the testing, classifying, registering, numbering, and herding that constitute the students' first involvement with the administrative machinery.

It is axiomatic that bright students take more time, not only in the classroom, in tutorial sessions, in the laboratory, but also in academic advising. They are eager to talk with a knowledgeable member of the faculty, not merely about routine matters, but rather in the hope of engaging in leisurely conversation on the educational ambitions, possible careers, and graduate and professional programs, as well as on ideas and insights that they are anxious to share. Students with this interest and this sophistication should not be put off with over-the-shoulder responses, short answers, or casual generalizations. They and their questions merit thoughtful, expert attention from a carefully selected faculty adviser, since such opportunities for discourse can result in academic counseling (and teaching) of the highest order.

Because the chief work of the academic adviser is to deal with major educational questions in a context meaningful to each student, he must be a good teacher. In general, faculty members with experience in teaching honors students make the best honors advisers. The adviser and his students need not have the same or similar fields of interest. Underclassmen, who are most in need of counsel and a friendly ear, are still tentative and uncertain about their educational and professional goals. The adviser should be seen as a representative of the institution as a whole, not as a recruiting officer for his department or his specialty. Later in his undergraduate career, the student will normally shift his loyalty to a member of the department in which he has chosen to major. But until this decision is reached, the adviser's function is to help each student shape an appropriate program of study and evaluate his experience critically and realistically so that he can make informed choices.

Although the number of advisers and how they are supported administratively will vary from campus to campus, some principles apply to all situations. First, not all faculty members should serve as honors advisers. Even on small college campuses where the main concern is with undergraduate teaching, some faculty members will not be interested in or qualified for advising honors students. On large university faculties, the need to select advisers carefully is much greater because there are more teachers removed from undergraduate concerns.

Equally important, students must be told who their advisers are and at what hours they are available. When a student taps apologetically on an instructor's door and is met by a questioning stare, the student-adviser relationship is off to an unpromising start. Unless students are reasonably confident that they are expected, they will tend to stay away.

Also, the adviser should be given time to meet the students' requirements. If advising is a responsibility added to the full schedule of an already busy man, it is likely to get short shrift. The honors student will be sensitive to any slight and will hesitate to bother his adviser with vague but important questions about the wisdom of switching from premedicine to political science, or the value of spending a year abroad. As a consequence, both student and adviser will miss many opportunities for timely, satisfying discussions on significant educational questions.

In addition to providing a welcome opportunity for students to converse, the faculty adviser needs to offer other services. For example, he should be reasonably knowledgeable about courses, prerequisites, and regulations, and, most important, how to get around them when circumstances warrant. To be really helpful to his students, the adviser must be authorized to substitute courses or waive requirements when the best educational interest of the student so dictates. One of the faculty adviser's most important functions is that of making judicious exceptions. Any clerk in the registrar's office can impose regulations.

When he talks with an advisee about program modifications, the faculty counselor should have immediately available a comprehensive, cumulative file of data on the student's background, preparation, and potential. Ideally, this dossier should include the admissions application, a profile of test scores, the latest college transcript, correspondence and other material concerning the student, and a running record of past interviews. Such a file will help the adviser answer specific questions the student may ask; it will also give him many happy leads for asking questions of his own that can make of the interview a satisfying and fruitful discussion.

Beyond their immediate usefulness, cumulative records are of continuing value as a means of giving students appropriate encouragement and indispensable recommendations for graduate and professional schools and for fellowships and scholarships. It is a tragic commentary on the inefficiency of bigness that qualified honors students sometimes get overlooked for nominations to Woodrow Wilson Fellowships, Marshall, Rhodes, and Fulbright Scholarships, and other significant awards. Equally sorry is the frequent complaint of seniors that "only my freshman English instructor knows me well enough to give me a recommendation for law school." The college's responsibility to give specific, evaluative support to its most promising graduates can be met more effectively if helpful data are available and used.

Other needs of honors students

At the heart of any honors program is the opportunity to encounter and engage first-rate minds. Special courses, seminars, tutorials, colloquia, and research projects are the major means of encouraging such encounters between honors students and the faculty as well as among honors students themselves. The specific advantages and the intellectual dynamics of these various educational approaches are described at length in other chapters of this book. There are, however, other desirable aspects of honors administration that further enhance the value of the program for the individual student. To what extent these are provided will often depend on the size and complexity of the honors program and the physical and financial resources on each campus.

No matter how large or small the program is, the responsible educational director must be a faculty man of stature who has a genuine commitment to honors and who has the confidence, respect, and support of his colleagues and of the administration. The program itself should be given quarters suitable to serve as an administrative and educational rallying point. If, in addition to the essential office and meeting space, there can be added an honors lounge or small library, so much the better. Such facilities will more than justify their cost by providing opportunities for honors students to meet their peers, their instructors, and their advisers in a more relaxed atmosphere than the classroom or faculty office. The informal, spontaneous discussions that can take place over tea or coffee (sherry is better still) are well worth the effort required to pry loose the extra space and funds from the dean.

The question of whether or not there should be special honors residential units sparks lively debate. Abler students are frequently unhappy over the nonintellectual tone of most college dormitories. On the other hand, many of them are reluctant to be set apart in special residences. Practically all vehemently oppose any *requirement* that they live in such an establishment. Perhaps the best resolution is to provide honors housing for those who want it, and to allow for easy transfer.

Honors students should be accorded special privileges designed to encourage a sense of discovery as a dynamic aspect of their education. What form these privileges take is limited only by student and faculty imagination and the resources of the campus. Those found particularly effective are special access to research collections in the library, assignment to graduate carrels, invitations to faculty seminars and colloquia, appointments as junior assistants on research projects, independent reading and research opportunities, annual publication of student research papers in an appropriate journal, opportunities to meet and to talk with distinguished visitors to the campus, and programs for travel and study abroad.

Still other possibilities should come from the honors students themselves. Informal student discussion groups on any subject, with or without faculty participation, are one fruitful manifestation of student resourcefulness. Another is the pleasurable use of the rich musical talent invariably present in a group of honors students, through organization of string quartets, recorder ensembles, madrigal singing, choruses, and folk music sessions.

To facilitate the creation and the development of such programs, it is usually desirable to set up a student committee to which the honors director and his staff give active support. Such a committee, in addition to acting as a clearinghouse for student-sponsored activities, can also serve as a valuable source of constructive criticism of the honors program itself. Joint meetings between honors students and the faculty engaged in honors teaching, advising, and administration can provide mutually profitable opportunities for analysis, explanation, and review.

Honors programs, realistically planned and effectively supported, are the most hopeful, promising means of reestablishing what is, after all, the primary and unique role of colleges and universities, namely, to provide students with the best education possible. The excellence of undergraduate education need not be compromised if each institution, especially the publicly supported university, is willing to reassess its program and to realign its values. The rising quality of the students it admits rightfully demands a high priority of imagination, resources, energy, and staff if teaching responsibilities are to be met successfully. Our bright, talented, eager young men and women expect intellectual engagement, a compelling challenge to reexamine their ideas and values, a deepening of their aesthetic sensibilities, and a vision of the exhilarating adventure of learning.

Chapter five / Honors

and the liberal arts

colleges / Walter D. Weir,

University of Colorado

IN 1900 about 4 percent of Americans between the ages of eighteen and twenty-one were attending college. In 1964 this figure was estimated at 50 percent. Our society has been sending more and more of its members to college in an attempt to realize the dream of providing equal opportunity for all and strengthening the democratic system by developing an educated electorate, and to meet the voracious appetites of the worlds of business, government, and education for men and women with skills that require a liberal arts college education.

At the same time, American universities have been shifting their primary emphasis from undergraduate liberal arts education to professional and graduate studies. The quality of liberal arts undergraduate education—particularly in the freshman and sophomore years—has suffered undeniably from this shift. To be sure, there have been countervailing trends, but the basic thrust has been toward development of what Clark Kerr, president of the University of California, has called the "multiversity." [1] Our most gifted under-

[1] See Clark Kerr, *The Uses of the University,* Cambridge, Mass.: Harvard University Press, 1963.

graduates have been the principal victims of this change of emphasis.

Honors programs in liberal arts colleges are a response to the phenomena of rising enrollments and the emergence of the multiversity. Swollen enrollments have brought a greater diversity of student ability, preparation, and motivation to the colleges. The rise of the multiversity has tended to produce, in President Kerr's words, a "cruel paradox" of a "superior faculty" with "an inferior concern for undergraduate teaching." Together, these two developments have created a crisis in those liberal arts colleges determined to give their best students the best liberal education possible. Honors programs were instituted in the hope that they might be a means of permitting the best students, at least, to participate in the real adventure of learning.

Of course, the basic problem is one of improving undergraduate liberal arts education for all students. But this will be an enormous and difficult task, one that has only just begun. In the meantime, our commitment to quality liberal arts education is visibly displayed in our honors programs. They can serve as testing grounds for new ideas and techniques and provide models for what might be done on a broader scale. They can become rallying points for the liberal arts colleges within the multiversity, helping them to reassert and strengthen themselves. And they can impart to the whole institution the liberal arts point of view, summed up by Montaigne's remark that "the object of education is not to make a scholar, but a man."

What kinds of honors programs are prevalent in liberal arts colleges now? What are some of their special problems? And how close do they come to fulfilling the role suggested above? This chapter attempts to suggest answers to some of these questions.

Today's liberal arts honors programs

Liberal arts honors programs today are as diverse as the hundreds of liberal arts colleges in this country. Each institution has necessarily built its program in the context of its own history and setting, its own faculty, student body, and administration. While there is no royal road to an all-purpose liberal arts honors program, the main paths taken by liberal arts colleges to meet the challenge of educating their best students can be mapped.

Following the traditional liberal arts practice of combining general education and specialization, four-year honors programs in many liberal arts colleges offer opportunities to honors students in both general studies and the field of specialization. While the usual pattern has been to emphasize honors in breadth during the freshman and sophomore years and honors in depth through specialization in the junior and senior years, many programs reflect an awareness that breadth and depth must characterize both studies in general education and work in the major field.

GENERAL HONORS PROGRAMS

If, in our age, a great specialist may be as ill-informed as a medieval peasant outside his particular field, it is partly because too much is known for any one man to know very much. The very words "sage" and "savant" sound almost archaic in our time. Nonetheless, it is the grave responsibility of liberal arts colleges and their general honors programs to find once again a rightful place for sagacity and wisdom on our campuses. We must all be specialists, but we must be willing to open doors, meet other specialists, and strive to become the best generalists we can. In order for this to happen, there must be a continuous dialogue among *and* between specialists on our campuses.

General honors programs have sought to achieve this dialogue by bringing together students from all disciplines, ideally throughout the four years of their college work. This cross-fertilization aids the student specialist insofar as it requires him to make the nature and significance of his specialty as clear as he can to those outside his discipline and allows him the opportunity to receive critical and sometimes imaginative insights on his specialty from highly perceptive peers. It also fosters a responsibility on the part of all the students to bring all the intelligence and knowledge they possess to bear upon problems of the whole man.

Offering special sections of regular introductory courses is an easy and relatively inexpensive way to meet the needs of the superior student, and this is therefore the most popular approach to general honors work in the freshman and sophomore years. Before the widespread adoption of four-year honors programs, most liberal arts colleges had special sections in mathematics, physics, chemistry, English, and foreign languages based on differences in student preparation for these subjects. With the honors movement came special sections in most introductory courses based on both preparation and ability, and an effort was made to place the best students in smaller classes taught by outstanding scholar-teachers. In many cases this new system of sectioning required a radical rethinking of the content and techniques to be used to realize the aims of liberal education. At least small classes made possible critical discussion of substantial reading and thorough review of the students' writings in these introductory courses.

The principal complaint against special honors sectioning comes from teachers who object that it drains the best students from other sections, making teaching the regular sections less interesting. Where special sectioning divides classes that are excessively large— and the trend in our colleges continues toward larger and larger classes—teachers must admit at least this benefit. And if regular sections are small enough to allow for some discussion on the part of the students, there is evidence to suggest that when superior students are removed another group of students assumes the leadership role, and often this group contains promising students who have not been recognized by the honors selection committee. However, it must be conceded that the teacher who uses the Socratic method and enjoys the give-and-take of discussion will usually find his honors section more intellectually stimulating than his regular section.

In addition to special sections of regular courses, most colleges now support general honors programs that offer a set of courses totally separate from departmental offerings. The University of Colorado, for example, has for many years presented thirty to thirty-five general honors courses to its honors students each semester. Limited to an enrollment of twelve, and ranging in subject matter from freshman courses in Introduction to Drama, Heritage of American Ideas, or The Concept of Energy to junior and senior courses in Shakespeare, The Tragic Vision, Existentialism, and The American Corporation, these courses are all part of a general honors program that seeks to broaden the vision of Colorado's superior students by placing them in honors courses outside their field of concentration. For example, seniors majoring in physics, anthropology, or economics explore in some depth a few of Shakespeare's plays and, hopefully, discover new dimensions of the human condition. Colorado students and teachers alike testify to the rewards of this conversation between specialists from many areas.

In other honors programs, such as that at Georgetown University, all honors students take a certain series of separate general honors courses, called a "core" honors program. At some universities, the core program has evolved into an honors college. The honors college at the University of Oregon is a "comprehensive, four-year program that endeavors to provide opportunity for the superior student to develop his potential in liberal education and specialized professional training. Its aim is to build within the university a select community of able and self-motivated students who actively engage in the independent pursuit of knowledge." [2] The University of the Pacific has established a small, independent honors college, Raymond College, which boasts its own faculty and residence halls. Such programs stress the development of a small community of honors scholars separate from and yet a part of the larger college and university community.

Occasionally this community within a community consists of a very small number of students who show most extraordinary potential. At Brooklyn College, for example, the Scholar's Program is available to about thirty entering freshmen of exceptional promise, whose ranks are augmented by a few additional students who demonstrate their scholarly caliber during the freshman year. (The regular Brooklyn honors program is a more flexible one open to many more students.) The Princeton University Scholar Program is "intended to provide a small group of especially qualified students with the maximum freedom in planning a program of studies that will fulfill their individual needs." [3]

Although not designed as a part of a general honors program

[2] Robert A. Ellis and Lucian Marquis, "Evaluation of the University of Oregon's Honors College," *The Superior Student,* Jan.–Feb., 1964.

[3] Richard D. Challener, "Princeton's University Scholars: A New Program for Outstanding Students," *The Superior Student,* Jan.–Feb., 1963. See the

and not restricted to freshmen of exceptional promise, the Harvard College Freshman Seminar Program, introduced in 1959, deserves mention here, for it reveals the importance of paying special attention to freshmen students and offers reinforcing evidence for the values of the seminar-conference-colloquium approach to learning. Over a thousand Harvard and Radcliffe freshmen students have participated in some 137 seminars, which have explored subject matter ranging from Prof. Oscar Handlin's "History of Liberty in the U.S." to the late Prof. Clyde Kluckhohn's "The Navajo Indian."

Many general honors programs now include interdisciplinary colloquia. The University of Colorado offers a four-year sequence of colloquia beginning with Greek Civilization and ending with the Contemporary Scene. Using the block-and-gap method, the colloquia take materials from history, literature, science, art, philosophy, and religion. Stress is placed on understanding the nature, problems, and spirit of past cultures and their relevance to the modern world.

The difficulties in conducting a successful colloquium are notorious. The brilliant, highly vocal student may antagonize his colleagues, monopolize the discussion, intimidate the shy and reticent, and bore himself as well as the other participants. The two or more faculty members assigned to guide and direct the discussion may prove inept in this capacity or dominate excessively, since it is easier to preach the overwhelming sermon than to ask the productive question. The line of thought in a two-hour discussion can easily become vague and tangled, a thread only superficially grasped.

But at its best the colloquium approach to learning stimulates

---

February, 1959, issue for a report on the Dartmouth Senior Fellows, and the December, 1959, issue for a summary of Yale's Scholars of the House Program.

students to read critically, to appreciate the joy of intelligent conversation, and to develop disciplined habits of expression. It asks them to explore the relationships of a given idea or set of ideas to other ideas, and to pursue the relevance of ideas to the world of values. Carefully directed colloquia can be useful instruments in the "complete and generous education" which, in Milton's view, "fits a man to perform justly, skillfully, and magnanimously all the offices both private and public of peace and war."

DEPARTMENTAL HONORS

I have emphasized general honors programs because they constitute the most revolutionary dimensions of the new honors movement and because, in my opinion, they represent a trend toward the strengthening of liberal arts education. It would, however, be a gross oversight to neglect the importance of sustained study of some well-defined area of knowledge to a "complete and generous education." Most liberal arts colleges have given their upper-class honors students a reasonable chance to explore in depth some limited area of knowledge by reviving and augmenting departmental honors programs. Through seminars, independent study, tutorials, and theses, departmental honors students are required to penetrate deeply a specific field of inquiry. Faculty mentors may guide them through the field, but the students must do their own plowing.

Unfortunately, students too often are asked to do their plowing while they are also expected to be sorting the fruits of four or five other courses. Students need to be given larger blocks of research time if they are to do really effective independent study. Brilliant student or no, the young scholar, like his teacher, will find it difficult to pursue independent research while he is preparing for many other courses. It is no accident that Ph.D. candidates normally write their theses after their course work is completed or that they often fail to finish their dissertations when they are teaching.

Even so, some research of merit has been accomplished by students in honors programs. At the University of Kansas outstanding honors students have been assisting senior members of the faculty in their work and have become real participants in the research effort. Amherst and Stanford have published meritorious essays by senior honors students. Students at the University of Colorado publish *Tangent,* a quarterly review devoted to creative and critical work of the students in the honors program. Prof. Harold Hantz reports of the work done by honors students at the University of Arkansas: "Some of the independent work has been clearly superior. There was the mathematics student who offered an outstanding paper on some proofs in topology as part of his Honors work.... There was the chemistry student who in her Honors research project contributed to the discovery of an isotope. The results of this work were published in the *Journal of Inorganic and Nuclear Chemistry.*" [4] This is but a sample of what can be done by honors students who are given the opportunity for research and independent study.

THE HONORS PROGRAM ABROAD

Honors programs can be enriched by giving students the opportunity to live in and study other cultures. America now sends hundreds of its college students abroad for a semester or a year. In some cases, the academic value of this experience is minimal. However, many colleges have developed overseas programs of some significance in connection with their honors programs. The Universities of Wisconsin and Michigan have sponsored a joint project to send

[4] Harold Hantz, "Observations on the Honors Program at the University of Arkansas," *The Superior Student,* Nov.–Dec., 1961.

forty to fifty honors students to France in their junior year. The program is open to "highly qualified undergraduates sufficiently competent in French to take full advantage of the regular educational offerings of a major French provincial university. Other criteria for selection include general academic excellence, maturity of educational purpose, and an appropriate field of interest." Dean James Robertson of the University of Michigan indicates the serious intent and high caliber of the Michigan program when he writes: "We are not interested in running a program which will be attractive and congenial to the casual dilettante, the dabbler in conversational French, the embryonic boulevardier."

Princeton University, in cooperation with Colgate, Columbia, Rutgers, and Swarthmore, sponsors a summer study program in Europe designed for the most able undergraduates of these colleges in the field of international affairs. The students prepare themselves during the spring semester for the summer in Europe. The entire group meets together in daily seminars for the first two weeks in Europe and then each student continues his study at a place previously determined as most appropriate to his concern. Whenever feasible, the student lives for one month with a host family. After two months the entire group reassembles for a final session of two weeks. Each student later writes a thesis in the field of his study.

The University of Kansas, in collaboration with the University of Costa Rica, offers a junior year in Costa Rica for exceptionally qualified students from the university of Kansas and other schools. Fordham University has long included a junior year in Paris as a possibility for its honors students. These are only a few of the many honors programs which include a year of serious study abroad as part of the opportunities made available to honors students.

Problem areas

Certain stubborn problem areas are common to many honors programs in liberal arts colleges. Questions frequently arise about grading in honors classes and granting honors awards at graduation, financing an honors program, obtaining and keeping faculty support for the program, and helping women students of honors caliber to overcome special obstacles to the achievement of their full potential.

GRADING AND GRANTING HONORS

There are two aspects to the problem of grading honors students. One involves the basic question of how valuable a measure of achievement grades really are. The second concerns how to ensure that honors students are not penalized because they choose to participate in honors programs that use grades as an indication of performance.

An increasing number of teachers admit that the best grade-getter is not always the most promising and creative student. It would appear that granting honors, or evaluating honors performance, on the basis of grades alone too often rewards the plodder, the memorizer, and the conformist. The point of an honors program is to encourage in students the "honors outlook" as opposed to pride in grades alone. If we are to develop in our students permanent habits of inquiry and critical thinking we must see to it that they find their reward in the learning process and not in the grade-point average. Perhaps one way to do this is to adopt the "pass-fail" system coupled with a carefully written analysis of each student's performance by his professor so that the honors director or council can evaluate the student's academic strengths and weaknesses and gauge the desirability of his remaining in the program. Another solution, that adopted by the Harvard Freshman Seminar, is to award no grades at all.

If grades are used, allowance must be made for the composition of the honors group being graded. Some professors grade honors courses as if they were regular courses containing the full range of student ability and motivation. When this is the case many bright students understandably steer clear of the honors program because they cannot afford to have grades appear on their records that do not truly indicate their rank in the educational institution as a whole. Until the conventional grading method now used across the country is revised, we must sympathize with the student who is concerned with how his grades will affect his future career. A necessary step in solving this problem is to get the faculty to recognize that students selected for honors would normally get an A or B in a regular class and that to establish new standards of grading (as distinct from new standards of expectation) is unfair to the student and is almost sure to undermine the program.

In spite of the rapid growth of honors programs in the past ten years, many colleges continue to award graduation honors on the basis of cumulative grade averages alone. Thus the student who manages to build a grade average of 3.75 or better automatically, in many cases, receives a *summa cum laude* citation whether he has participated in honors programs or not. Other institutions now grant honors recognition on the basis of successful completion of work in the honors program. Still others require something more than participation in the honors program.

An example of this last system can be found at the University of Colorado. Here a student must have participated in the honors program to become a candidate for honors, but he must also take comprehensive written and oral examinations. A faculty examining committee reads the written comprehensive, conducts the oral examination, and then makes a recommendation to the Honors Council. This latter group, representing all the departments of the college, reviews the recommendations of the examining committee along with the examination results, reports of faculty who have had the student in honors classes, grades, and any other materials that might be relevant to an assessment of his college work. The Honors Council then decides if he should receive honors and, if so, what degree of honors. It is interesting to observe that of the ninety students who take honors work in their senior year at Colorado only about sixty elect to take the examinations for a degree with honors, and of those, about forty-five are finally awarded honors degrees. At some institutions, as at Swarthmore, faculty members from other colleges are brought in to conduct the honors examinations.

Maintaining a separation between participation in honors and the receiving of an honors degree emphasizes the accumulation of knowledge and skills rather than of course credits, and it allows the insecure or examination-shy student to take advantage of honors work without fear of being subjected to a set of rather awesome examinations.

FINANCING THE PROGRAM

A liberal arts honors program, no matter how carefully conceived and flexible it is, will not last long unless the college administration is willing and able to give it adequate financial support. The chief item in an honors budget is faculty time. Honors counseling, courses, tutorials, and colloquia are expensive. Even the special honors sections of regular classes are likely to be far more expensive than other sections because they are smaller and involve the time of senior faculty members. (Professor Angell of the University of Michigan estimates that the annual cost per student in the honors program of the College of Arts and Letters is $165 more than the average instructional costs of $500 for nonhonors students.)

Most honors programs do not have a line budget for faculty time; they depend on departmental release of faculty to honors. Sympathetic department chairmen and/ or a wise dean can do much to provide the necessary manpower for the liberal arts honors program. Even so, staffing honors is a problem in most institutions. Large regular classes, research and publication obligations, and business, government, and community needs all vie with the honors program for faculty time. The problem becomes particularly acute in recruiting faculty for participation in general honors courses and colloquia. Even departments committed to broad liberal education and thus to general honors must consider the demands of the regular introductory courses in their disciplines, as well as courses for majors and graduates—demands which make it difficult, if not impossible, for them to siphon off faculty time into the general honors program. They may lodge a request for additional staff with their dean and he may pass the request to the university budget committee, but such requests are not often granted in full. The net result is a chronic understaffing. In the years ahead a continuation of this pattern may provide a serious threat to the growth of effective honors programs.

One answer may be the establishment of a special honors instructional line budget which would enable the honors program to reimburse departments for time released to the program. This would allow honors to count on faculty and departmental support and would give effective control of selection of honors faculty to the honors director and his council. Other partial solutions may lie in deliberately increasing our already large lecture courses so that the small honors classes can be supported, or in changing the frequency of class meetings. (An honest appraisal of this last possibility may reveal that we cling to the fifty-minute, three-hour-a-week course out of habit only, and that too much faculty time is spent in routine classroom instruction.) Or we may consider reducing the number of courses offered within the entire university, eliminating those that play no essential role in fulfilling educational objectives. A final possibility is to redirect some of the funds now spent on remedial work to honors programs.

GAINING FACULTY SUPPORT

An adequate honors budget does not in itself guarantee a successful liberal arts honors program. The viability of any academic program depends in the end on the understanding and support of the faculty.

Much has been written about those ladder-climbing, globe-trotting, and prestige-seeking professors who scramble noisily in the academic marketplace, and very little is said about the thousands of dedicated scholar-teachers who fill the majority of positions in our liberal arts colleges. To be sure, college teachers are not monastic saints willing to surrender the joys of this world for eventual recognition in paradise. Nor are they the paragons of reason and logic that they are sometimes fancied to be by awed undergraduates. They are subject to all the human frailties, not the least of which is pride. And yet, as an occupational group, they are probably more aware than most how much happiness depends on satisfaction in one's work. Most teachers enjoy teaching and are excited by their subject matter. If honors programs involve, as they do, an interaction between students and faculty who *both* enjoy ideas, inquiry, research, and discovery, most teachers will welcome the opportunity to teach in honors when they understand what is involved.

The first steps in gaining faculty support for an honors program, then, must be to explain the aims of honors to faculty and then to bring them into contact with honors students. Also necessary is to see that honors courses are not assigned on an overload basis, but are undertaken as part of the regular course load. And it is imperative that faculty participating in honors be recognized for their contributions and given appropriate promotions and salary increases.

REALIZING THE POTENTIAL OF TALENTED WOMEN

One of the most challenging problems facing the liberal arts college today is that of ensuring that its women students, particularly those of honors caliber, develop their talents to the full. Many of us are alarmed at the fact that so many talented women fail to realize their intellectual potential, for we have become increasingly aware of the consequences of failure for both the individuals involved and society. Honors teachers and directors are in an especially advantageous position to help gifted women students with this problem.

A survey of a national sample of graduating seniors conducted by the National Opinion Research Center in 1961 revealed the following: Even women who had participated in honors programs tended to be more conventional, conforming, and cautious than their male counterparts; though better grade-getters, women honors students felt less adequate in their field than the male honors students; about 65 percent of the women had received no psychological or vocational guidance in college; though they considered the guidance received from their parents as far more important than did the honors men, they agreed with the men that academic and faculty advising was important.

These findings suggest that faculty members engaged in honors programs should spend more time counseling their women students. Since honors students tend to trust in the advice of the faculty more than in that of professional counselors, our honors teachers need to become more familiar with the problems of women in our culture, to better understand the conflicts and concerns of their women students, and to know more about the life patterns available to women in our society today. They should then undertake to convey this knowledge to their honors students, both male and female, so that these students can more realistically appraise the problems women face today.

Honors teachers can attempt to reassure talented women students about their capacities and encourage them to be less cautious. Honors directors can try to get more faculty women who are models of both femininity and scholarship to teach in the honors program; they can establish honors courses dealing with the problems of women; they can bring their students in contact with women who have successfully combined marriage and career. If a liberal education means an education for the whole man, it also means an education for the whole woman.

Impact of honors on liberal arts colleges

It is still too early to say very much about the ultimate significance of the liberal arts honors movement. We shall have to strengthen our current honors programs much more before they can even be considered to have had a fair trial. Nonetheless, the data of educational researchers and the testimony of faculty and student participants in honors indicate that honors programs, in one form or another, are not only here to stay but are already making substantial contributions to liberal education.

W. J. McKeachie's survey of experimental studies in the procedures and techniques of teaching provides evidence to support the advocates of small conference classes. His summary of research findings shows "the superiority of lectures for information learning and of discussion for achieving higher level objectives." [5] The ends of a liberal arts education, these findings indicate, are best satisfied by a judicious combination of lecture, discussion, written work, and independent study. Insofar as we are attempting to develop in our students habits of critical thinking, self-exploration, concept formation, evaluation, and articulate oral and written expression, we will want to use the methods of honors.

But perhaps the single most important verification of the beneficial impact of honors programs has come from studies of the role of a peer group in student learning. Sanford reports that recent investigations "leave no doubt that what students learn in college is determined in very large measure by their fellow students, or, more precisely, by the norms of behavior, attitudes and values that prevail in the peer groups to which each student must belong." [6] We are just coming to realize the importance of the student culture in education. If faculty values are to influence students, they need, as Theodore Newcomb suggests, to be transmitted in some way to a student peer group. He writes:

[5] See W. J. McKeachie, "Procedures and Techniques of Teaching: A Survey of Experimental Studies," in Nevitt Sanford (ed.), *The American College,* New York: John Wiley & Sons, Inc., 1962.

[6] See Sanford's introduction to the section "Student Society and Student Culture," and Theodore Newcomb's "Student Peer-group Influence," in *The American College.* See also Newcomb's *The American College and Student Personality,* Social Science Research Council, New York, 1960. P. E. Jacob's *Changing Values in College,* New York: Harper & Row, Publishers, Incorporated, 1957, enlightened many of us and was responsible for many ensuing studies on the student population.

In the typical large university, it is hardly more than a chance occurrence if a set of students whose personal relationships are close find themselves simultaneously excited by the same lecture, the same book, or the same seminar, with resulting reverberations in their peer-group life, so that they reinforce and sustain one another's excitement. Such outcomes are predictably more likely if arrangements concerning college (or sub-college) membership, living-group membership, and classroom experience are so dovetailed that groups of individuals who are important to one another come to share many interests, including intellectual ones.

Honors programs tend to provide just such environmental conditions. They offer the framework for development of a peer group through the give-and-take of small classes and through a core program which usually expands classroom contacts into social contacts out of class. An Arizona State College student expressed the importance of contacts with other honors students this way:

> To be an intellectually curious undergraduate in a small, isolated, state-supported college sometimes can be a very lonely affair, and oddly enough, those who are interested in matters of the mind frequently never meet each other. An honors class, because of its very orientation and physical makeup, tends to bring such people together. They begin by discussing outside reading in class and soon find they are gathering together in groups outside of the classroom.

Formation of an honors peer group can also make possible the contact between faculty and student groups that Newcomb indicates is necessary if we are to see a greater influence of the faculty liberal arts culture upon the student body at large. Honors students usually have much more contact with the faculty than other students; at the same time they tend to play leadership roles on campus. The leadership influence of students in the honors program, however, is possible only as long as they are not too cut off from the student body at large. Thus it is important to provide an environment that makes for formation of a real honors peer group but does not prevent that peer group from interacting enough with other groups on the campus so that its members may still play major campus roles.

Most honors programs can do more than they are now doing to increase the students' sense of identification with an honors peer group. Honors classes, particularly those in large state universities where many different student subcultures compete for the student's allegiance, cannot alone create peer groups of the kind needed. Some colleges are now realizing the advantages of establishing "honors centers" as a way of solidifying such peer groups. In these centers students discuss, argue, and meet other honors students, as well as study.

We can best judge the impact of honors programs from what honors students themselves say about them. A group of these students from colleges all over the country meeting at the 1960 ICSS Western Invitational Conference at Berkeley summarized the benefits they received from participating in honors programs as follows: the opportunity for direct contact with enthusiastic, exciting, and dedicated teachers; the excitement of doing research and working with professors; the sense of being treated as scholars by their instructors; the relief from ordinary routines and requirements; the interdisciplinary character of honors courses leading them to broader intellectual horizons; the rigorous examination of assumptions and generally held values; contacts with other able and questioning students in small classes; and the constant challenge from both teachers and fellow students to do their best work.

The planks of this student summary might well constitute a manifesto on the goals of a liberal education. Those who have pronounced the liberal arts dead may want to test its pulse again; if honors can confer these benefits upon young scholars, the liberal arts are still very much alive within our multiversities, and our best talent is not being neglected.

Chapter six / Honors and

the university / Dudley Wynn,

University of New Mexico

THE PURPOSE of this chapter is to attempt a survey of institutionwide honors programs in some institutions of higher education in the United States, to discuss some specific features of these programs, and to point out the ways in which all-university programs in comprehensive institutions can contribute to educational effectiveness. Previous chapters of this book have established the necessity for particular concern with the unusually talented and able student: to keep him from getting bored and indifferent; to challenge him to increased effort; to lead him to acquire a healthy appetite for knowledge and facts and their subsequent use in evaluation and judgment; to encourage him to look for correlations and strive for some degree of originality and audacity in his thinking. There is no reason to repeat here all the good and acceptable reasons for almost any honors program, regardless of the modesty of its aims or which unusual corner of a university it appears in.

Nor is it necessary any longer to apologize for the cost of honors programs, for all of us have always known that good education is expensive education, that somewhere along the line there ought to be the kind of student-teacher ratio that permits the teacher to look and see if the student is really developing, growing, learning to be critical, acute, and self-impelled.

Another basic consideration that recent experience with honors programs seems to have taught us is that a program should not be merely a device to increase prestige or to enable us to do a little better what we have been doing, but rather should grow out of a recognized need to shift educational perspective. An honors program should be carried on, if possible, in an aura of experimentation and excitement and new expectations. Good honors programs have behind them the conviction of teachers that it is time to look at the product and to ask ourselves if we cannot pay more attention to what at least the very able students really believe in and what they really know about the world and the society they live in—about modern technology and the science behind it; about what science can legitimately profess and what its limitations are; about the legitimate claim that the humanities can make for the attention of the person and the citizen.[1]

Can the science major tell you anything coherent or relevant about the scientific tradition, the scientific method, the place of science in modern culture? Can the humanities major give an engineering or pharmacy student a convincing, historically oriented, critically sound reason why any potential C. P. Snow or Buckminster Fuller should pay the slightest attention to William Butler Yeats, Bernard Shaw, Tolstoy, or D. H. Lawrence? What kind of aesthet-

[1] "... The motive to study is inevitably lacking in at least three out of four classes when so conducted, that is, when the listener is not addressed as a person or a citizen, but only as that dreadful model of our age: the useful member of society who must be clothed in qualifications and armed with licenses to practice."—Jacques Barzun, *Intercollegiate Press Bulletin,* March 16, 1964, p. 166. Without sharing *all* of Professor Barzun's aversion to professionalism and our times, one can—and I shall—make use of his felicitous phrase: "[the student] addressed as a person or a citizen."

ics does the fine arts major profess? Is the pharmacy graduate an educated man, or is he just a yarn swapper destined to go out and sell pharmaceuticals? Can the social science major defend or justify his discipline on any but either the most utilitarian or the most sentimentally humanitarian grounds? Does any of these know enough of principles, aims, excellences in the other disciplines? Since four years is not a very long time, does any of these have any desire to start or to continue learning something of the other disciplines? Has his formal education, even when continued beyond the baccalaureate, equipped or motivated him to continue his education?

When a few teachers start asking themselves questions like these, they know that they have to start paying attention to *students,* to students writing, students talking, students living in noisy madhouses known as dormitories, students making decisions between going out for "contacts" and going out for intellectual growth and self-realization. And when a few teachers on a campus do ask such questions as well as the completely respectable academic question, that is, how they can better fulfill their academic, scholarly obligation to intellectually superior young people, then there is soil for an honors program to flourish in.

This simple concern that the elaborate system of education really educate, that the mind be engaged, was stated very aptly by Prof. Joseph W. Cohen in an address to the Association for General and Liberal Studies in October, 1963, in Chicago. Professor Cohen said:

> I choose the example with which I am most familiar, my own institution, the University of Colorado. I think it was at the time typical enough of all that both our movements seek to mend. I go back to my earliest impressions, as a young instructor of philosophy

from the University of Toronto in Canada, of the students as a whole, but particularly of those who were graduating with the honors award for high grade averages. I recall my shock, naïve perhaps, with how little they really knew, responded to, or could command even in their own fields for all their courses and high grades; how bleak their awareness of historical, theoretical, social, imaginative or value perspectives germane to the beginning stamp of an educated person; the absence of a sense of connections or of the power orally to cope with the setting of what they did know. It was clear how the pedantry of encapsulated facts had too long ruled the educational roost.

My curiosity as to causes led me to explore on my own the Dean's cards of many such students. I wanted to discover the prevailing patterns of their schedules, to estimate the time they spent in basic requirements and electives and in the major fields. I began to realize the degree of haphazardry in the former and of over-emphasis in many of the latter, and the general imbalance between them. But I noted above all the absence of an adequate reigning concern with the quality of the total outcome—an absence due, I felt, to routine counseling, the dominating criteria of grades in separate courses, and strictly departmental competence.

I suppose we might say that if there truly has been a resurgence of interest in the state of the mind and culture of graduating students, particularly the abler ones, it could be attributed to a kind of *appallment*—appallment of the teacher at his own failures; appallment of the student at how little has been expected of him and how little responsibility has been put upon him for his education; appallment of the educated public at the limited and partial carry-over from formal education into everyday, actual life.

At the risk of repetition, I wish to affirm my faith that, however desirable it may be that large multipurpose institutions have what I shall call an all-out, all-university honors program, the more important thing is the spirit prompting any efforts, even partial ones, that appear to be succeeding. This chapter, by the nature of its topic, will have to deal with methods, devices, procedures, formalized programs, machinery; and I wish simply not to lose sight of the fact that the dedication of teachers to the problem of increasing breadth *and* depth in good students is more important than machinery, more significant than any paper comprehensiveness or fullness of program. Intellectual climate, not a beautiful synthetic scheme, is what is important. A good honors *program* seeks to deprogrammize the student's education and to resist constantly its own tendency to formalize and blandly institutionalize itself.

The university honors program

An ideal honors program in a large, multipurpose institution, in my view, would seek to increase significantly the depth and breadth of the education of a certain percentage of the abler and more apt students who are capable of responding and persisting. It would also have as a purpose the supplying of some kind of intellectual, educational core or center to the institution's multiple purposes. It would, in short, have a departmental honors program available to undergraduate students following any of its major curricula. In at least the larger undergraduate professional colleges (agriculture, business, education, engineering, fine arts, health sciences, etc.) there would be all-college, interdepartmental honors colloquia and seminars as well as honors sections of basic professional offerings. Use would be made of some or all of the familiar devices of departmental honors: independent study, summer reading, senior thesis, tutorials, research apprenticeships. Centered in the college of arts, letters, and sciences, but not directed or staffed exclusively by that college, would be a *general* honors program extending through four undergraduate years. Honors candidates in all colleges of the university not only would be eligible for enrollment in this *general* honors program; they would be strongly urged to enroll in it, even required to do so. Professional colleges should be prepared also to make their contribution of ideas and of staff to the *general* program.

Depth *and* breadth; a strong complement of *departmental* or disciplinary honors programs; a *general* honors program that would throw students from all areas together for a significant part of their time in the four undergraduate years for the purpose of focusing their attention upon matters that concern them as *persons* and as *citizens*. Concentration-distribution; specialization-general education —there's nothing very new here except that we are rethinking the educational problem in terms of the unusually able and at the same time hoping for some new intellectual energy that might spill over to the whole process.

It is probably a great deal easier to serve depth than breadth. Learning *is* departmentalized, and as it increases it will probably become more so. The aims of a departmental, disciplinary, or professional college honors program are clearer, the staff are more of one mind, the students are more definitely committed to the subject matter offered them. I would go so far as to say that in the areas of specialization, of training in techniques and technologies, the American university system is succeeding much better than at the level of general education. We are probably turning out the world's best lawyers, physicians, engineers, scientific researchers (insofar as their technical competence is concerned); but somehow the tone of the enterprise, the tone of our national life, is not what we could wish.

We seem to have lost the capacity for overview. Multiplicity and pluralism are, on one side, healthful and vital; but on the other side there are distraction, unfulfillment, frustration from lack of any central aim or view.

Because it is more difficult to serve breadth than depth (this is, of course, ultimately, a false dichotomy), because good departmental honors programs are probably more likely to spring up spontaneously and find their aims naturally, achieving a proper balance requires strong emphasis upon *general* programs.

A *general* honors program can and ought to make use of all the resources of the university. This is not easy, but it is not impossible. In a state university no larger than New Mexico we have frequently offered a sophomore general honors seminar in Legal Concepts, taught by members of the law school and not open to students who intend to major in the social sciences or go into the study of law. This offering has been popular. It has the reputation of being extremely difficult and highly valuable—an eye opener, the students call it. There is no textbook; not even paperbacks are used; the staff prepared their own materials, which run to nearly 800 pages mimeographed.

We once had a sophomore general honors seminar in Science Fiction, taught by an electrical engineer and not open to engineers or science majors. A professor of art has given a sophomore seminar in How to Look at a Painting. The professor of physiology in the recently established school of medicine will be giving a sophomore seminar in Some Landmarks in the Development of Scientific Thought. Members of the faculty of the colleges of education, engineering, fine arts, law, and medicine have participated in one way or another in the general honors work of the freshman, sophomore, and junior years, often as instructors in various sections of the freshman colloquium.

Getting this kind of participation by busy faculty members from a variety of colleges is not easy, as I said. But there are devices that help make it possible. Sometimes a man simply relinquishes one of his specialized courses for a semester in order to teach in general honors. Sometimes out of the general honors budget we are able to supply a man with an extra research assistant or extra help for paper grading in his large-enrollment courses; or in certain instances where a competent off-campus replacement is available we pay for a temporary replacement. Rarely, an off-campus person is given a temporary part-time appointment to work in an honors colloquium or seminar, usually in cooperation with a regular full-time staff member. Lest someone get the idea, however, that our path is made easy by an abundance of ready funds, I should add that our honors budget provides less than $5,000 a year for this purpose. It is obvious that we have to rely mainly on time released by departments for our purposes, since no general honors offering is made by way of overload on the instructor. And since there probably never has been such a thing in academic life as an overstaffed department, it is obvious that honors does not always get what it wants when it wants it or needs it. Perpetual beggarly improvisation is the only answer— but a remarkable advantage is that it keeps people stirred up and honors-conscious all the time, and it keeps the director of general honors constantly in search of appropriate staff with good new ideas.

The idea that the staff for a *general* honors program can be drawn from a variety of areas within the university will probably not disturb as many people as the thought that it enrolls students with a variety of specialized interests, with the result that there is no common specialized knowledge from which to start and that therefore everything has to be off-the-cuff, glib, thin, and general. It is not the purpose of this chapter to answer this objection, but it must be glanced at. Excluding courses in science, mathematics, and certain highly technical fields (engineering, pharmacy, accounting, and the like) where there is an obvious, step-by-step progression from the simpler to the more complex, in what *regular* courses does any conscientious teacher ever escape the annoying awareness that he is always having to start from scratch, that the necessary common background for any of his courses cannot be presumed but must be provided within the purview of the particular course? This problem, it is true, may be slightly greater in a general honors offering, but the differences are not very great, and there are compensations:

1. Able students can orient themselves quite rapidly.

2. Because the class is small, dialogue can be maintained, values and assumptions probed and tested.

3. The disciplining power of practice in writing and oral expression can be brought into play more often and more thoroughly.

4. The big general questions *are* important, are at the root of liberal education, and liberal education is good for anybody if we have the time and the money for it.

5. There are some pleasant and also some unpleasant but valuable surprises in store for any teacher who temporarily gives up an advanced course in his field, where he is addressing the already committed and sometimes the sycophantic, and takes on a general honors course, where there will be give-and-take between himself and the uncommitted, the hard-to-convince, the pragmatic but apt

and nimble young mind whose presence in the class is contrary to its present convictions.

This can mean that some fundamental and sometimes disarming questions have to be faced. Instance: a young premedic, intent upon hanging up an "A" record in as much biology, chemistry, and mathematics as she could cram into her program, ambitious, strongly motivated, career-oriented, tough-minded, frankly and vigorously pragmatic, and with a 3.77 average as a freshman honors student, was put against her will into a sophomore seminar (How to Look at a Painting) reluctantly undertaken by a man who, because of administrative duties, had not taught a lower-division course in recent years. That instructor frankly admits that this student and more of her kind (she was not the most aggressively hostile) gave him a bad time for a part of the semester. But here is the unsolicited and unexpected testimonial she sent to the director of honors after the grades were in:

> I have noticed several signs of doubt concerning the value of the Sophomore art seminar, both among the students and those in charge. The thought that this class might not be tried again distresses me, because it was an experience which enriched my life more than any other class I have had at the University. I had never discovered a whole world which can offer the difference between "just living" and "life." Of course I am not referring just to art, but to the Arts or Humanities.
>
> I am afraid that many science majors are in the same boat I was in, and will resist attempts to help them see this as I did. The very fact that a person enjoys the clean, useful logic of science implies that he may scorn the Arts, but it doesn't mean he has to. I know that [the instructor] was frustrated with us, because he didn't quite realize what he was up against at first. Instead of discussing

what the various values of art are, he had to first convince most of us that art has value. Naturally this is sometimes impossible, but if it can happen to only one or two students, a great deal of effort will be well justified. I think [the instructor] did a very difficult job well, and I wish I had some way to thank him (and the Honors program) for what he has given me.

I believe that studying one of the fine arts will help students like me more than the study of literature or other more direct humanities (which are more easily accepted), but, whatever the humanities section may be please don't allow students to get around it. I took the art seminar "against my will," and I found that this former attitude of mine is quite common. I hope that no one will be too discouraged by student resistance, and specifically that [the instructor] wasn't discouraged by his class last semester. I hope that what he has to offer will be made available to many, many more students.

To many teachers, I am sure, this kind of experience gives equal reward with that of sending one of one's own kind farther along in one's own field.

Another great advantage of a *general* honors program is that it can conceivably provide some kind of center to a large institution's "multiple purposes." It is an important question how far an institution can go in multiple purposes, in serving almost everybody's wishes—mortuary science, cosmetology, etc.—and still keep as a central purpose the general or liberal education of persons and citizens. Probably a majority of academicians gave up on this problem long ago and have resigned themselves to tolerating almost anything under the big tent as long as they are free to pursue their specialty and recruit apprentices. Nevertheless, a kind of moral stubbornness afflicts us all, and we get resurgences of the philosopher's desire for unity, coherence, and centrality. The moment you wonder how it would be to spend a week shipwrecked on a small island with only a Bachelor of Mortuary Science for a companion, you begin to ask yourself what you think the intellectual experience and the formal education of B.M.S.'s, bachelors of chemical engineering, bachelors of arts who are going to teach English in high school, M.D.'s, LL.B.'s, etc., etc., should be. What do they need to know in common as "persons and citizens" in addition to, and as a basis for, their skills and their professional ministrations? The question keeps cropping up, and we get an occasional Meiklejohn or Aydelotte or Hutchins or Reed College, as Mr. Cohen points out in Chapter 2 of this book. We get general education movements, often abortive; we hear speech after speech about the decline of liberal education, accompanied by increasing emphasis upon the technical and the technological; large state universities (Illinois, for example) establish divisions of general studies, hoping to provide thereby a semblance of curricular core for the thousands of students interested in the many specialties and vocational branches.

But even in the midst of increasing pluralism, vocationalism, and professionalism, there lingers the hope that for more than a mere elite there should be education that goes beyond training, that is basic, liberalizing, that has to do with man's concern for his role as person and citizen. But this hope is often combined with a considerable skepticism that neither snippets of graduation requirements nor specially devised general basic courses (all to be gorged down and gotten out of the way in the first two college years) provide what is wanted. General honors offerings are not the perfect or complete answer, but properly devised and carried out through the four years of an undergraduate's life, they at least throw attention back to where it belongs: Some teachers assume a kind of responsibility for the able student's having been faced with some of the questions relevant to him as person and citizen. And if it is possible for a modern large university to become again a "community of scholars," what can contribute more effectively than a deliberate enterprise in which teachers in the liberal arts and in professional schools try to explain and justify themselves to one another and to students in various fields? When and how are we going to bridge the "two cultures" if we do not put articulate students of science and technology to arguing with equally able students of literature and art? The dialogue has got to be started, and the university campus is the place to start it.

Within the last year I have witnessed the following reciprocity as the result of a general honors program: Junior honors students— majoring in such diverse fields as anthropology, biology, English, political science, and journalism—taking a seminar in architecture under a professor of architecture had their eyes opened to the fact that architecture is more than drawing house plans and has to do with slums and poverty and mass housing and highways and planning and aesthetics and the inevitable problems of political consent to the taking of socially desirable action; and the senior colloquium, taking a project that involved Henry Adams and Allan Temko on French cathedrals and that moved on into *Communitas* by the Goodmans and *Slums and Social Insecurity* by Alvin Schorr and books by Jane Jacobs and Lewis Mumford, found it possible to bring Allan Temko and Nathan Glazer to the campus for two days with a resulting stimulus to the department of architecture that it admits it had not had in many a day. Through this reciprocity, liberal arts majors got insights from a professional department, and that department picked up something decidedly valuable to itself out of the somewhat innocent and impractical academicism of the two English instructors who were teaching the senior honors colloquium. There is now a strong chance that all this will spill over from the campus into the community. Interdepartmentalism, cross-fertilization don't just happen; they have to be worked at. But the best result of all is that, where something is going on, where some instructors are resolved that students shall somehow be intellectually engaged, and where departmental members are willing to start from scratch with intellectually alert students, interesting and valuable things happen—serendipities, I believe they are called today.

I will not argue that a general honors program will suddenly and miraculously turn a large, amorphous, multipurpose university into a kind of Swarthmore or Reed with an intense, central liberal-educational purpose. But it is a good beginning. If you can cause some liberal arts students to see the *rationale* of a profession, if you can cause a student in an undergraduate professional college to recognize some of his social responsibilities and some of the gaps in his cultural equipment, if you can get staff members of all sorts interested again in missionary work among very receptive "natives," you have made some kind of start.

By way of summary: An ideal honors program in a large, multipurpose institution would offer *departmental* (or college or divisional) honors work to qualified undergraduate students in every major curriculum for at least the junior and senior years; and it would offer a *general* honors program of four years' duration to qualified students in every division of the university; and this *general* honors program, while having liberal or general education as its major aim, would make use of the resources of the *whole* university and would make an effort to serve as a kind of fructifying intellectual center for the university community. Equal stress on the importance of both kinds of program—departmental and general—would be about right; but the spirit behind a going program, even if it is only a partial program by our ideal standard, is infinitely more important than mere completeness in a prospectus. Kansas and Michigan, for instance, with spirited and effective departmental honors programs, give less attention to general honors as I have described it here. Colorado has a strong general program, and does not so strongly or universally emphasize the departmental. All three, by present standards, have the reputation of being strong programs.

Honors in the multipurpose institution today

Having discussed some of the characteristics of what might be an ideal honors program for a large, multipurpose public university, let us examine the nature of programs actually in operation throughout the country. This is more difficult than it appears, because the devices and procedures used and the stages of development at different institutions are so varied. To try to get something of an accurate picture, the rest of this chapter will summarize and comment on replies to a survey of honors programs in multipurpose institutions, review very briefly some honors efforts that extend beyond the liberal arts college, and describe some arbitrarily selected programs in enough detail to get from them whatever valuable lessons, pointers, or suggestions they seem to offer.

SURVEY FINDINGS

The survey was made by sending a questionnaire to the director of the honors program at the sixty-one institutions listed in the ICSS inventory of institutions having programs extending beyond the liberal arts college as of April, 1964. Forty-five directors answered, but seven said their programs were not all-university. Survey findings, therefore, are based on replies of thirty-eight institutions. These are mostly state universities, ranging in size from the very large (Illinois, Michigan, Michigan State, Washington) through medium size (Arkansas, Kentucky, Tennessee) down to the relatively small (Hawaii, Nevada, New Mexico). All have one or more undergraduate professional colleges.

The questionnaire [2] was aimed at obtaining as precise an answer as possible to two questions: (1) Has your institution accepted and tried to foster an "honors philosophy"? (2) To what extent has an honors philosophy been implemented throughout the institution? It also included a general evaluation question intended to find out what directors of programs felt about the impact of these programs on students, faculty, administration, and the public regardless of institutional philosophy or degree of commitment.

Answers to the first question were for the most part very encouraging. For example, the honors philosophy as conceived of in this chapter implies acceptance of certain principles, among which are that an honors student's performance should be judged on other bases than the grades he earns in a collection of separate courses, and the quality of the education of honors students in any division of the university should be the business of faculty of all divisions, who should establish and apply universitywide standards. Questions about program policies and features in the questionnaire measured to what extent these basic principles were accepted. The answers were quite gratifying. In a majority of the institutions "the ability and performance of students ... is formally judged by representa-

[2] I am extremely grateful to Prof. R. D. Cuzzort, research associate in the ICSS office, for his very valuable help in preparing and interpreting the questionnaire. He deserves credit for its merits; I deserve all the blame for its many shortcomings.

tives from outside as well as inside the student's specialty." Likewise, a large majority answered that "requirements for graduation with honors are determined by the university as a whole rather than by specific schools and colleges." Also, a solid majority denied that their programs were a collection of autonomous college or divisional programs. In these respects these institutions have accepted the idea of honors as *more than* (not opposed to) a departmental or college concern.

To which students in the university is honors work open? Thirty-four out of thirty-seven replying to this question said that "the honors program is open to students from all or most of the undergraduate colleges and divisions"—although it is impossible to tell whether this meant departmental or general honors. A large majority have "special honors program course offerings"; in other words, honors is not an extra burden placed upon instructors, but instead there is a formalized program of courses for honors students. This indicates that a large majority of the institutions are committed in some degree to *implementing* the honors idea, even though some still rely heavily or exclusively on honors sections of regular courses.

Another important component of the honors philosophy is that the honors program in a large university should involve, in addition to departmental work alone in the junior and senior years, an effort to improve the general education of students in the undergraduate professional schools by extending the honors program into the earlier years. To discover if this principle was being accepted, the questionnaire asked if honors in the professional colleges was being used only to intensify professional training, or if it was also being used to extend and improve the student's capacities as person and citizen.

The replies to this question were divided about equally. Nine directors said their honors programs were used to intensify professional training only, eight said theirs were aimed at general education, nine said they had both kinds of programs, and six said they did not wish to generalize on the point. In short, in these institutions (and even more so in the many institutions that do not claim an all-university program) the purpose of an honors program is still in question. There is, as yet, among institutions in general no consistent dedication to the idea that honors must serve to improve a student's general as well as his specialized education. However, as many institutions (approximately) respect both aims as respect only one or the other, and this, no doubt, represents a tremendous gain in recent years.

Basic to the honors philosophy is the concept of interdepartmentalism. Interdepartmental offerings should allow the student to see beyond his particular discipline, exploring its relationships with other disciplines and its place in his scheme of things. Such a program should generate a drive toward the introduction of interdisciplinary courses in which the attempt to discover unifying or integrating concepts will play an important part. Additionally involved in the interdisciplinary concept, if only by implication, is the idea that since the approach is nonprofessional (at least in many circumstances it should be), the material may be offered to students with heterogeneous specialized backgrounds—i.e., students from a variety of disciplines can be thrown together into seminars and colloquia where problems that relate to them as persons and citizens can be presented, discussed, and argued.

In an attempt to see if this feature of the honors philosophy was taking hold in the institutions, we asked whether or not the director felt that the honors program in his institution was "characterized by constant effort to provide interdisciplinary offerings." Twenty-four said yes, six said no, five were uncertain, three did not reply. Apparently, then, in a large majority of the thirty-eight institutions the interdisciplinary concept is alive. Seeking then to distinguish between interdisciplinary offerings in allied fields (as in history, literature, philosophy) and in disparate fields (as when a teacher of the history of science and a teacher of the history of art give a course together), we asked: "Would you say that your program encourages allied or disparate interdisciplinary offerings *for the most part?*" Eleven said "allied," none said "disparate," twenty-two said "some of both," five said they had "no interdisciplinary offerings," none was uncertain, and none failed to reply. Since this is the type of question that any director would answer cautiously, the eleven who said "allied" and the twenty-two who said "some of both" add up to a rather remarkable majority of institutions in which the interdisciplinary concept in its more modest phase is no longer radical or unacceptable. (The answers, however, came from directors of programs who may be a few jumps ahead of many of their colleagues—they are all familiar with ICSS thinking. Even so, enough of their colleagues must see eye to eye with them to get *something* started, as their answers to the question about "constant effort to provide interdisciplinary offerings" show.) The acceptance of the honors philosophy appears to mean acceptance of the interdisciplinary concept, and in a few instances acceptance on its "wilder" ("disparate") side.

To the open-ended question "Which single feature of your honors program has been found, in your opinion, to be most successful?" the most frequent reply by far was colloquia and seminars of the more or less general type, i.e., enrolling students from a variety of disciplines. Equally gratifying was the second most frequent reply: junior-senior departmental seminars. Again we must remember that these answers come from directors of programs who presumably have been reading the party line in the ICSS newsletter. But they are not saying that general honors colloquia and seminars are *theoretically* fine and indispensable; they are saying that these are the most successful features of their going programs *now.*

The questionnaire asked only for a rough evaluation by directors of the impact of their programs. But their responses are interesting and, I believe, valuable. Directors of programs very strongly agreed that their programs have given honors students increased opportunity to write and to discuss ideas and have brought them into much closer contact with teachers. (These benefits are tangible and are rated high.) They agreed less strongly (but still strongly) that their programs have helped increase student dedication to intellectual activity; have promoted intellectual contacts between colleges and divisions of the university; have helped students in professional schools get a better liberal education; have improved the status of the university within the community, state, or nation (but thirteen are uncertain on this proposition and eleven disagree); and have played a significant role in promoting concern for improved educational standards on the campus. These accomplishments, if true, are very great indeed, and directors of programs, being human, should not be expected to be any more disinterested in their replies to such questions than anyone else in a similar situation would be. And yet they do not appear to be restrained in making critical responses where they feel these are justified. They are, on the whole, not averse to admitting that students who have succeeded in the honors program would have succeeded anyway, that the honors program may have promoted some undue grade consciousness, and that honors may have professed integration without achieving it. They are highly uncertain whether honors has improved the quality of majors and specialists throughout the university. None of these more or

graduate) are enrolled in the liberal arts college during their first two years at least and sometimes longer, and admitting further the possibility that many students who select honors work (when offered the opportunity) are also those who select the liberal arts college in preference to an undergraduate professional college, this is still an enormous disparity. The table does not show whether pro-

Table 1   Honors enrollment and honors graduates, liberal arts colleges versus all other undergraduate colleges, total of eighteen selected universities *

	Total enrollment,† semester 1 or quarter I, 1962–1963	Enrollment in honors programs, semester 1 or quarter I, 1962–1963	Honors program graduates, June, 1963
All colleges of liberal arts	75,073	4,308, or 5.8% of total	513, or 0.68% of total
All other undergraduate colleges	97,983	1,590, or 1.6% of total	236, or 0.24% of total

* Arkansas, Brigham Young, Colorado, Denver, Hawaii, Illinois, Kansas, Kent State, Kentucky, Massachusetts, Miami, Michigan, Michigan State, Ohio (Athens), Oregon, Texas Christian, Utah, and Wichita. Some of these have reputedly excellent programs, and many have large enrollments.

† The questionnaire asked for total enrollments in FTE (full-time equivalent), but some institutions clearly gave us a head count. However, assuming that each institution counted the liberal arts enrollment and the enrollment in all the other undergraduate colleges in the same manner, using the total figures to derive percentages should produce valid data, even though as absolute quantities these figures are quite undependable.

fessional students fail to participate because of a lack of departmental or disciplinary programs within their colleges or because they have no access to *general* honors work within their institutions. It is fairly obvious, I believe, that *both* reasons apply. At Michigan, for example, the undergraduate professional student has no honors program open to him in his junior and senior years unless he is in music or liberal arts. Nor will he have access to very much *general* honors work, for Michigan's upper-division offerings in honors, like those in many other institutions, are pretty largely departmental.

This general lag in the development of honors work for, or acceptance of the honors opportunity by, professional college students is, with its implications, the most unpalatable aspect of the whole honors picture. It forces us to face the basic problem in honors, which is, after all, very much the problem of general or liberal education. Most undergraduate professional schools do not encourage or permit time for their students to take a detour from their professional work, and most of the students are unduly modest about their ability to hold their own in the give-and-take of colloquia and seminars. And yet their knowledge and their values could be made important ingredients in any balanced view of modern society and the application of intelligence to its needs.

Answers to other parts of the questionnaire supplied additional evidence of this lag. To the proposition that the honors program has a disproportionate number of people drawn from the arts and science faculty, directors replied: yes, twenty-two; no, twelve; uncertain, three; no reply, one. Since those answering were largely arts and science people themselves, no strong personal or professional bias can be said to be at work here. Of more significance is the fact that, to the open-ended question What single feature of their program had directors found least successful? the most frequent reply was failure of professional colleges to develop programs. (The second most frequent reply was honors sections of multiple-section regular courses. And this is the kind of honors work that freshman-sophomore professional students, although they may be technically enrolled in the liberal arts colleges, have the most opportunity to engage in.) In all the large public-supported institutions in the country as a whole, at least one-half of the undergraduate students and probably at least one-fourth to one-third of the highly able ones are enrolled in professional colleges. To realize that only 1.6 percent (approximately) of these students are participating in honors tempers any assumption that there is nothing more to do on the honors front. We are doing much better than we used to, but we are not yet doing well enough.

PROGRESS TOWARD HONORS IN PROFESSIONAL COLLEGES

We asserted at the beginning of this discussion that we were more interested in any signs of originality and enterprise than in statistical compilations or fine prospectuses. The fact is that although the survey findings indicate that the amount of honors available to and participated in by liberal arts students far outweighs that in professional colleges, there are many places in which able students in undergraduate professional colleges are getting honors work in their specialties, in general studies, or in both. There is not space to go into all of these in detail, but our emphasis would be completely warped if we did not call attention to some of them.

For example, Washington State has a rather fully developed program, which emphasizes liberal or general education in the first two years. A substantial component of the honors students are from engineering, pharmacy, home economics, veterinary medicine, and other professional colleges, and there are "departmental" junior-senior programs in many of the professional areas. "As each year goes by, the number of professional students participating in the program has shown a steady increase," the director reports. Illinois (discussed in more detail below) has made an amazing achievement in the development of specialized or departmental honors work in a large number of the undergraduate professional colleges. The program in the college of agriculture, for example, is notable for the interdisciplinary emphasis revealed in the list of general seminars offered: on the agricultural resources of the world—the use made of them, their potential development; on the contributions made to agriculture and related sciences by certain great men; on the application of science to feeding, clothing, and sheltering large populations; on the impact of social, moral, and political issues on the family; on American literature and the rural scene; on the role of agriculture in our agricultural-industrial-service economy.

Lehigh has a full departmental type of program in all three of its colleges (arts and sciences, business, and engineering) and also an interdepartmental honors program. The departmental program for many years has offered courses in "readings" or "problems" for superior students on a project, seminar, or independent-study basis, all augmented by devices for acceleration, independent but closely supervised research, and a senior thesis. The interdepartmental honors program makes use of limited-enrollment seminars (called creative concepts seminars) in the four major areas of life sciences, natural and physical sciences, social sciences, and humanities. To graduate with interdepartmental honors a student must successfully complete three of the four creative concepts seminars, write an acceptable thesis, and pass his senior comprehensive examination with distinction. In June, 1964, there were 12 interdepartmental and 32 departmental honors graduates out of a class of 530.

At Utah, the comparatively new honors program is closely and carefully coordinated with the MA-3 (three-year master's degree) program sponsored by the Ford Foundation. The program involves students from business (6 students in 1964), education (15), engineering (16), fine arts (7), mining (4), and nursing (5), as well as from the usual departments of the liberal arts college (111 students). These students are exposed to both departmental and general honors with an emphasis (because of the MA-3) upon the student's going into at least one year of graduate study. For this reason also, foreign language study, research apprenticeship, and the preparation of a senior thesis (as a warm-up for the master's thesis) are all strongly emphasized. On the general honors side, the student takes an honors section or a special honors course in each of three general education areas; he also takes two honors reading courses, although these "general honors" requirements are frequently modified for professional college students with crowded programs of study.

A list of specialized or departmental honors opportunities in large institutions would be almost endless: honors in engineering at Colorado, Purdue, Carnegie Tech; in medicine (this of course is not an undergraduate professional college) at Washington, Northwestern, Western Reserve, Kansas, Michigan; in education at Wisconsin, Michigan State, Western Washington State; in music at Michigan. If the total picture of the development of honors work in undergraduate professional colleges is not as encouraging as one could wish, one cannot look at the whole scene without feeling that a tremendous leavening is going on, that many undergraduate professional colleges are eager to establish that the work their students do is a kind of interdisciplinary effort in itself with an important contribution to make. At the same time, these colleges admit readily that their approach heretofore has often lacked breadth, integration, and a sufficient theoretical foundation. Professor Cohen of the ICSS has constantly said that some of the most original and creative thinking about honors programs that he has discovered has been in the professional areas, where teachers are often more inclined to look at their efforts in total perspective than are those in liberal arts. Fifteen years ago, honors work in undergraduate professional colleges in large public institutions was practically unheard of; today there are many notable examples of broadened perspectives and close attention to excellence.

FIVE PROGRAMS IN LARGE INSTITUTIONS

Perhaps the best way to get a picture of honors programs as they have developed or are developing in large, multipurpose institutions is to describe a few characteristic programs. I have chosen those at Colorado, Michigan, Illinois, Michigan State, and Oregon. Except for Colorado's (of which I have some firsthand knowledge), I know these programs only from conversation, printed descriptions, brochures, and articles, and I may not have seen all printed materials on them, especially the more recent. Inadequate and incomplete as these brief descriptions are, however, they may lend themselves to some crisp comparisons and highlight certain excellences.

The Colorado program is very clearly divided into a general program and a departmental one, with an honors council supervising both. A student may graduate with honors, high honors, or highest honors in either general studies (the general program), a departmental field, or both. The program has always been largely for liberal arts students, but the general program is open to any undergraduate student, and there are now programs in nearly all the liberal arts departments as well as in the colleges of engineering and business. In cooperation with the liberal arts college, the nursing and premedical curricula also offer their students fine opportunities in honors work.

In deciding upon citations, the council considers over-all grades, grades in the major, graduate record examination scores (area and advanced), written reports of all instructors in honors courses, a written comprehensive examination (general), an oral comprehensive (general), and such requirements as departments may demand and the council approve. The system is flexible; it is clearly designed to emphasize the importance of general honors without denying citations to more departmentally minded students.

The general side of the program is stronger than the departmental. The strength of the general program lies in its colloquia and honors theme groups. The freshman colloquium deals with Greek civilization. The junior and senior colloquia can deal with anything the instructors choose. The honors theme groups appeal greatly to students from all colleges, undergraduate professional as well as liberal arts. For many years, honors offerings at Colorado were not available to non-liberal arts students; this privilege was extended as a result of a demand by the professional college students themselves. Honors theme groups have been taught by faculty members from nearly all colleges—liberal arts, education, music, architecture, architectural engineering. The teacher chooses a topic out of the area of his specialized competence (or sometimes a special side interest) and conducts his course as an introduction to the topic or field. Students can take only those honors theme groups that lie outside their specialty; they can take them in any or all semesters of their four undergraduate years.

The whole Colorado program is pervaded with an air of excitement. More than thirty years old, it has not lost its verve. It helps make the Colorado campus, in my opinion, one of the most stimulating for undergraduates in the whole country. In recent years I have had the opportunity to observe (in regional interviewing for fellowships) that, as Colorado has sought to strengthen its graduate program, the Colorado students have become stronger in their specialties without losing their breadth of interest and general intellectual awareness. There is little doubt that the honors program at Colorado, with its long tradition, has attracted good students and has contributed immensely to the broadening and deepening of their education. (Incidentally, Colorado honors students do exceedingly well in scholarship-fellowship competition.)

The program at Michigan owes much of its repute to the insistence of Prof. Robert Angell—a sociologist and for some years its director—that its accomplishments be constantly evaluated, and to the interest of staff members that leads them to write about their program. Associate Dean James Robertson, long concerned with all aspects of student counseling, has helped the honors program achieve its present high level of advising.

Freshmen in honors have access to honors sections of most freshman courses. What might be called general honors is open to freshmen and sophomores from all undergraduate colleges, but there are full-fledged departmental programs only in liberal arts, music, and medicine. Nevertheless, the backbone of the program is the junior-senior departmental seminars; these, in the words of the director, "give it most substantial structure, continuity, and measurable achievement."

Departments frequently devise special honors offerings for non-majors, and students continually request more of these. Indeed, one of the strengths of the Michigan program is that outstanding professors have been willing to give these special offerings or to teach an honors section of a regular introductory course. Prof. Theodore Newcomb, the psychologist, who has also had an important role in studies aimed at evaluating this program, is a notable example. Major interdisciplinary efforts in recent years have been a course by an English teacher in the Renaissance (history, literature, art, science) and a course by four scientists (a physicist, an astronomer, a geologist, and a biologist) built around the concept of evolution. The Unified Science program, although not specifically an honors project, appears to be a valuable adjunct of the general honors or interdisciplinary idea. This program emphasizes mathematics and some relationships of the sciences to one another, with concentration in a particular science in the last two years. Outside of arts, letters, and science, there is a junior-senior program in the school of music and, more recently, an honors program in medicine. The latter is a cooperative program with the liberal arts college. It permits attainment of the Ph.D. degree from the school of medicine, with some medical courses counting toward the bachelor's degree of the liberal arts college; among its aims are some acceleration and a more thorough grounding in basic science. On the extracurricular or cocurricular side, the honors student organization sponsors lectures on a variety of topics.

Judged against ideal standards, the Michigan program involves too few of the undergraduate professional college students and perhaps does not offer enough broad general honors in the freshman-sophomore years. But its students are strongly motivated, and there is a wholesome absence of pretentiousness of any sort. The junior-senior departmental program is an old one at Michigan, but it has taken on new life recently under criticism from students that it was not challenging enough. Imaginative interdisciplinary efforts and the willingness of many departments to provide honors offerings for nonmajors may have helped in this revitalization of honors at Michigan in recent years.

On the departmental side, the honors programs at Illinois probably offer the most comprehensive and complete slate in the whole country. The office of the university honors programs issues a valuable detailed report annually, the most complete I have ever seen. The 1961–1962 report lists active honors committees or councils in the following colleges of the university: agriculture, commerce and business administration, education, engineering, fine and applied arts, liberal arts and sciences, library science, and veterinary medicine. The 1962–1963 report backtracks a bit and says that "a few undergraduate colleges still lack full honors programs as such as well as college honors councils," and withdraws education and veterinary medicine from the list. But this is still the most impressive battery of honors programs in professional colleges within any university in the country. The staff is fully aware that general honors work is neglected, and there is constant evaluation and development. The director is a patient and persistent explorer, and he has a large staff of testers and counselors.

The whole program is administered by an all-university faculty honors council, but citations are made in the colleges, where programs are mostly junior-senior operations, highly autonomous and more or less isolated from one another. There is a vigorous recruitment program. Freshmen honors students come directly into the college of their choice where, apparently, there is often nothing in the freshman or sophomore year to let them know that they are honors students except possibly some honors sections of courses they take in the liberal arts college.

The 1961–1962 report mentions some successful lower-division honors courses and colloquia in the college of agriculture (described above) and intimates that these ought to be open to students of other colleges. The 1962–1963 report, however, states:

> Almost no effective interdisciplinary courses or colloquia have been organized for undergraduates....
>
> ... here lies the most serious failure of University Honors Programs. We should like to see colloquia sponsored by one college attended by honors students from many colleges. Some of the trouble lies in the wishes of the faculty. Some of it lies in tight curricula, with no time for electives.
>
> Now that a general education requirement has been made obligatory for all colleges, perhaps something effective could be done. We hope that the Division of General Studies will be given a chance to show what it can do for superior students in this way.... Honors programs at Illinois flourish in departmental aspects; they languish in interdisciplinary and integrative aspects.

And yet in this atmosphere of vocationalism and extreme departmentalism, the honors programs perform exceedingly well many of the supplementary functions an honors program should interest itself in. The honors office recruits good students for all colleges and curricula; it runs an excellent testing and record-keeping program; it has an adequate counseling arrangement for its James Scholars; it makes great use of advanced placement and other forms of acceleration; it has excellent relations with the graduate school; it seeks to identify potential candidates for graduate and professional scholarships and fellowships; it lends all aid and encouragement to the departments, divisions, and colleges in their desire to improve and intensify departmental work. But a program that is very largely a collection of departmental honors programs, although it can speed up a student's career and aid him in many other ways, leaves many possibilities for enriching his education untapped. Fortunately, the director of the programs and the faculty members most interested in honors work are fully aware of the deficiencies of their program.

Illinois's problems are those of any large multipurpose, public-supported institution. Other universities might profit from adopting Illinois's assumption that there is no harm in making a virtue of necessity. The 1961–1962 report states:

> It should be possible to make an intellectual asset, not a detriment, of the vocational orientation of superior students in engineering, commerce, agriculture, the natural sciences, and the preprofessional curricula in law and the health sciences by judicious mixing of them in appropriate colloquia with other superior students.

The next year's report also reminds us that even liberal arts enrollees are not "all intent on a pure, scholarly undergraduate education":

> Quite the contrary, a large majority comes in with a strong vocational orientation—about a quarter of them in either the chemistry curriculum or the physics curriculum; about one-sixth of them in one or another of the health science preprofessional curricula; about one-seventh in a teacher-training curriculum; and about one-tenth in a pre-law or pre-journalism program. Our faculty in honors work must therefore try to instill academic and intellectual values into a group of students who are, by and large, pragmatic and vocationally oriented.

It is good to be reminded that, in a state university at least, the orientation and the state of the mind and culture of liberal arts enrollees and students in undergraduate professional colleges are similar in more respects than they are different. It is also well to remember, along with the director of the Illinois programs, that the pragmatism and vocationalism of American culture and the American educational system, though often lamented, do offer opportunities of interdisciplinary approach and of understanding of the relationship of technology, science, and the professions to the whole culture that are relatively new in human experience and that probably will prove exceedingly valuable. The professional student is very often strongly motivated toward success and tangible results; it is folly not to exploit this motivation, to urge the student toward excellence, even though excellence in this case may mean only better and broader professionalism or even vocationalism.

Michigan State and Oregon are notable examples of large public institutions that have gone all out to establish an honors college. These programs are all-university in the truest sense of the word: They get their authority from the entire university faculty; they enroll students whose major or specialized work may be done in any undergraduate college of the university; they strongly emphasize either a specific common core or at least a minimum quantity of work in general education for all honors students.

The Michigan State honors college enrolls students at the end of their freshman year or in their second year. There are honors offerings for freshmen; honors students are selected as sophomores on the basis (partially at least) of their academic performance as freshmen. The program relies mainly upon guidance. The student's adviser is an honors-college adviser, but he represents also the college in which the student will do his major work. He and the student lay out a program which must be approved by the honors-college committee and by the honors committee of the student's major field or college. One of the nine regular colleges grants the student his degree and is responsible for his honors work in his specialty. The honors college as such serves mainly to recruit and advise. There are specific honors courses within the regular colleges, but the honors college itself provides only cocurricular colloquia, that is, discussion periods in the evening that are not required and do not carry credit. Honors sections of elementary courses are open to freshmen, and to those honors-college students who wish to take them.

The adviser has a great deal of authority. He can waive any requirement except that of total number of hours for graduation. He is responsible for the student's general education. Any student at Michigan State must take at least one-fourth of his hours in general education. The honors handbook strongly encourages honors students to take more than that amount and to seek breadth. Although the emphasis is on flexibility and the student's program is supposed to be designed to fit his needs, abilities, and desires, and to provide for him the best education he is capable of achieving, a regular college or departmental honors committee must approve each student's program. This requirement makes possible a good relationship between the honors college and the various departments and colleges of the university, but it could possibly inhibit an adviser in providing for breadth in the student's program.

The advantages of relying so heavily on the advisory system are clear. Individual student wishes can be met, no hard-and-fast "core" curricular requirements are set up in advance, advisers can often arrange substitutions or omissions in the sometimes very demanding prescribed curricula of the professional schools. In a highly pluralistic, multipurpose university with strong professional and vocational colleges or divisions, to have adviser and student select already-existing courses as the chief means of giving breadth to the student's program is probably a practical and feasible device when an honors program is just beginning. Ultimately, I believe, persons with experience in honors programs will hold that the undergraduate professional student should also have a chance to "mix it up" with other highly able students in colloquia in which all are subject to the discipline of doing a great deal of reading, writing, and discussing. Michigan State apparently depends upon voluntary or "cocurricular" colloquia to perform this function—further evidence of the philosophy of no regimentation that prevails in the honors college.

Another benefit of Michigan State's free system is that it appears to strongly encourage advanced placement, the challenging of courses by examination, and acceleration generally, although the literature of the program emphasizes enrichment over acceleration and exhorts the student to get a good general education. The overall impression of the program that an outsider gets is that it is providing an excellent opportunity for students in an amazing variety of subjects to find their way individually to some kind of self-fulfillment without prescription or coercion. However, so much freedom —this, too, is merely an impression that the outsider gets—may take its toll in that the honors program is not so clearly evident or "visible" at this institution as it is in other places, and honors students may tend not to feel any identity with the honors college or with one another.

Oregon's honors college developed out of its sophomore honors program, which was in turn, to an extent at least, Oregon's reaction to the "general education" movement. The honors college at Oregon offers a four-year program leading to the B.A. degree (honors college) with departmental or professional college honors work in the junior-senior years. Just as the older sophomore honors program was built on an attempt to give at least the very able students a basic understanding of the major areas of intellectual effort, the honors college carries on the idea of a "core" for all able students, but provides means for the student to demonstrate his knowledge and capacity without necessarily taking courses. More than in any program with which I am familiar, the Oregon faculty have decided what it is that a student needs to know as citizen and person and have prescribed this for him, although allowing him to get as much of it for himself as he wishes. This is admirable—and it is unusual in a large state university.

The "core" program includes work in separate honors courses (not just sections of regular courses) in literature, history, philosophy, social science, and mathematics and science. Although the student may prepare to satisfy these requirements by taking courses in all of them, he must pass the comprehensive examinations in these areas, or most of them. Proficiency equivalent to that attained in a second-year college course in a foreign language is also required. Honors sections are given in second-year French, German, and Spanish. The honors-college student takes a one-term honors composition course and two terms of composition tutorial, in which he submits to an English instructor for review all the papers written for other honors courses. The rest of his program is largely the conventional departmental type of honors work in the liberal arts college or in a professional school. However, in his junior and senior years he must take two terms of a colloquium. The brochure describes colloquia as "small discussion courses designed to enable groups of students of different backgrounds and interest to focus their attention on a common topic outside their major fields."

In almost every detail the honors college at Oregon fits one's idealized conception of what a program in a multipurpose public institution ought to be: It is available to students intending any major or specialty within the university; it provides departmental or disciplinary intensification; it strongly emphasizes general education; it throws together able students from varied disciplines in its colloquia. In addition, it provides a small liberal arts college of very high quality within the walls of a large university, combining the advantages of both kinds of institution. There is an ample honors-college center, where students, instructors, and visiting scholars meet in the "Monday Night Discussion Groups." The formal scheme is complete, so to speak. More important, the director is very alert to the role an honors program should play in providing intellectual stimulation on a campus; he is also alert to the danger that the program will merely intensify and add prestige to routine and traditional concepts of academic excellence—having the students work harder, overcome more hurdles, and gain more applause from faculty and peers.

Since the Oregon program is so thoroughly what a liberal arts man would order (if he could) for all students in a state university, one might question whether it appeals to business, engineering, nursing, medical, or law students. As of now, the question is answered by the statistics that went into the totals in the table on page 117. These show that Oregon's honors college is drawing and retaining a significantly larger share of students from undergraduate professional colleges than the eighteen institutions collectively. It is exceedingly gratifying to observe that a rigorous, demanding, complete honors program attracts undergraduates in the non-liberal arts areas of a characteristic state university.

The Oregon and Michigan State examples together illustrate what can be done through an honors college. The two institutions have perhaps gone further than any others (except possibly Illinois) in providing junior-senior programs for students in all or most of the professional areas. In addition, Oregon and Michigan

State have faced the general education issue rather squarely—the former, for some tastes, with perhaps a little too much restrictiveness, the latter with possibly too much freedom. But both illustrate that an honors college, with the freedom it provides from the curricular restrictions that too often plague students in undergraduate professional schools, has definite advantages. Of course, as we have already stressed, a program can have verve, be stimulating, and serve as a center of intellectual enterprise on a campus without having the comprehensive structure or the freedom in advising that the all-out honors college has.

The Colorado program shows what long adherence to the general honors concept can accomplish. The Michigan program shows that a solid departmental program in a liberal arts college can, with proper leadership, encourage exploration into the general and interdisciplinary fields and ultimately take the lead in extending honors work into other undergraduate colleges. The Illinois program illustrates the excellent possibilities in the field of departmental honors in a great variety of undergraduate professional colleges and also the inevitable concern of a perceptive director and faculty that the program develop more in the general and interdisciplinary directions. The Michigan State and Oregon honors colleges offer fine examples of all-out honors efforts within a comprehensive, all-university structure.

Looking back over our beginning general observations, the results of the questionnaire, and the descriptions of characteristic honors programs, I believe that the following conclusions are justified in the light of the pooled experience of directors of programs and the students, faculty members, and administrative officers they have worked with over the past few years:

1. That despite some laudable examples to the contrary, the departmental type of honors program has not developed sufficiently in the undergraduate professional colleges in large public institutions. (This is also true of many departments of many liberal arts colleges.)

2. That students of the undergraduate professional colleges also do not take full advantage of the opportunity to participate in general honors offerings even when they are available; and this is true even in institutions that claim "all-university" programs.

3. That however inevitable it is that the departmental type of honors can flourish more naturally in the strongly departmentalized climate of our American public institutions (especially where there is strong emphasis on graduate work), the really strong honors programs have, on the whole, moved increasingly to provide also *general* honors colloquia, seminars, interdisciplinary courses; students have requested these; faculty have been stimulated by them; lively departments (and individual teachers) have welcomed the opportunity to provide special courses for able nonspecialist students.

4. That an honors program with some degree of balance between its departmental or professional and its general aspects will almost invariably improve student performance in the conventional sense (which can be measured in terms of awards, scholarships, fellowships, etc.), as well as provide the intellectual stimulation needed to shift emphasis from grades to intellectual curiosity, from accumulation of facts to the use of knowledge in judging and evaluating. Although a great deal more research will be necessary to prove this point, if it can ever be proved, students and faculty members who have been involved pretty generally agree that this effect on honors students "spills over" on to the whole university enter-

prise. Honors students set a higher expectation for themselves; other students emulate them.

5. That an honors program (and indeed the entire educational process) will flourish best when attention is paid to *all* aspects of the drive toward *excellence*—recruitment of able students, recognition of academic achievement, recognition of and reward for spirited and lively teaching that is solidly grounded in intellectuality and the desire for intellectual and cultural growth, provision of proper atmosphere and tone on the nonacademic side of campus life. Properly led, the public will accept, support, and take pride in an institution's drive toward excellence. This requires administrative understanding and support at many levels and in practically all areas of the university structure. When an institution lets it be known that it is seeking out good students, good students begin to seek it out. It is the same with a good honors program within an institution.

6. That although there are many devices, schemes, and plans worthy of emulation, no institution should think of taking over bodily some other institution's program. The agony of creative improvisation must be undergone.

7. That all our students, but especially our ablest ones, deserve to be addressed as persons and citizens in addition to being trained in what they think they want or society thinks it needs from them.

Chapter seven / Departmental honors

at the University of Kansas:

a case history / George R. Waggoner,

University of Kansas

MORE THAN A GENERATION has passed since departmental honors programs were first instituted in the United States, but although the number of programs has multiplied many times and the basic pattern has been greatly modified, the philosophy behind them and their essential form have remained much the same.

The first departmental honors programs were developed out of a concern for the most gifted students and a belief that if given the opportunity some of these students could and would search more widely and deeply than their peers in behalf of their own education. The form of the traditional departmental honors program during the 1930s and 1940s, particularly in the large state universities, was much influenced by that of the Swarthmore program, though what was copied was not so much the organizational details as general goals and procedures—for example, honors work beginning in the junior year and carried out under the supervision of the division in which the student's major department fell.

This chapter discusses the departmental honors program at the University of Kansas from its beginning around 1930 to the present

—the patterns of programs offered by the various departments, the early programs of the 1930s and 1940s, the newer responses to pressures of increased enrollments and growing concern with the superior student, and some challenges raised by recent developments and requirements. Because it was one of the earliest honors programs in a large state university, because it was typical of many others, and because I have had direct experience with it as an undergraduate between 1934 and 1936 and again as a teacher and administrator since 1954, I shall use the Kansas program as a basis for describing and evaluating the departmental type of program during the past thirty-five years. The history of the Kansas program illustrates vividly both the strengths and weaknesses of an honors program that relies entirely upon academic departments.

Patterns of departmental programs at Kansas

Honors at Kansas began in and is still confined to the college of liberal arts and sciences. From time to time a student in the school of education or journalism may choose to do a departmental honors program in arts and sciences, but the professional schools of the university have never offered any formal programs leading to graduation with honors.

The general rules of the college of liberal arts and sciences regarding departmental honors have been simple and flexible. Candidates for honors are required to have an over-all grade point average of 2.0 and a departmental average of 2.2 (where A is 3.0 and B is 2.0). The only other requirement is that the student carry through a program that gives evidence of scholarly distinction and that the department certify to the dean and the registrar that the student has successfully completed this program. The departments can make any additional eligibility requirements they wish and design their programs in their own way.

Before the 1950s the science departments participated little in honors; this was on the whole typical of honors programs in state universities during this period. In the social sciences and the humanities, programs emphasized independent study, the tutorial, and comprehensive examinations. I can best illustrate the pattern and the kind of changes that have taken place over the years by describing the English and political science programs at Kansas in the 1930s and at the present time.

In the 1930s both departments showed their concern for independent study as a major element by using the term "reading for honors." In political science eligible students were permitted to enroll during their junior and senior years in from six to twelve semester credit hours of individual work with several professors in the department. There were weekly sessions with the professor and, occasionally, when several students were doing reading for honors with the same professor, the meetings took the form of small, informal seminars. The students received grades for each semester of honors reading, but to graduate with departmental honors they had to pass a comprehensive oral examination given by three professors of the department in the spring semester shortly before graduation.

The political science program now is much the same except that honors students must enroll in the departmental honors seminar (still for six to twelve credit hours) and the student must present "an acceptable honors thesis" before finishing the seminar.

In English in the 1930s reading for honors consisted of three or four semesters of tutorial: Each semester dealt with a specific topic, and the student wrote a major paper on some aspect of the topic. At the end of the program, the student took a comprehensive examination on a reading program administered by a committee of three members of the department. In the 1930s, when standard courses still took the form of panoramic surveys of periods of literature, these English tutorials usually represented intensive reading programs. One student, for example, devoted his three tutorials to the complete political prose of Milton, the whole work of Tennyson, and the whole work of three twentieth-century poets. Another read all extant English plays up to 1600, the eighteenth-century periodical essayists, and the major twentieth-century essayists; a third studied English translations in the Renaissance and nonorthodox literature of the eighteenth century.

The present English program is more formally organized. The required grade point average in work in the department has been increased to 2.5; the student enrolls for credit in three honors seminars; in the last semester before graduation, if he has received a grade of A in at least two of the seminars, he enrolls in independent study for the honors examination. This examination has two parts: a written examination ("a test of the candidate's critical and analytical powers") based on two major works announced at the beginning of the semester, and an oral examination based on a list of important literary works given to the candidate when he begins his honors work in the junior year. To graduate with departmental honors the student must successfully complete all of these aspects of the program.

The English department awards a substantial prize each year to the student who completes the program with the highest degree of distinction. The award is presented at a dinner or luncheon attended by all seniors graduating with honors and all students completing the sophomore year who appear to be eligible for the honors program. Because the spring of the sophomore year is the point at which students are about to declare their majors, this event serves to recruit the best English majors to the honors program and also to bring outstanding students into the department.

Programs in other departments in recent years show diverse patterns. Candidates for honors in philosophy must take more regular courses than the minimum required of other majors. The heart of the philosophy honors program is an honors essay which the student does in the senior year. An interesting aspect of the program is that students who have held an undergraduate assistantship in the department may substitute this experience for the extra course requirement. In the foreign language departments the older reading for honors pattern still prevails. Sociology, psychology, and anthropology require a year of senior research. Economics requires an honors dissertation and a comprehensive examination. The programs developed by the physical and biological science departments in recent years have always involved senior research. The mathematics department has developed an honors seminar, but bases its award of honors upon the student's completion of four key courses with a grade average of 2.5.

Honors at Kansas: 1930–1954

The faculty first authorized the granting of departmental honors at Kansas in the late 1920s, and thereafter the catalogue regularly described the general college rules for honors participation. As was true in most state universities at the time, there was a real possibility for a while that the program might exist only in the catalogue. However, from 1930 to 1954 the program at Kansas continued to grow, even if slowly, and was gradually extended to new departments. During the 1930s fifteen students from three departments completed honors programs successfully, most of them in the department of English. In the 1940s forty-seven students in six departments graduated with honors, two-thirds of them in political science.

During this period the honors program was concentrated in a few departments and took its impetus from the efforts of a relatively small number of faculty members. However, although the Kansas program derived much of its vigor from the departments of English in the 1930s and political science in the 1940s, it was never so clearly based on the activities of a single department as the University of Colorado program (where Prof. Joseph Cohen and his colleagues in philosophy were a major force) or the University of Texas program (where Plan Two depended heavily on the efforts of Dr. Harry Ransom and the department of English) seem to have been.

In most public universities during these two decades the trend was away from a direct concern for the needs of the most gifted segment of the undergraduate body and toward "democratizing" education, which meant in part placing major emphasis upon enabling the weak students to survive. Remedial courses and dropouts received more attention than the talented. Concurrently, especially in the 1940s, theories of general education calling for reductions in the excessive power of departments and integration across departmental lines engaged that active segment of faculty committed to educational experimentation. In the few state universities where there was a concern for the talented student, the outstanding honors programs usually combined this concern with an interest in general education, as seems to me to have happened at both Colorado and Texas.

It is difficult to understand why the honors program at Kansas kept to the earlier departmental tradition and was not influenced by experiments in general education. The reason probably relates to a third type of program that also developed during the 1930s in Kansas, the Summerfield Scholarship program. Through this program, which began in 1930, scholarships are awarded each year to some twenty boys who are seniors in Kansas high schools, selected from among the outstanding students nominated by high schools throughout the state. They are chosen on the basis of tests administered in regional testing centers and two additional days of tests and interviews on the university campus. The winners are guaranteed whatever financial aid is necessary during their undergraduate years, subject only to their maintaining a minimum academic performance roughly equivalent to that required for election to Phi Beta Kappa. The Summerfield Scholarship program has always been directly administered by a faculty committee made up of outstanding professors, on the whole those who have also been most influential in developing experimental education programs in the college. Additionally, the group of Summerfield Scholars (usually totaling sixty-five or seventy) have always met eight or nine times a year at dinners with the faculty committee. At these dinners the seniors usually present papers for discussion by the scholars from the other three classes. These meetings both supply an interdisciplinary program for the outstanding undergraduate group and demonstrate for faculty members the great capacity for individual work of this group of exceptional students. After World War II an identical program for women scholars was established; over the last several years the two programs have been merged, and they now have the same faculty committee, selection system, and program of on-campus activities. The arts and sciences members of these scholar groups have always made up a very large proportion of the departmental honors groups.

Despite, or perhaps partly because of, the presence on the campus of this group of publicly identified outstanding students, the departmental honors programs remained small, existing only in the catalogue in many departments until the early 1950s. The disruptions of the depression and of the war, the GI bulge after the war, and the lack of an overriding concern for quality on the part of many faculty members also worked to keep these programs small. Perhaps a more fundamental reason is that because the student body during these decades was smaller and pressure from graduate programs and research upon faculty members not so heavy as was the case later, the outstanding student often received the attention he needed in informal ways.

The sudden postwar growth in enrollment made it necessary for the public universities to use many less qualified instructors than in the past and to abandon many traditional teaching patterns geared to smaller classes. It was no accident that in the 1950s there appeared simultaneously experiments in new techniques of mass education, like that of educational television, and a new concern for what was happening to the most gifted portions of the vastly increased student bodies.

Before discussing the impact of these developments on honors programs during the 1950s, I should like to attempt to convey a sense of what the programs of the 1930s and 1940s meant to the students who participated in them. In the spring of 1964 I wrote to all students who had graduated with departmental honors in arts and sciences at the University of Kansas asking them to tell me, if they could, what had led them to participate in the departmental program, what the program consisted of, what they thought of it at the time, how they evaluated it now, how they thought it might have been improved, and what their own subsequent activities had been.

Respondents most frequently said they had selected honors because they wanted freedom and flexibility in choosing courses, the opportunity to try independent work and to pursue a topic in depth, and a chance to work more closely with professors. A graduate of the class of 1940, now a professor in the University of Minnesota, wrote:

> I believe I registered for work in departmental honors as soon as I was permitted to; that is, early in my junior year. I had, I suppose, several reasons for trying the honors program: (1) I had even then decided that I would go on to graduate school, and I felt that the program of independent study which the honors course entailed would be excellent preparation for the later work; (2) I wanted to study intensively certain facets of literature which were not offered—at least not in an intensive way—in the usual program of courses; (3) I especially welcomed the opportunity to study under the close personal supervision of certain members of the faculty: they welcomed me to their homes, spent a great deal of time going over my work and in conversing on unrelated matters which I found illuminating; (4) I wanted to win honors for the sake of my record and (further) professional standing.

An executive in a chemical company mentioned his desire to study under a particular professor and his pleasure at discovering that he could do honors work with him:

> I suspect that the opportunity to sit at his feet to explore a subject of interest encouraged me as much as anything. I also recall that I felt it would be a mistake to pass up an opportunity to be graduated "with honors." Just why that seemed important to me then is not really clear today.

One point that these responses make clear is that the reason most students participated in an honors program was not because they read an announcement in the catalogue but because they were directly invited to do so by a department, a professor, or an adviser, or urged to do so by fellow students. True, most outstanding students felt the "almost inevitable desire to avail myself of what honorific opportunities were open" that an editorial writer for the *Chicago Tribune* cited. But the stimulus of a faculty member and the enthusiasm of other students were all-important. A professor of economics at UCLA comments that "it was the thing to do in my circle." A professor of political science in a Western state university, now responsible for planning a new honors program, emphasized the influence of fellow students:

> As I can reconstruct it now, my major academic interests were developed along lines suggested to me by my reaction to the subject matter of the courses I took and by the quality of the faculty members I met in these courses, but the most important factor was the interests of my friends. I was motivated to work hard and be a good student, in part because I had been so motivated in high school and in part because I had a scholarship and had to do well to retain it. But the direction in which my interests went was a matter largely of the student friends I made.... I have referred to my own student experiences in the years since whenever I have thought about the problem of arousing student interest and motivation.... My particular circle of friends I acquired largely because of the extracurricular activities which seemed most important to me at the time. For example, I joined the student co-ops, partly because I thought the theory of cooperative self-help attractive, partly because it was the only interracial housing set up on campus at the time.... Most of the leaders in these groups were political science majors who

were good students, and I fitted in well.... It was simply assumed by most of us that we would take honors programs and go on to graduate school.

Most of the programs described by respondents were essentially reading programs, combined with tutorial sessions with professors. Written or oral comprehensive examinations were important. Perhaps two-thirds of the letter writers were extremely enthusiastic in retrospect; they described their reactions to the program at the time of their participation as "enjoyable," "exciting," "stimulating," and "challenging." They praised most often the welcome opportunities for individual study, introduction to research techniques, freer and better use of library facilities, a chance to learn something about scholarship, the meaningful association with departments and faculty members, and freedom from the "anonymity," "boredom," or "slow pace" of regular classes.

Viewed with the hindsight of from twenty to thirty years, the programs still earned the approval of almost all respondents. An enthusiastic psychologist wrote:

> The honors course, and what I learned from it . . . left me with no fear of graduate courses.... Orals and faculty status were just hurdles and had nothing to do with what I wanted to learn and retain.... Today I would say that the University of Kansas could have charged a million dollars for that whole experience and still have been underpaid, as far as what it meant to me. It was there that I found out that I had potential.

Those who felt grateful for and enthusiastic about the experience specified most often that it served them well as preparation for graduate study, influenced their decisions about graduate study, led them to make the preparation in foreign language that they might otherwise have neglected, and helped them to discover their own potentialities and to develop confidence, independence, self-discipline, and a critical sense. An editorial writer for the *St. Louis Post-Dispatch* commented:

> The honors work at K.U. was more than merely relevant to my present work; it was, in method at least, almost the same thing. Possibly men in other professions also would recognize the value of a study system which allowed latitude but required the discipline of fact finding before opinion, or research before conclusion.

A writer for another major metropolitan paper made the same point with more personal detail:

> In a way my entire academic period is largely irrelevant to my present work; none of my colleagues or superiors has been through the graduate school process, which obviously is not prerequisite to the kind of work I am doing. Yet I think my academic conditioning contributes directly to my daily work. Though I do not write monographs, I write constantly. . . . In conference, I represent informally the sub-culture of books and eggheads, as well as of the "liberal" cast of mind, which in this immediate context is non-conformist. . . . Though in an improbable kind of work, I feel that it is work to which everything that I have ever learned (including what I learned in the undergraduate honors program) makes a usable contribution.

When asked to criticize, a few respondents found that participation in honors was not as significant in terms of prestige as the holding of certain scholarships. Also, if the honors program consisted, as in mathematics, only of taking certain special advanced courses, it was not seen as really different from what the students would have done on their own.

The respondents did not hesitate to say that in some cases they and their peers should have been subjected to higher standards, and more required reading. Some found themselves appalled in retrospect by the quality of their papers, describing them as "too speculative for an undergraduate," "superficial," or "merely a rough draft." Others wished they had been more restricted in their choices of reading and subjects for investigation. A number of respondents judged the programs too flexible in terms of the freedom given to students to select their own problems and methods of work. One writer insisted that the English honors program should cover the major periods of English literature in sequence and minimize the value of a major final paper on a particular author. Some, however, urged greater attention to research papers dealing with very specialized topics, while still others asserted that the absence of a thesis or major paper is the best feature of an honors program.

These comments indicate that the fundamental question troubling many respondents as they tried to suggest improvements is the persistent one of how to ensure that students somehow cover what is generally regarded as "basic," or "classic," or "essential for a given discipline" while avoiding so much structuring that "flexibility," "freedom," and "creativity" are lost. "I know of no magic formula for balancing these things," wrote one political science graduate of 1949–1950. "If there must be errors, I would certainly opt for error in favor of intellectual excitement at the expense of the basics." All respondents agreed that the key to success in any honors program is a close relationship between students and faculty.

These letters from honors graduates of fifteen to twenty-four years ago are full of evidence of the fact that gifted people never stop growing or lose their vigor and creativity. It is of course impossible to determine quantitatively the results of the departmental honors experience for these respondents. (One New York securities dealer commented: "I am glad that you did not insult us by sending a questionnaire to be marked with a special pencil so that it could be processed electronically.") But their interest in and enthusiasm for honors work and independent, creative intellectual activity for superior undergraduates are clearly manifested. This is especially true of those graduates of the 1930s and 1940s who chose university teaching as a career. Almost all of these respondents reported some kind of activity in honors programs in their own colleges and universities in recent years. These data conform to the generally held impression that Rhodes Scholars have played a key role in many honors, tutorial, and independent-study programs in our colleges. The experience of the University of Colorado, too, indicates that many of the honors graduates of the 1930s who have stayed in the academic field have been leaders in the new honors movement of recent years.

For a variety of reasons, then, the small but valuable honors programs of the 1930s, 1940s, and early 1950s in the state universities never flourished as much as they should have; too small a proportion of talented students participated, and the programs did not take root in the arts and sciences departments. About 1954, however, a new period of growth and development of honors programs began. The traditional departmental program continued, but it interacted with a whole series of new kinds of honors activities stimulated by a growing national concern for special treatment of gifted students in large public universities with ever-increasing enrollments.

Honors at Kansas since 1954

During the 1954–1955 academic year the administrative committee of arts and sciences attempted to analyze why participation in honors had been so insignificant despite the high quality of a portion of the student body, as evidenced by the Summerfield Scholarship program and the equivalent Watkins program for women. The committee concluded that one reason might be that students who passed through the standard freshman-sophomore program established certain academic habits that indisposed them to seek out the little-publicized honors programs of their major departments during the junior year.

As a result of this analysis several changes and innovations were made in the departmental honors program. In the fall of 1955 the members of the administrative committee each took four incoming freshmen as advisees; these students were Watkins or Summerfield Scholars or had been finalists in the selection process. The committee agreed to approve any variations from college rules that might put talented students into programs requiring them to do work more suited to their level of ability. It was also hoped that this close counseling process, combined with curricular flexibility, would stimulate students to make long-range plans appropriate to their talents. The committee guessed that one test of the effectiveness of this special counseling program for freshmen and sophomores would be to bring them to their majors in the junior year ready to enter enthusiastically into the departmental honors programs.

At the same time, during the first two years of this program, efforts were made to persuade departments to create special honors sections of multisectioned freshman and sophomore programs. A general education program some ten years old was of special value in this new lower-division college honors program. This course, known as Western Civilization, was required of all sophomores. It used a reading list of great books in social, political, and philosophical thought from the Renaissance to the present. The course met in small discussion groups of five or six students one hour a week for a year. The students received two credits for the year of discussion and four additional credits when they took a comprehensive examination. Honors students in the freshman year were enrolled in Western Civilization discussion groups, each group of advisees being kept together in an honors Western Civilization section.

During the next two or three years honors sections were created in almost all freshman courses; the Western Civilization program for honors freshmen was continued; and, as more honors classes became available, the necessity for radical experimentation in omitting prerequisites, placing honors freshmen in advanced courses, and so on decreased. With the beginning of the National Merit Scholarship program a year or so later, eligibility for the freshman honors program was broadened to include all National Merit Scholars and finalists enrolling in the college of arts and sciences.

Table 2 indicates the effect of these changes on participation in honors. Enrollments of the early 1950s are similar to those of the 1930s and 1940s. Four years after the first honors program for freshmen was established, however, the number of graduates with departmental honors, as well as the number of participating departments, increased markedly, and both have continued to grow. By 1962 the number of graduates with departmental honors had risen above fifty, and in the two past years this figure has remained relatively constant. Seventeen or eighteen departments now graduate students with honors; the only major omissions are four professional or semiprofessional programs—physical therapy, home economics, medical technology, and radiation biophysics—which give only the Bachelor of Science degree.

Considering both the general minimum grade standards set by the departmental honors programs and the numbers of honors students who continue in arts and sciences instead of transferring to a professional school in the junior year, we can estimate that from 8 to 10 percent of the graduating seniors in arts and sciences may be the maximum number of students able to participate successfully in the honors program. A study of those graduating *with distinction* in arts and sciences—an honor based entirely upon over-all grade point average—indicates that a reasonable number of good students are not taking departmental honors. Nevertheless, the present pattern of completion of departmental honors is very different from the pattern before the general lower-division program was instituted in arts and sciences.

Table 2   *Graduates with departmental honors, 1950–1964*

Year	Number of students	Number of departments represented
1950	9	4
1951	9	3
1952	4	3
1953	5	4
1954	11	5
1955	6	3
1956	5	3
1957	7	4
1958	18	6
1959	15	8
1960	31	10
1961	29	13
1962	54	17
1963	55	17
1964	58	18

Just as the freshman-sophomore honors sections in elementary courses have been the basis for much experimentation with content and methods of teaching, so the honors students have been those to whom much other activity aimed at increasing the quality of the undergraduate experience has been directed. Broadly defined, honors activities include more than the honors programs described above. For example, two important areas of opportunities open to honors students are research and international programs.

A grant from the Carnegie Corporation in 1955 permitted the development of an undergraduate program in research that has been a great stimulus to many of the honors students at Kansas. This program provided small stipends to students in all fields of arts and sciences, originally to some thirty students each year, more recently to seventy or seventy-five. Later the National Science Foundation Program in Undergraduate Research made possible a sharp increase in the research program through a concentration of other funds in those fields not included in NSF grants. *Search,* a publication of the best undergraduate research papers issued annually since 1961, has provided a healthy stimulus to the research program. Some of these papers find publication in regular scholarly journals. Another annual publication, *Versuch,* publishes translations from German literature, translations from English poetry to German, and original creative work in German. *The Bulletin of the Museum of Art* has also begun to publish a good deal of scholarly work in the history of art by Kansas undergraduates. (A semimonthly honors newsletter modeled after the one that has been produced for a number of years in the honors program at Michigan State University gives honors students another means of communication.)

Honors sections in foreign languages have stimulated several developments in the international field. For example, students who do outstanding work in the first-year course in French, German, and Spanish are invited to participate in intensive summer sessions lasting nine weeks in France, Germany, and Spain during which they complete the second-year language course. Participants are chosen on the basis of merit; then those with financial needs are aided by a combination of scholarships and loans. The directors of these programs have been aware of the criticisms made of many study programs overseas and have felt that there was good reason to focus on language training, the results of which can be measured objectively by such tests as those devised by the Modern Language Association. These summer language institutes also allow students to complete the language proficiency examination for the B.A. degree before they begin their sophomore year.

There has been a great deal of pressure from students for junior-year programs abroad. An academic-year program was established in Central America in 1959, but otherwise the university has been slow to create this traditional type of program. A junior year in Germany has recently been established as well as an agreement to share in a program organized by the University of Colorado in France. One result of these various activities in European modern languages has been the high percentage of students graduating with honors in these departments: in 1964, 21 percent of the Spanish majors, 18 percent of the German majors, and 8 percent of the French majors.

Kansas has also experimented with teaching courses outside the language departments in a foreign language. Sections of the introductory course in art history have been taught frequently in French, German, and Spanish; an introduction to Latin-American history and a course in botany have been taught in Spanish. These classes were all successful in terms both of students interest and enrollment, as well as academic results, but as yet no program of offerings on a regular basis has developed.

The growth of foreign area programs in Slavic, Latin-American, and Far Eastern studies, as well as the development of programs in Chinese, Japanese, and Russian language and literature, has been indirectly related in important ways to the honors programs. The large group of honors students in the freshman and sophomore years has been the major source of support for these programs. The area committees have felt that at the upper-division level their major students should all have a second major in a traditional discipline. Thus, no honors programs have been offered in the area majors, but many students participate in honors in the department of their second major.

Another important recent development in the international area has been an experimental program with basic courses in the social sciences and the humanities. Some sections of these courses have been remodeled to include a large comparative element, drawing especially upon the areas that the university has concentrated upon outside of the traditional studies related to Western Europe and the United States—i.e., the Soviet area, the Far East, and Latin America. These experimental sections in sociology, political science, theater, economics, etc., have been taught as honors sections of the regular courses or in the same organizational pattern. The largest experiment in this program grew directly out of the lower-division honors program. Many freshmen in the honors program enrolled in their sections of the freshman Western Civilization discussion program petitioned for a similar kind of discussion group for their sophomore year. It was clear to the honors committee that a new program of discussion groups concerning major themes in Eastern

Civilization would fill this need. Beginning with an experimental section in 1962, the program grew to a dozen sections in 1963–1964. The planning group hopes eventually to merge the Western and Eastern Civilization programs.

There has been no attempt at Kansas to organize all of these various honors activities in any formal way. Instead, the college administrative committee, the offices of the deans in arts and sciences, the departments, and the area programs all offer activities for honors students, and these are very loosely coordinated. The group considered as honors students is itself flexibly defined; it includes students from the original freshman group, participants in departmental programs, and those named each semester to the honor roll of the college (the upper 10 percent). This loose coordination of a flexibly defined group through the usual departmental and college administrative channels has sometimes been called an "antiprogram" or a "nonprogram" in honors, designations meant to indicate a general flexibility that aims at offering outstanding students a constant variety of intellectual challenges.

In addition to stimulating the growth in participation in departmental honors programs and the development of several experimental undergraduate programs, the general freshman-sophomore programs have had another important effect—one anticipated by the committee that set them up in 1955. This is a substantial increase in the percentage of arts and sciences graduates going on to advanced study. It was evident that those admitted to the freshman honors group were qualified to attain a Ph.D. or equivalent professional degree. The committee believed that the advisory system should encourage such students to plan for advanced degrees, while recognizing that some fields of work into which many talented people choose to go require only a bachelor's degree.

The percentages of students going on to postgraduate work have increased every year; the administrative committee now feels that in a university without selective admission it is hardly reasonable to expect them to rise further. In 1962, for example, 62 percent of the graduates in arts and sciences planned to go directly to further study, 9 percent expected to go into military service, and 27 percent expected to seek employment immediately. Of the 62 percent continuing their studies, 31 percent planned to enter graduate school in the United States, 4 percent to study abroad, and 27 percent to enter professional schools, chiefly law and medicine. Perhaps out of a biased interest in its own profession, the committee has followed closely in recent years the results of the national Woodrow Wilson Fellowship competition, a program designed to give graduate fellowships to the most able college seniors who have an interest in a career as a college or university teacher. In the 1961–1964 period the University of Kansas, with between seventeen and twenty fellowships each year, fell within the top ten universities and colleges in numbers of fellowships. Because admission to all of the other schools in this group was selective, the administrative committee was disposed to credit some of the university's success to the effectiveness of the honors program.

Challenges to departmental honors

The recent experimentation that, by enriching the departmental honors program at Kansas, has encouraged participation in honors and contributed to the increase in numbers of students going on to graduate school, has not answered all the questions raised by a departmental honors program. Among these are: What should be the relationship of an undergraduate program in a large university to the graduate school? What interaction should there be between the programs of each department and those in other departments within the college? Both questions involve a discussion of the claims of breadth and depth in undergraduate education.

The presence of a graduate school within a university affects the honors program of the upper division. One can seriously ask whether departmental honors programs and other honors activities in the junior and senior years are necessary if appropriate graduate courses are open to gifted juniors and seniors. On the other hand, graduate courses are often more specialized and narrow than a talented junior or senior wishes. In one way the problem is that of the choice to be made at all levels of education between enriching or accelerating the talented students' program. The most practical answer seems to be to offer a sound departmental honors program that enriches the standard major program, at the same time recognizing that the interests of an occasional talented student may be best served by placing him in graduate courses for which he has both ability and preparation, provided they are not too specialized.

Comments by recent graduates with honors indicate the complexity of the problem and the necessity for flexible, individual solutions. A 1960 graduate with honors in history writes enthusiastically about specialization and a combined use of graduate and honors courses, explaining that in his senior year the university appointed:

...a visiting professor from the Rheinische Friedrich-Wilhelms-Universität Bonn for the spring semester, Professor Hubatsch. I enrolled in both his lecture course and his graduate seminar which, with the honors course, formed my semester's work. I wrote my honors paper under the guidance of Professor Hubatsch on Justus Möser. It is no coincidence that after three years at the University of Minnesota I am now in Bonn writing my doctoral dissertation on

"Justus Mösers Staatsauffassung" under the guidance of Professor Hubatsch. All of this I consider relevant to the departmental honors program at K.U.

A graduate with honors in English, also from the class of 1960 and now an instructor at Hunter College with a recent Ph.D., writes suggesting that the English department require a senior thesis in the departmental honors program but indicating, at the same time, the manner in which the same purpose was served by graduate seminars in which she enrolled as a senior:

> ...a senior honors paper should be added to the requirements or substituted for the examination. Friends of mine who did such papers at Yale, Radcliffe, Smith, and other schools seem to have gained much from the experience. Particularly they became initiated into the standards of scholarship demanded in graduate work. (I gained such an initiation by taking Dr. Quinn's graduate seminar in Donne and Marvell and Professor Orel's graduate course in the Irish Literary Renaissance.)

A graduate with honors in philosophy in 1961, now in the Yale Graduate School, takes a completely contrary position toward both the senior thesis and premature specialization:

> The chief advantage of the honors program in which I took part was that it was no program at all. The lack of a senior thesis (or whatever it is called) which has since been added in philosophy was in my case a real benefit. The big problem with undergraduates is that there is too much pressure to specialize. If the senior paper were to take additional time from other subjects outside the major field for a dry run at a graduate course, then I would be opposed to it. I would think there might be an option available to write a senior paper if the student desired. The strength of the whole honors

program at K.U. has been, however, that the student who is uncertain about his interests and future is exposed to as many areas as possible. Early specialization should be discouraged whenever possible, particularly in such a field as philosophy. A departmental honors program is of great value if it enables a student to investigate, under the more or less direct personal supervision of a professor, a topic which is normally not covered. If the honors program narrows, rather than broadens the student, however, then it would be better not to have a "program" at all.

Most honors students want both discipline and freedom, both professional and scholarly competence and the values of liberal education; however, these desires are not felt by all gifted students at the same time or in the same degree. Respect for the student's wishes, necessary if he is to work with the deepest motivation, demands individual flexibility of program and the most effective combination of regular and honors undergraduate courses and of independent research and suitable graduate courses.

Since 1960 a new set of programs supported by the Ford Foundation has been developing rapidly the goal of which is to integrate the work of the last two undergraduate years with the master's degree program. This is called the Three-year Master's Degree Program, or the MA-3. Because these programs emphasize independent study and writing and close orientation with faculty members, and because they recruit students of high intellectual quality, it is always assumed that there should be a close relationship between the MA-3 and departmental and college honors programs. The leader in this movement, Dr. Oliver C. Carmichael, describes the goals of the program as:

> Restoration of meaning of the master's degree and the production of qualified teachers short of the Ph.D.; provision for accelerating

progress toward the doctorate; identification of the gifted student early and requiring of them more rigorous intellectual training; better articulation of undergraduate and graduate work; and finally, a marked reduction in attrition, and hence of waste, in the graduate schools.[1]

These programs are so new that it is not yet possible to know whether they will bring about any change in the traditional pattern of looking upon the completion of the bachelor's degree as the point at which students shift from an undergraduate college to a graduate school in another university. Most gifted undergraduates, it may be guessed, will probably not stop short of the Ph.D. The other goals of the MA-3 program are little different from the goals of good departmental honors programs or from those set by the Woodrow Wilson Fellowship program in terms of the kind of students it encourages universities to prepare and nominate for awards. Finally, the movement to expand honors programs from the traditional departmental programs of the upper division to full four-year programs, by minimizing the break between lower- and upper-division undergraduate work, will probably make the MA-3 pattern less appealing to colleges. Those involved in good undergraduate four-year honors programs are likely to feel that such programs can achieve the major goals of the MA-3 programs in four rather than five years.

As important as the relationship between undergraduate honors and the graduate school is the horizontal relationship between the departmental program and other aspects of honors in the upper division. The University of Kansas has not as yet developed a general

[1] "Three-year Master's Degree Programs," *The Superior Student*, March–April, 1963.

university honors program at the upper-division level of the effective kind that has long existed at the University of Colorado, and, more recently, in other university programs. To fill the need that many staff and students have felt for greater breadth than can occur in a departmental program, two different directions have been taken. First, in the B.A. program there are limitations on the degree of concentration a student may have in a single department, and hence the student has many electives. A majority of the honors students in recent years have chosen to complete two or three majors, often, but not always, doing the honors program in each major. For example, in 1962–1963 of the total number of junior-senior majors in arts and sciences 318 students were doing double and triple majors, frequently choosing their second major without reference to whether it directly supported their first major. Double and triple majors are much more common among honors students than among nonhonors students.

The first student to complete a triple major (mathematics, political science, and German) was a member of the class of 1961. He later received an Oxford degree in jurisprudence and is now a graduate student in political science at Princeton. His current attitude toward his undergraduate program is mixed:

> My case is particularly complicated by the fact that I took a triple major. The novelty of this has been of great advantage to me in several respects, but I would suggest that it was not, perhaps, educationally the best thing to do. Honors students should be encouraged, especially in their junior and senior years, to improve the quality and not only the quantity of their work. The senior thesis in political science partially performed this function.... In mathematics the quality element was provided by the increased element of competition with graduate students.

One of the more interesting reports came from an honors graduate of 1960 with a double major in English and mathematics:

> After graduation I took an M.A.T. in mathematics at Harvard.... As an undergraduate I had been unable to decide whether I wanted to teach English or math; so I applied for the M.A.T. program at Harvard in math and at Vanderbilt in English. My decision, then, was that I would prefer Cambridge to Nashville.

The multiple major is not the only solution to the problem of breadth in the upper division. The honors committee at Kansas supplemented the small Western Civilization discussion groups of the freshman year and the Eastern Civilization groups of the sophomore year with two additional levels of interdisciplinary seminar-discussion groups in the upper division. For the junior year there were created three seminars, one each in the humanities, the social sciences, and the natural sciences. All upper-division honors students were eligible for each seminar except those taking majors in the area it covered. For seniors an honors seminar in contemporary intellectual issues was established; this seminar, open to all honors students in their last year, is a very flexible discussion group in which the students themselves plan much of the program. The junior seminars have sometimes been a major influence upon individual students, but on the whole they have commanded less interest than the senior interdisciplinary seminar.

The recent rapid growth in honors programs, both departmental and general, in colleges and universities is a sound development in the continuing effort to improve undergraduate education. All of the data on the departmental program at the University of Kansas indicate that it is in a healthy state. Graduates with honors are enthusiastic over their experiences. They emphasize the importance of the quality of the professors involved in the programs; they insist upon the value of freedom, flexibility, and independent work. They feel that their program could have been more rigorous and demanding, and they are concerned about the need for both depth and breadth in education, although they disagree on the relative emphasis each should receive. On the whole, however, they make no demands for radical changes. Most earlier graduates who are already in university teaching are actively working to develop programs in their own departments; and those who are still in graduate school may be expected to do the same.

Much of the increase in quality of higher education in the United States in recent years is attributable to the new emphasis on excellence which both students and teachers have shared. The most important channels for the exercise of this impulse, particularly in the large public universities, have been undergraduate honors programs like the one described in this chapter.

IN DISCUSSING what an honors course in science might or should be, one must keep in mind constantly that science is now very mobile. Boundaries between disciplines are always shifting, new models are constantly being proposed and accepted, and well-established concepts can be swept away in a surprisingly short time. The interval between discovery and exploitation of discovery is becoming remarkably brief. An inevitable consequence for education is the shrinking of the interval between discovery and incorporation into course content. This has almost precipitated a crisis in textbook preparation (perhaps an obsolete occupation in any case), in the preparation of teachers, and in the communication of research results. Whatever it does, or is, the honors course in science must reflect and meet the challenge of the complex interaction of intellectual forces that is producing this ever-changing pattern.

Many scientists will maintain that their courses are inherently honors courses. By this they mean to say that their students are already selected to some degree and that the course content is "solid." Moreover, a vertical structuring obtains in the sciences—course A must precede course B; this is not so often the case in the humanities or social sciences. A vertical structuring does not always make a true honors course. A course in science may be difficult, even exhaustive, but unless it presents a subject as a portion of current intellectual enterprise, it most certainly is not an honors course.

Scientists do not always agree with their colleagues in other disciplines concerning the value of honors courses or honors devices. In part, this may arise from a difference in attitude toward research. Undergraduate participation in research in the sciences has been reasonably common for a generation. Moreover, during this time the majority of scientists have been caught up in the scientific enterprise—they have been activist and research-oriented. In contrast, teachers and scholars in other disciplines more easily identify with the intellectual and contemplative tradition.

Another factor may also enter. In the humanities, the term "scholar" connotes approbation, and the role of critic is considered a valid and commendable one. In science very few men who are not originators of knowledge enjoy genuine esteem. We are all aware that some colleagues, intent on writing or investigation, have managed to exclude the student rather effectively, but this is not the general case. Most scientists seek a position where they must contend with the attack of youthful intelligence. In science, then, the honors device must be openly designed in the interest of *both* student and faculty member. What will be wanted is a device for a more productive and more enjoyable association between a highly trained and educated man and a group of critical and intelligent neophytes.

It is also true that the majority of those teaching undergraduate science are strongly motivated to ensure acceptance of their students by graduate schools with prestige. In science, success often requires uninterrupted progression through the Ph.D. and even postdoctoral training. It therefore follows that emphasis will be placed upon professionalism, at least in the sense of preparing students for graduate experience. This emphasis is by no means as strong in humanities and social sciences, where the Ph.D. is often earned over a much longer time span during which a man or woman often takes a teaching position. In the sciences there is great pressure to move students into and through graduate school as rapidly as possible. It may be assumed that students deserving honors will be precisely those who will go to graduate school.

The honors course in science has often been discussed as a device for proselyting young scientists. This is unrealistic for the following reasons. First, those who become scientists very frequently elect a discipline during their period of secondary education. Second, the young scientist is so amply rewarded that most college freshmen are aware of the financial and social benefits to be derived from a scientific career. Third, it is commonly observed that students will flow to centers of activity and excitement, of change and challenge. The research laboratory today is such a center, and the problem is not to interest the student but rather to ensure his fitness to participate.

To avoid meaningless generalities, we must recognize that there are a number of requirements within the science enterprise. Begin with the biased view that honors work in science shall be designed to produce, most efficiently, successful scientists. One major consideration appears immediately—how much time does the student have to achieve success? If he is to do theoretical work, the time is very short. His most important contributions are expected before age thirty-five. The experimentalist has five to ten years more. The professional in medicine and engineering supplies a service function that will extend to the end of his life. Certainly, no single honors program can serve students in each of these categories adequately. The incipient theoretician must be set upon his own path with the utmost dispatch, the experimentalist must be engaged in research at the earliest moment, the professional will require contact with the demands of the microsociety within which he will work.

Relatively little has been done for the theoretician. Perhaps the best thing to do is to develop reliable selection rules and then stand aside. It may be noted that the development of mathematics majors is very different from the development of those in the experimental sciences. The latter, in contrast, require substantial and complex support. Such support is partly furnished at present by the National Science Foundation Programs in Undergraduate Research Participation and Undergraduate Independent Study. In order to increase the effectiveness of this support and to acquaint students with scientific undertakings, gifted high school students are also offered programs during the summer, and no doubt the sophistication of students who have attended such programs has increased markedly.

What is honors in the sciences?

It is a moot point whether such programs are truly honors programs, because there is so little agreement as to what constitutes honors. It is my own bias that whether a course or program is honors is partly determined by intent, and that if the intent is simply to provide an intense exposure to science per se calling it honors means very little. Many of the so-called honors courses in science are a college analogue of the secondary-school track system. The existence of such courses is not a function of commitment but a function of money. The average instructor in science will continue to wince at the term "honors" precisely because it presents him with a welter of conflicting emotive symbols. As a group scientists tend to be quite egalitarian. To label a course that he teaches well for professional reasons an *honors* course, and hence to hint at elitism, is a social error. Scientists are weary of the elitist label so often given them. They are eager to be part of society—and resist being further differentiated.

What is quite patently an honors course in science is one that attempts to develop cross links within science and external to science. Even here there is some confusion. The course entitled Physical Science Survey has not earned the respect generally accorded to the Survey of English Literature. One is terminal, the other not. One is a spectator course, the other induces participation in an intellectual venture. In the college analogue of the track system the Physical Science Survey has been delegated to the service of various curricula. Its counterpart in the first track must now be called something else. It is supposed to accommodate students majoring in all areas, and there is a growing demand that it serve as part of a science sequence so that it not be mandatorily terminal. In addition there is an implicit admonition to relate science to a variety of modes of thought. All of the aspirations of the liberal arts seem to be included in the paradigm. The description is not that of a course but of a way of life. Strangely enough, one does not hear loud clamor for a course in economics that relates to science as part of the liberal arts—nor are such demands made upon history, sociology, or psychology.

An attempt to furnish a course that might meet some of these demands has resulted in the development of the interdisciplinary course. This variation of the survey course abandons the concept of a course as a collection of information to be passed on or as propaganda for the good name of science. Rather it attempts to follow a concept with its tributary ideas without regard to the territorial claims of the disciplines. An admirable example is the one-semester science course for sophomore nonscience majors at the University of Michigan.[1] It results from the cooperative lecturing of an astronomer, a geologist, a physicist, and a zoologist. These particular disciplines were chosen because they were appropriate to the theme of the course, the theme of evolutionary processes. Anyone familiar with Blum's *Time's Arrow* or Wiener's discussion of irreversible time will see at once that such a theme can call into play a wide variety of important ideas. Such a course avoids the offense of superficial treatment, and it also avoids the episodic nature of a block-and-gap organization. It is limited in appeal only by the imagination and energy of the participants and the funds at their disposal.

One noteworthy feature of this course is that it offers no laboratory experience. On this matter there can be no unanimity of opinion among educators or students. One point of view insists that the natural sciences are primarily experimental. Without denying this, it may be held that an interdisciplinary course like the one described above may be jeopardized if the quite considerable teaching problems encountered in the laboratory are added. Another type of course may be developed to provide the encounter between the concept and the object, but in such a course the number of ideas handled must be substantially fewer.

What most of us desire fervently is that the student learn how to achieve a synthesis of the many modes of thought to which he is subjected. This probably cannot be done vicariously, as in a course, but there are various devices to facilitate such an endeavor. One of these, though not designated honors, is the freshman seminar at Harvard. In many other schools colloquia are offered in the later

[1] *The Superior Student,* Sept.–Oct., 1958; July–Aug., 1960.

years. Another is the departmental seminar which, in the sciences, tends to promote synthesis within the discipline.

We all agree that excellence in teaching is an important concern, but the question remains of how to achieve it. The science teacher has been bombarded in recent years with materials and with suggestions for good teaching. It would be understandable if the average college teacher concluded that society had lost faith in his competence to teach. Even less respect is accorded the high school teacher. The spirit of the age is that a few master teachers should teach everybody, or at least set the norm. This has resulted in biology texts and materials emanating from the American Institute of Biological Sciences, a national televised course in physics, a physics text for high schools prepared by a team at MIT and financed by NSF, and two projects in the presentation of chemistry for secondary schools—the Chemical Bond Approach and the Chem Study Program. It is only a matter of time until college freshmen will be accorded the same—the Very Best from the Very Few.

The honors approach opposes such a development. It insists that any subject can be viewed in a very large number of ways, and that each instructor is not only entitled but expected to develop his own view. In chemistry and physics, and to a lesser extent in other sciences, a tension develops that has a greater intensity than in other fields. The science instructor wants his honors course populated by majors, and occasionally the majors cannot meet the general requirements for honors. The result is that he will wish an honors course to admit honors students and majors, a practice that tends to augment the intensity of the course and to reduce its breadth.

An examination of the sixteen points characteristic of a full honors program (shown in the Appendix to Chapter 3) indicates applicable demands that are met by an excellent science department in a college or university. For example, good students are selected early for research participation and special counseling. The laboratory is the physical facility that brings students into contact over significant periods of time. The important characteristic that cannot be provided by any one department is exposure of the student to different modes of thought.

The last point is probably the most significant in discussing what an honors program in the sciences should be. The relation of scientific ideas to the general intellectual activity, and the communication of this relation, is perhaps the most difficult teaching commitment that one can assume. It is a synthesis that, ideally, the student should make for himself, but all indications are that this has not generally occurred and probably will not to any extent without help.

During a conference on science and contemporary social problems that I attended in June–July, 1964, informal conversation revealed that a number of experiments have been tried and are being tried to meet this problem. The seminar or colloquium format seems best in many cases, especially when the goal is to inculcate attitudes or awareness rather than a discrete body of knowledge. There seems no special virtue in restricting such seminars to any segment of the college career—e.g., to freshmen only, to nonmajors only—precisely because it is so difficult to offer the course at the right time.

In the hands of a skilled instructor a more formal course may serve. In 1963 Dr. G. Holton presented a paper at the International Conference on Physics in General Education [2] in which he detailed proposals for a connective physics course. In his view, "the important topic is not to what extent science is separated from other activities, but rather how we may define and transmit culture in such a

[2] See *The Superior Student*, Sept.–Oct., 1963.

way that the sciences are seen to be valid components of our culture." He proposed a course in which concepts in physics would be discussed not only in their relation to other ideas in physics but also to their use in chemistry or biology and their impact on philosophy or on foreign policy; and in which the developments in physics would be handled as a history of ideas to be correlated with other historical material. The student would be urged to write essays so that he would actively participate in exploring these interrelationships. Holton has emphasized that the type of course being urged would be quite soundly *in* physics and not just *about* physics, and that it would involve development and use of the elements of calculus. Moreover, the instructor would seek advice from colleagues in other disciplines, and the course would "help to cement the bonds of colleagueship across departmental frontiers."

Doubtless a course like this would receive the endorsement of many staff members; however, it is equally likely that few people would be found who could execute it properly, or, being capable, would devote the time. It is to Professor Holton's credit that he observes the development of such a course by one department only as hardly sufficient: "It will be when many fields follow our lead and adopt the method sketched ... that our culture will be seen, by teachers as well as students, to have the coherences which indeed already exist, but which so far have not been nurtured, conveyed, and championed enough in our time." Somewhat similar suggestions were made concerning courses in chemistry by Drs. A. B. Garrett and C. Leake at a conference on chemistry for nonscience majors at Montana State College in 1960. Again the purpose was to explore relevance of the subject to other disciplines.

It is debatable whether a single course or a seminar can accomplish what is wanted—which is, after all, a change in educational philosophy. The relations to be explored are so numerous that anything less than a total educational milieu may fail. Such a climate was extant during my undergraduate years at Reed College thirty years ago. There liberal arts education was understood to demand synthesis of knowledge of all kinds, and many courses were explicitly related to one another. Successfully introducing such a program on a large scale in a university is a difficult task. (At the University of Oregon the Honors College was established in the hope that progress might be made more rapidly with a smaller group. Presumably changes of attitude will then diffuse throughout the university.)

In the sciences there is a real danger that those interested in promoting general educational activities will be walled off and pejoratively termed "college" people. The "university" persuasion of intense specialization also involves research participation, often of a high caliber. In most university science departments today there is pressure to develop research men as rapidly as possible and to distinguish, more and more, courses for "majors" from courses for "nonmajors." Thus, education becomes training and training under high pressure. This is only to be expected in a society that honors the utility of science so much and does not put a high economic value on those types of learning that are "nonscientific."

Bentley Glass has stated that "A liberal education is not a matter of choosing this or that curriculum; it is a progressive liberation of the mind." [3] Much earlier Whitehead wrote: "If we are finally to sum up in one phrase the peculiar impress on character to be obtained from a scientific training, I would say that it is a certain type of instinctive direction in thought and observation of nature, and a

[3] Bentley Glass, *Science and Liberal Education,* Baton Rouge, La.: Louisiana State University Press, 1959.

facility of imagination in respect to the objects thus contemplated, issuing in a stimulus toward creativeness." [4] Instead of bewailing the polarity of the scientific and humanistic viewpoints it would be far better to exploit this tension. The dreams of the humanist can be enlarged and his creativeness increased by a knowledge of science. But for this to happen there must be the proper intent and adequate goodwill. If the liberal arts college cannot manage this it must indeed cease to pose as a repository of culture. Furthermore, in a world where man has nearly attained control of his natural environment—"the world of nature"—but has not come close to mastering his own nature, there must clearly be concern for matters that lie outside the boundaries of science.

Honors in the sciences today

Turning from a general to a specific discussion of honors in science, we can attempt to see what is actually being done today. The data in Table 3 for seventeen varied institutions selected at random illustrate several points about current honors activities in science. A majority of the institutions report honors of some kind for freshmen; it is less clear that sophomores are heavily engaged. Most institutions have well-developed departmental honors for juniors and seniors. Undergraduate research may provide a continuing activity. And science for the nonspecialist is a source of concern and the object of experimentation in a number of institutions.

SCIENCE HONORS IN LIBERAL ARTS INSTITUTIONS

A look at honors programs in science in various colleges and universities reveals the great diversity that might be expected. An hon-

[4] Alfred North Whitehead, *Essays in Science and Philosophy*, New York: Philosophical Library, Inc., 1947.

	Freshman seminar or freshman honors	Science as part of honors college	Departmental honors	Under-graduate research	Independent study	Science for non-specialist
Amherst College			jr.–sen.			
California Institute of Technology	+			+		
University of Colorado	+		jr.–sen.	+		+
DePauw University			jr.–sen.	+	fr. soph.	+
Harvard University	+			+		
University of Idaho	biol.		jr.–sen.			soph.
University of Michigan						+
University of Michigan Medical School				+		
Montana State University	+		jr.–sen.			
Newark College of Engineering	+		jr.–sen.	+		
University of North Carolina	+		soph.–jr.–sen.			
University of Oregon	+	+		+		+
Oregon State University	+		jr.–sen.	+		
Princeton University			soph.–jr.–sen.			
Rutgers University			jr.–sen.		fr. soph.	+
University of Washington School of Medicine			sen.			
Wesleyan University					+	+

ors program for freshmen and sophomores at Yale, which arose from a more general program, is called Directed Studies in Science.[5] Through this program nonscience majors, or those who have not chosen a major, can participate in special courses that provide a sound background in mathematics, physics, chemistry, biology, and geology during the first two years.

Brown University continues experimentation with "IC" courses —courses belonging to a program of Identification and Criticism of Ideas.[6] Freshmen and sophomores participate, and the classes are limited to twenty students. Each course is rooted in a classic, such as Darwin's *The Origin of Species,* or a concept, such as that of energy. Science courses in the program are offered by the departments of biology, physics, psychology, geology, and mathematics. Courses like these clearly invite the finest kind of teaching and present an opportunity for genuinely close student-instructor relationships.

Another freshman-sophomore program offering courses in science to selected students is found at Princeton. A substantial percentage of the students (called University Scholars) in this program are anticipating a degree in mathematics or natural sciences.[7] In this program the exceptional student is allowed to specialize as much as he chooses. The faculty and administration are confident that the student will recognize his own needs for breadth and will undertake to fill those needs with the advice and guidance of a faculty member. No faculty member is allowed to advise, officially, more than one University Scholar in each undergraduate class.

A two-year program is being tested at Wesleyan University. The interdisciplinary course for the first year is not meant for superior

[5] See *The Superior Student,* Nov., 1959.

[6] J. R. Workman, *New Horizons of Higher Education,* Washington, D.C.: Public Affairs Press, 1959.

[7] *The Superior Student,* Jan.–Feb., 1962.

students only but does employ honors practices.[8] It is designed for the student who is not anticipating a career in the sciences or who is poorly prepared to choose one. Each formal class presentation is followed by a period devoted to independent readings or laboratory work. A second-year course concerned with life, man, and society involves the departments of biology, psychology, philosophy, and mathematics.

A very different type of emphasis has characterized an experimental program at Providence College.[9] Here the intent is to involve the superior student in research as deeply and as rapidly as possible. A few selected students are allowed to move as quickly as they can through science courses, finishing most of them in the freshman-sophomore years. They then devote the final two years principally to research.

The Swarthmore honors program in science is confined to the junior and senior years. The division of natural sciences specifies a rather more organized program than do the humanities and social sciences. Successful completion of honors depends on the ability to pass final comprehensive examinations which involve outside examiners.

In this connection might be mentioned the intense reaction of some graduate schools to any program that departs from the traditional and well-established grading system. Occasionally the science student who participates in a science honors program finds his choice of graduate schools somewhat narrowed. At the present time the policies of some of the university graduate schools must be considered a real deterrent to honors programs in science except those that are frankly departmental and devoted to early specialization.

[8] *The Superior Student,* Oct., 1960.
[9] *The Superior Student,* May–June, 1960.

Finally, an excellent brief review of honors programs in chemistry in various institutions is supplied in articles by B. R. Willeford, Jr., R. W. Parry, and W. B. Guenther in the *Journal of Chemical Education*.[10] And a survey of honors programs in psychology in forty colleges and universities, both state-supported and private, as of 1962 is reported by J. W. Cohen in *The Superior Student*.[11]

SCIENCE HONORS IN THE PROFESSIONAL SCHOOLS

Various kinds of honors arrangements have also developed in professional schools. It has been contended that technology is the bridge between science and the humanities.[12] For this to be true those designing the professional curricula must moderate the demands of the basic sciences and attempt some appreciation of the nature of man. The evidence shows that a very large number of compromises along these lines are possible.

A survey of honors programs in engineering recently published [13] notes that the engineering curriculum has taken on some of the aspects of a game—a situation easily understandable in view of the fact that the average engineering curriculum contains three to four thousand items. The selection of strictly scientific subjects is a complex problem, but, in any case, the institutions surveyed generally agreed that about one-fourth of the work of honors students in engineering should be in the humanities and social sciences. Despite some popular misconceptions, neither the engineering faculties nor their students seem disposed to eliminate man as an object of study.

[10] *Journal of Chemical Education*, vol. 39, pp. 110, 114, 118 (1962).

[11] *The Superior Student*, Sept.–Oct., 1962.

[12] See, for example, K. Denbigh, *Science, Industry and Social Policy*, Edinburgh and London: Oliver & Boyd Ltd., 1963, and Eric Ashby, *Technology and the Academics*, New York: The Macmillan Company, 1959.

[13] F. Kreith and J. M. Allen (eds.), *Honors Programs in Engineering*, Boston: Allyn and Bacon, Inc., 1964.

The demands of professional schools, particularly those training people for professions that are science-oriented, have always posed difficulties for the university. The curricular prejudices of the scientist or scholar who is primarily preoccupied with creating new knowledge will forever differ from the beliefs of those who wish to use knowledge to control the environment and for the benefit of man generally. In the great centers of technology such as MIT or Cal Tech the "liberal arts" are considered an adjunct to the main business of scientific technology—but an adjunct that, though subservient, is indispensable. In the more diversified type of university the structure of departments and schools is such as to strengthen the resistance to "service courses"—and with good reason, since it is difficult to design courses that will satisfy the several professional schools within the resources available. At the same time the professional schools are making a demand—one that is altogether reasonable—for some kind of integration of view, some consolidation of attitude, within the humanities and the social sciences. If pride and vested interests are put aside, there would seem to be no obstacle to fulfilling this demand. Fundamentally it involves the same approach as that desired for honors in the liberal arts curriculum.

One of the recommendations agreed upon in the study of honors in engineering mentioned above is that a course in the "history and philosophy of science and technology" should be required of all engineering majors. Hopefully, this course would *contain material on* the philosophy of science, the history of science, and the history of technology. Quite apart from this quibble, it would seem profitable to include such a course in any honors curriculum. In general, science faculties do not manage much enthusiasm for such courses because they consider them to be "about" rather than "in" science. As yet the number of men and women capable of teaching such a course is quite small. However, the steady output of the few excellent departments now in operation will undoubtedly increase the stature of the field so that the flavor of scientism and antiquarianism will disappear.

The medical school curriculum is, like that of engineering, also in flux. To compound the difficulties already mentioned, the medical school is often separated physically from the main campus of the university. Some of the needs of a broad program are filled by proper premedical curricula and wise counseling, but often attempts to emphasize nonscience subjects severely reduce the student's opportunities for participating in research. An attempt to remedy this is exemplified by the honors-type Special Studies Program at the University of Michigan Medical School. This program is intended primarily for students in the first two years of medical school, but does not exclude those in the last two years. The University of Washington School of Medicine maintains an honors program for students in the top 10 percent of the fourth-year class. They are given the privilege of organizing their own programs of study, and can choose to remain at the University of Washington or study at any other university. Moreover, they may spend their time in course work or research in a basic science department. The honors program at the University of Kansas School of Medicine is chiefly characterized by the establishment of a tutorial system involving the faculty member as tutor. Stanford University School of Medicine intends to establish an honors system to promote more extensive collaboration between those in medicine and those in social science of the behavioral cast. The School of Medicine at the University of Arkansas maintains an honors program which the student can enter in the sophomore premedical year and which encourages independent study and research.

Some attention is also being given to honors in schools of agriculture—for example, the College of Agriculture at the University of Illinois has established programs covering the first three years. During the first two the selected students are required to participate in special seminars; in the third year they participate in honors courses in one of the other colleges of the university.

EVALUATION OF TWO SCIENCE HONORS PROGRAMS

Finally, we can look at honors in science from another perspective by examining the results of two recent evaluations of honors-type activities in science.

The first of these is the survey of the National Science Foundation Undergraduate Science Education Program made by the staff of the ICSS.[14] Questionnaires were sent to both students and faculty participating in this program in a variety of institutions throughout the United States. Some of the conclusions were as follows: Rarely did students express disapproval of the program; they appreciated in particular the opportunity to engage in some measure in a research project. Most of the students who participated already contemplated a research or teaching career, and hence the program had only an occasional impact on motivation; the research experience unquestionably reinforced their career plans but significantly altered those of only a few. A similar pattern emerged for plans to do graduate work; nearly 70 percent were already contemplating the Ph.D., but the program reinforced the intention to proceed. This was particularly true in physics and biology, less true in chemistry and mathematics. The faculty felt that participation in the program made the students more independent and confident, increased their curiosity, and developed professional maturity.

[14] *The Superior Student*, July–Aug., 1963.

The second evaluation is one made in 1963 of the freshman seminar [15] offered at Harvard since 1959. Unlike the highly diversified program described above, the freshman seminar was instituted to solve a more parochial problem. This was to induce self-awareness, to orient the freshman as an independent being, to provide a special kind of general education. It was explicitly stated that the program was not honors. Nevertheless, we note it here because the same activity in a state university, or in many colleges, would be part of an honors program. Obviously the selection of students and the size and character of the seminar would be modified accordingly.

The Harvard seminars are elective and ungraded; they are intended to engage the student in the life of the university. Typically, each enrolls from eight to ten students and meets once a week. Subject matter, degree of specialization, and depth of inquiry all vary greatly. According to a report dated February, 1963,[16] the program has been declared a success. However, it is noteworthy that the science seminars were generally less satisfactory than those in the humanities and social sciences. Not only were the demands on faculty time felt to be more serious, but it seemed to be difficult to provide the right seminar at the right time. It is no surprise that the

[15] It is necessary to note here that the terms "seminar" and "colloquium" no longer have unique meanings. To the social scientist a seminar often signifies a small upper class or graduate course with an instructor and students. To the scientist the seminar usually signifies a series of regularly scheduled meetings with a different speaker and a variable audience at each. To the student "to have a seminar" often means "to hold a bull session." Thus "freshman seminar" must be understood in terms of the folkways of its sponsoring institution.

[16] Byron Stookey, "The Freshman Seminar Program," *A Report to the Faculty of Arts and Sciences,* Harvard University, Cambridge, Mass., February, 1963.

greatest difficulty lay in providing science seminars for those not originally intending to pursue science as a career. More experimentation was urged in seminars relating science to other areas.

In the science seminars as in no other, preparation was found to be a crucial factor. Those students with a good background and enthusiasm for science did benefit from association with a working scientist. Those who had no such background, and consequently needed the experience more, found the problem of "language" a severe handicap. The seminars were not intended to substitute for science courses but rather to enhance the significance or function of those courses. Yet the report observes:

> The constituency and impact of seminars in the sciences will continue to depend upon the way in which the credit granted by the seminars gets related to curricular requirements—to some extent on its relation to departmental requirements, but principally on its relation to General Education. To the extent that an appropriate seminar in science can help to meet the lower level General Education requirement it will attract the less, in addition to the more, committed.

The future of honors in science

It is tempting to predict that departmental honors in science will continue to expand and that research participation will also expand as long as governmental subsidies are forthcoming. As high school instruction continues to improve and advanced placement spreads, honors programs for freshmen will also be encouraged. This in turn will predispose toward four-year programs. Just how the faculty will respond to such pressures is not certain. With growing student bodies, more pressure to do research, and increased difficulty in keeping current in one's specialty, it is difficult to know what compromise may prove the best. The temptation to accept honors students is great because they are the students who are most stimulating.

Less predictable is the future of science courses for the non-science major. Any solution to this problem requires much more time and money than currently seems available for such a purpose. It is quite possible that such courses will eventually be taught by faculty specially trained for this purpose. For an excellent collection of thoughts on this subject, the reader is referred to the report of a conference on "Education in Science for the Undergraduate Non-Science Concentrator," held at Rochester, Michigan, in 1962.[17] In the final session of this conference seven resolutions were agreed upon; in abbreviated form they are:

1. All college students should take two one-year courses in science; these should include physics, biology, and the elements of calculus.

2. Colleges and their faculties must recognize the necessity of science *teaching* and its support.

3. Support must be sought for *general* science courses.

4. Both small-scale and large-scale programs in science education should be supported.

5. Better high school practices are crucial to a solution of college problems in teaching science.

6. Pluralism, not randomism, in science education is to be encouraged.

7. A continuing conference on science instruction for non-science students should be established.

[17] R. Hoopes (ed.), *Science in the College Curriculum,* Rochester, Mich.: Oakland University Press, 1963.

The seminar or colloquium style seems well adapted to the honors approach in science, and use of it will probably increase, particularly where funds are available for visiting speakers.

Science activities are expanding so rapidly that the difficulties already inherent in the pedagogy have become greatly magnified. At the same time very large numbers of students are now being taught rather well. Despondency about the future of honors in science does not seem justified. All present signs point to adequate subsidy to ensure well-educated scientists.

Beyond mere survival of honors in science, however, is a more central concern. This is well stated by Raymond Aron: "In a democratic regime, public opinion must be sufficiently informed to permit the rulers to listen to the advice of the scientist. In this sense, democracy in our era remains more than ever a wager on the capacity of man to learn and to understand." [18]

Epilogue

In the above I have attempted to describe what *is* or what is *intended;* but now, separately, I want to state what I believe *should be.* Unquestionably such a statement will reflect personal bias, but it may be valuable if only as a basis of argument. Thus, in what follows I set forth my own prejudices.

The fundamental thesis is simply that higher education should be devoted to the cultivation of the intellect. A university education should provide a large number of opportunities for students to work toward becoming intellectuals. It should persuade students that statesmanship is worth striving for, that social responsibility re-

[18] R. Aron, *Daedalus,* 1962. See also Gordon Brown's chapter in this issue.

quires a perusal of many value structures and an understanding of many kinds of men. In short, some students should develop an appreciation of the privilege of joining in the great stream of intellectual effort that constantly reforms our culture.

But even in the finest universities only a small fraction of the students will be exposed to such an education, and of those only a fraction will respond. In the ideal university there would be no need for an honors program—but we work in nonideal institutions. It is my prejudice that the honors program should be structured to serve the ideal—the ideal university, the ideal student, the ideal professor. If the nonideality of the environment is great enough, then the honors group will take on some of the character of an elite just as the science group has done in some institutions. In a pluralistic society this should be unremarkable.

An esteemed colleague of mine has noted that the state universities have initiated very few interesting honors experiments. The record will verify this. Many of the programs called "honors" are quite recognizably attempts to increase the student's proficiency in a professional discipline. It is the state university, which hovers in the focus of anti-intellectual forces, that must avoid every appearance of limiting egalitarianism. Thus, the state university is a very unlikely harbor for any but the lonely intellectual.

Yet some of us believe that even the intellectual should be assimilable by the multiversity if the university is to persist. The question is whether the university administration can, and will, find the means to support an intellectual enterprise vigorous enough to retain and challenge the potential intellectual.

I am assured by many that the scientist today is accorded great respect. It is a pity that he is really respected as a technologist rather than a scientist: He is looked upon as a man who helps make nature subservient to man. We will always need such technologists, and this need will grow, requiring our universities to produce more and more people so trained. Undoubtedly the trend is toward professionalism at all levels. The multiversities have become increasingly involved in "training" students, with gratifying results if we consider only the output of useful citizens.

Because of this emphasis, many institutions will probably attack the problem of teaching science to the nonscience major by instituting *training* programs. A knowledge of science will be so necessary to earning a living that no education philosophy will be involved. What forces will then promote an *understanding* of science among honors students?

I raise this question because the nature of the scientific enterprise is now such that some public *understanding* of scientific doctrine is imperative. In their own self-interest, if not for less selfish motives, scientists must engender sympathetic reception of their proposals. What better audience could be asked than a group of honors students? Here, in mind-to-mind combat, the scientist may play the field and in a variety of modes.

In brief, it is probably pointless to attempt a formal solution to the problem of teaching science to nonscientists. Each man who undertakes this task should improvise according to his talents, taking into account his audience and the educational environment. He has no hard core of subject matter to impart, but rather an attitude toward the world, some working hypotheses. In our less-than-ideal university it is unlikely that such difficult teaching will be rewarded, but fortunately even less-than-ideal universities have a few professors who like to teach.

In the last analysis the honors enterprise is rather self-contradictory. We must aim to produce intellectuals, reflective individuals. At the same time we must attempt to handle as many likely candidates as possible. Somehow the intensive demands of the individual and the extensive demands of the *class* of individuals must be conciliated. For the scientist who is intellectually involved the problem is no greater than for the nonscientist.

Chapter nine / Challenging the

superior student in the small private

college / William E. Cadbury, Jr.,

Haverford College

EDUCATIONAL INSTITUTIONS of all types are faced with the problem of how to ensure the best possible education for their best students. One way to meet this need is to establish special honors programs for these students. There are also other ways, some more suitable to one type of institution, and some to another. This chapter describes what the independent liberal arts colleges are doing about this problem. It also considers some of the broader implications for the liberal arts colleges of the emphasis on excellence and the methods used to promote excellence.

The Inter-University Committee on the Superior Student has been influential in promoting excellence on all kinds of campuses, but it was initially conceived to serve superior students in the large state universities and colleges, and its point of view has been predominantly that of the university. Although the Committee has been hospitable to ideas from the smaller colleges and has reported much information on these institutions in *The Superior Student,* its work and the views expressed in its newsletter have not had as much influence among the colleges as among the universities.

191

In January of 1960 a small committee, the College Committee on Outstanding Students (CCOS), was formed to collect information and to raise questions about the way colleges were meeting the problem of challenging the superior student. Like the ICSS, the CCOS was supported by a grant from the Carnegie Corporation. In March of 1961, it called a national conference to discuss this and related problems.[1]

Following this national conference, the Committee held a number of meetings and sponsored several regional conferences to discuss problems that arose out of, and after, the original conference. The ideas developed in these conferences form a basis for much of the material presented here.

The college and the university

Although in attempting to meet the needs of superior students the colleges and the universities encounter many of the same problems, differences in such characteristics as size and homogeneity may require quite different approaches to solving these problems.

The liberal arts college is a single unit; all of the students enrolled in that unit presumably have roughly similar goals. The university has many units, of which one, whether called the college of liberal arts or something else, is like a liberal arts college. Usually, most of the work in honors within the university is done in the college of liberal arts. When I compare the independent college and the university here I am speaking of the *whole* college and this *part* of the university.

The students in most small colleges are all liberal arts students—if

[1] For a report of the conference, see W. E. Cadbury, Jr., "Outstanding Students in Liberal Arts Colleges," *Liberal Education*, December, 1961.

not by inclination, at least by formal enrollment. In universities containing other undergraduate schools (for example, education, business administration, and pharmacy) any course, especially at the lower-class level, taken by liberal arts students may also enroll students from other parts of the university whose goals, both immediate and long-range, and whose points of view are quite different from those of students in the liberal arts college.

There is also a significant difference in the roles played by faculty in the two types of institutions. The faculty member in the small college teaches only undergraduates, the best of whom are obviously the best students he encounters. His counterpart in the university may well teach students enrolled in other undergraduate colleges in the university along with students in the liberal arts college. He also teaches graduate students to whom—because of their maturity, their specialized interest in the discipline, and their singleness of purpose, and because of the special nature of graduate teaching—he gives a great deal of attention. Usually, therefore, the able student gets more individual attention from the best professors in a college than he would from comparable professors in the university. The important difference, then, is not so much one of the number of students as of the focus of faculty attention.

The quality of an educational institution has little to do with size. There are strong and weak institutions both large and small; neither type has any monopoly on quality. Although the degree of homogeneity of an institution's student body can markedly affect the way the problems discussed here can be attacked, the effect of selectivity on such problems can easily be exaggerated. One or two critics of the original plans of the CCOS maintained that since the colleges then involved were selective, all of their students should be "outstanding" and none needed special consideration. But, obviously, no college is this selective; some students are always better than others, and even if abilities were identical, differences in such particulars as motivation, health, and freedom from economic stress would bring about marked differences in performance. Even a very selective college or university has some students who stand out above the others.

Differences among the colleges

The forty-five colleges represented at the first CCOS conference were a fairly homogeneous group of small liberal arts colleges with selective admissions policies and high standards. The group was deliberately kept homogeneous so that the discussions would have a common base. There are many other small (fewer than 2,000 students) private colleges devoted to the liberal arts across the country, some of them like those in the original group, some quite different. Where there are major differences in selectivity, or in resources, there are obvious implications for honors work.

In colleges where both students and faculty are excellent and teaching loads light, opportunities for giving the best students all the attention they need are abundant, whether or not special programs are provided for them. Where resources are meager, special efforts may be needed to do justice to the most able.

At many small colleges, twelve hours a week is a normal teaching load; at some others, nine hours or less is normal. Where the load is fifteen hours a week or more, faculty members have to struggle hard to find the time to meet special challenges. But perhaps it is under these circumstances that special efforts are most needed in order to do justice to good students.

The *ideal* honors program is expensive, calling as it does for small groups and often individual attention. However, something can be done even if large amounts of money are not available. Often special funds can be found, but even that may not be necessary. Breaking away from routine does not necessarily involve added expense. At the very least, sections of courses can be arranged with careful attention to ability and interest. A good many less prosperous colleges are doing this much and more without special funds.

Conceptions of honors in the small colleges

The granting of honors awards at graduation, either for general excellence or for more than normally successful specialized study, goes back a long way in American education. Honors *programs,* as contrasted with honors *awards,* are of more recent origin.

Even today, the award of honors at graduation implies to many, and often correctly so, that the recipient is being "honored" for achievement; the award of honors is a reward for academic virtue. However, to win honors may equally well mean successful completion of a particular program. The justification for calling a particular program "honors" is usually twofold: Only able students are allowed to take the program, and it is thought to be more difficult than the regular one. In many cases, however, difficulty is not the distinguishing characteristic of the honors program. In some honors programs, student independence is encouraged. In others the program is more specialized than standard fare. In still others, interdisciplinary subject matter is emphasized in an attempt to counteract specialization.

At some institutions a distinction is made between honors awarded by the college and honors awarded by a department, where college honors (the title may be different) are awarded for over-all excellence—usually measured by general average—and departmental honors are awarded for excellent work, and often extra work, in the major department.

It was undoubtedly departmental honors that Joseph Cohen had in mind when, in addressing the CCOS conference, he referred to "your characteristic honors pattern" as "junior-senior-departmental, independent study, senior thesis." This is the traditional honors pattern at the small college. Details, of course, vary, but a typical program would call for the student to decide whether or not, at the invitation of his major department, and as late as the junior or even the beginning of the senior year, to try for honors. He would be expected to do extra reading, to maintain a high average in his major subject, quite possibly to participate in a senior research project, and in many cases to perform exceptionally well on a comprehensive examination required of all majors in his field. At many small colleges honors candidates also undergo an oral examination, sometimes conducted by outside examiners. Programs of this kind, more or less traditional at the stronger small colleges, are not so widely used in the universities. Very few universities require major comprehensive examinations of all seniors, although many of them do require such examinations of honors candidates.

The award of college honors is usually limited to those who have earned departmental honors, in the belief that only a student who has achieved considerable mastery of some field deserves academic honor, and that he only deserves the honor from the whole college if, in addition to mastery in his major field, he can demonstrate a high level of competence in other fields.

Honors awards like these are designed to encourage excellence by rewarding the student who achieves it, and although details of such awards have changed at many colleges in recent years, the idea is fairly old. The use of honors as a means of taking advantage of ability to promote excellence through a *special* educational program, however, is more recent. It was in a small college, Swarthmore, four decades ago, that such an idea was first tried successfully. The Swarthmore program, described in more detail in Chapter 2, encouraged many of the best students in the college to undergo, during their last two years, a very different—more rigorous, more independent, and more specialized—kind of educational experience than was encountered by the other students. Following Swarthmore's example, some other colleges and universities established clearly defined honors programs, but few of these flourished for long.

The award of honors for general excellence, and of departmental honors for excellence in the work of the major, has continued, but there was a considerable gap, ending only recently, in the development of honors *programs*—that is, in a special kind of education for the better students—and it has been principally in the universities where the rebirth of interest in honors programs has occurred.

Attitudes and patterns in the colleges

The March, 1961, CCOS conference had two objectives: to find out what was being thought and done in the colleges, and to discuss what might or should be done. Nobody knew how representatives of the colleges really felt about what J. W. Cohen has called "the honors approach." It soon became apparent that there were various points of view. Participants disagreed most sharply over whether special programs should be set up for the best students, or whether their needs could be met by individual arrangements.

THE SUPERIOR STUDENT

But who are these "best" students? Who are the students for the quality of whose education we need to feel concern? Are we talking about the top 1 percent, the top 10 percent, the top 25 percent of the student population?

At the conference a consensus gradually began to emerge that the problem is not one of percentages at all, but rather one of the student's relationship to his intellectual environment and opportunities. The question is whether the intellectual fare offered in a particular institution challenges all of its students, even the best, or whether some students are *not adequately challenged*. If so, then these are the "best" or "superior" or "outstanding" students for whom something special must be done. As William C. H. Prentice, then dean of Swarthmore College, put it at the conference: "The problem of educating the outstanding students is ... a question of educating any and all students in our colleges who are not yet being stretched to their limit."

THE SPECIAL PROGRAM

At many colleges, it is felt that the normal courses are substantial and flexible enough so that even the best students can be adequately challenged, and further, that more would be lost than gained by isolating them. At other colleges, just as strong as those in the first group, it is felt that even though the ordinary fare may be good, it is worthwhile to offer a different challenge for the best. As illustration, consider a statement describing the College Scholar Program at Franklin and Marshall College, which points out that while the regular program attempts "to give its students the best possible liberal education," there is always room for improvement, and "while the present curriculum is serving most ... students well, there remain some highly gifted students who are not being sufficiently challenged to make their fullest possible commitment to higher education because their intellectual needs are greater or different from those of most students."

One of the advantages of a special program often cited is that it serves as a focus for innovation and experimentation in the college. It is more difficult to try something new with a group of students that is large and somewhat heterogeneous than with a small and homogeneous group, and the faculty involved may be stimulated by a group of especially good students to try different ways of doing things. The colleges without such special programs may have to make special efforts—and many of them do—to keep an experimental attitude alive.

CHALLENGING THE STUDENT WITHOUT A SPECIAL PROGRAM

Among the colleges there is some opposition to honors programs in general. Some of it arises from complacency—the college is satisfied with what it is doing and sees no reason to change. Some is caused by lack of financial resources—the college knows that special programs tend to be expensive and believes that its limited resources can be better used in other ways. A good deal of the opposition arises from a genuine conviction that there are better ways to meet the problem of challenging superior students.

One major objection is that where a special program is established for the best students, their influence is missing from the standard classes. It can be argued, although evidence on this point is contradictory, that taking the best students out of a course will lower the value of that course for those who are left. "Spillover" from an honors program may raise the level of the institution's total intellectual environment, but it is also possible that the existence of such a program will suggest to students not participating that they can be content with second-class standards. Perhaps *every* student needs to be challenged to his limit.

This point of view was eloquently expressed by President Howard F. Lowry of the College of Wooster in his address opening the CCOS conference. He said:

> What we do for the gifted student should take place as far as possible within the framework and opportunity that we offer to all our students alike. The inclusion of everyone ... is an essentially healthy thing for a campus where ... the gifted are not restrained, where the sky is their limit and every encouragement is given to them, but where one has the fun also of enjoying some of the fine surprises that come to men and women who would never have the nerve to propose themselves for honors. ...

I suppose that the most important phrase here is "where the gifted are not restrained." Too often freshman courses are not challenging enough for the most able student; too often college requirements force him to repeat work he has already done; too often a student coming to college with enthusiasm for a subject is prevented by college regulations from studying then and there what really excites him; too often an able student loses his enthusiasm before his college career is well begun. A possible answer to many of these defects is the establishment of an honors program. But Lowry's point is that if such restraints on the gifted can be avoided, every student at the college should be included in the best education it can offer.

It is easy to say that a small college needs no special program because it can readily give special attention to the special needs of individual students. However, it is not always obvious whether anything appreciable is in fact being done for the ablest students. Still, many at the CCOS conference felt that a good number of the small colleges without special programs were adequately challenging their best students.

Doing so requires imaginatively conceived standard courses and individual, flexible guidance. Where there is an honors program the student identified as outstanding normally takes much of his classroom work in the company of other students also so identified. Where there is no special program, where reliance is placed on individual arrangements, the student must be placed in courses that will challenge him. These are often courses designed for a level higher than his, but which contain students of all ranges of ability represented in the college. How successfully such a system meets the needs of the able student depends on the quality of the courses. Merely putting a bright student in a course for which he is not ready, and so making him work harder, may keep him from becoming bored, but it doesn't contribute much toward a good education. In many fields that are not sequential, such as English literature, the idea of an "advanced" course in this sense doesn't apply. And even though a course may be advanced, the presence of too many dull students will inhibit the development of a student much brighter than they. So we return to the point that if the standard courses are dull, or even if the spread of abilities among students is too wide, a special program may be the only answer. Most of those who oppose special programs do so because their experience is with sound and imaginative courses offered to relatively homogeneous and competent student bodies.

In addition to appropriate courses, the colleges with no special program for the ablest students must provide good individual guidance and a great deal of administrative flexibility. To place the student in courses or sections where he will be adequately challenged requires the availability of adequate information about him and thorough consultation and advice. Beyond selection of courses, whatever special treatment seems to be called for may be permitted. How effective this is depends upon how realistically the student is able to judge himself, on the wisdom of those who advise him, and on the flexibility of the machinery of the college and of any department concerned. The kind of flexibility I mean might include the following: making provision for a major program other than those specified by the separate departments; granting instructors the right to waive prerequisites for their courses; allowing a student to do extra work for extra credit in a standard course; making it possible for the student to study under faculty supervision and for credit a subject not treated in the regular course.

Among those colleges which do not offer honors programs there are some where the lack results from inertia rather than conviction. Others, though, are genuinely concerned about the best students and provide the kind of flexibility discussed here. In these colleges the benefits of this flexibility are not limited to a small list of selected "best" students, but are available to all who are prepared to profit from it, of whom most, of course, would be the "best," but among whom there would be some who, as Dr. Lowry put it, "would never have the nerve to propose themselves for honors."

RESEARCH

A growing educational feature in the small colleges that is often, but by no means always, limited to honors students is some experience in research. In the university, where graduate students demand so much of the time that faculty members can devote to supervising research, it is more difficult to make research experience an important part of standard undergraduate education. In the colleges, where there are no graduate students—or at most a few candidates for a master's degree—teachers with an active interest find it possible to supervise research for students who want it.

These, then, are some of the attitudes toward and general patterns of honors and other means of ensuring that the ablest students in the small liberal arts colleges are allowed to fulfill their potential. If the college decides that it needs a specific program to do this job, it encounters some problems: the difficulty of selecting the participants; possible social difficulties for the group thus singled out; the question of how to assign fair grades; possible impoverishment of other classes from which some of the best students have been removed; the chance of serious consequences to those students who should have been selected and were not, as well as to those whose abilities fall just below the level required for selection; and many others. These are not, however, problems that only small colleges will encounter; they arise in all attempts at honors and therefore are discussed more fully elsewhere in this volume.

What the colleges are doing today

What has been the effect on the small liberal arts colleges of the recent emphasis on excellence in education and of the ideas spread abroad by the ICSS? What are some of the specific programs offered by these colleges to their ablest students? [2]

[2] Many of the special programs developed recently in the colleges, and a good many specific courses of an honors nature, have been described in the pages of *The Superior Student*. Some reports of special interest are on: Colorado College (March, 1961, and April, 1961); Elmira College (October, 1960, and November–December, 1962); University of Redlands (March, 1960); Stetson University (May–June, 1959, April, 1960, and December, 1960); Wesleyan University (October, 1960, and May, 1961); and Williams College (November–December, 1962).

There has been much less change in the colleges than in the universities along the lines recommended by the ICSS. Although, as we have seen, there are exceptions, the tendency in the colleges is to concentrate honors work in the junior and senior years. Only eight or ten of the forty-five colleges represented at the first CCOS conference have "comprehensive" honors programs—that is, special programs, not limited to the major field, which include students in freshman or sophomore classes as well as upperclassmen. The proportion of all small colleges in the country offering a special program outside the major field is probably no larger, and may even be considerably smaller.

Haverford, the college I know best, has an honors program largely limited to the upper-class years and to the major department (although college honors are awarded). I will describe it here to illustrate a typical small college honors program and also to show how the interests of the best students can be looked after informally, using, as appropriate, several devices: advanced placement, early admission, waiver of requirements, special advising, independent study.

The "formal" part of Haverford's honors program is not very formal. Each department sets its own standards for honors work, but almost all honors candidates, and many others as well, take "project courses," which may range from a program of independent reading to truly original research. College honors are awarded by the whole faculty to students chosen by a special committee from among the recipients of departmental honors; to get college honors these students must perform well on a special oral examination which emphasizes knowledge and understanding outside the major field.

In addition to the formal honors program, Haverford participates in the Advanced Placement Program, and occasionally will accept a student who has not completed high school. Especially in mathematics, the sciences, and languages, it places freshmen students in sections, or courses, according to ability and previous preparation. Individual faculty members are permitted to waive prerequisites for the courses they teach. Such special arrangements as a junior year abroad are permitted. A special three-man committee—one member is replaced each year—has responsibility for the best students in all classes. These faculty members are alert to learn which students are especially promising; they check the ranking lists, but more important (since high grades don't tell the whole story) students are called to their attention by other faculty. Committee members meet informally with these students and discuss their needs, their aims, and their criticisms. The committee may make recommendations for exceptions to regulations, if necessary. Its principal service, however, is to advise these students on how best to take advantage of what the college has to offer in the light of their special talents. Through this contact with able students, these faculty members can keep the rest of the faculty informed of what good students seem to want and need.

Wooster College is an example of a college that believes in trying to challenge all students without any selective special program. In his speech already referred to, President Lowry indicated what is done there:

> "Introduction to Liberal Studies" [a freshman course] introduces students, through the reading of certain important books, to the things that are likely to be the staple of liberal education.... In the last two years ... we have a scheme of "independent study," that is in some ways more of a tutorial. One-fifth of a student's time goes into the work of his major field in this independent or

tutorial way for the last two years. In [the] junior year this can be—and often is—a seminar out of which independent work arises and has the kind of community that I remember Dr. Cohen's saying he thought one of the things normally lacking in independent work. There are papers and projects in the junior year that culminate in the senior thesis ... the heart of [this program] is that it is for all students in the college, and not just for honor students alone.

Among the more highly organized programs are those at Franklin and Marshall and Beloit. Students at Franklin and Marshall are admitted to the College Scholar Program during the second semester of the freshman year. Then, and again in one semester each year thereafter, they participate in a course specially designed for them, a seminar characterized by "some specificity of subject matter ... going beyond the usual range of the colloquium"; each Scholar must "produce written work demonstrating intensive study as well as take part in discussion of a more discursive nature." Scholars are freed from normal curricular requirements; they can receive only two grades—"honors" and "pass"; the Scholar will "by-pass most of the introductory courses in the various disciplines and move immediately into advanced courses" wherever possible. College requirements are waived for Scholars (there is a danger here; presumably advisers prevent unreasonable combinations of courses), and only certain designated advanced courses are open to them. The Scholars do not "major" in specific departments; they do, however, take comprehensive examinations in an area or areas of knowledge of their own choosing.

Students in the Porter Scholar Program at Beloit [3] take special interdisciplinary seminars in place of some of the regular college courses. They can begin in the fall or join the program (or leave

[3] See *The Superior Student*, Oct., 1958; May–June, 1959; May–June, 1962.

it) at the end of the first semester. The emphasis is on "wide-ranging intellectual curiosity" rather than merely more and harder work. Freshman Scholars choose "one of several two-hour-a-week courses which are interdepartmental in their implications." In the second semester each Scholar takes a three-hour interdisciplinary course. The Scholars are expected, in addition to taking these special courses, to participate during either the junior or senior year in one of the following: a two-hour colloquium, study abroad, the Argonne Semester (see below), the Washington Semester, or an approved independent study project. In his final semester, the Porter Scholar participates in an informal colloquium consisting of six or seven dinner-and-discussion meetings in faculty homes.

Many of the features of this program are being carried over into the regular curriculum, and the whole program may very well one day become in large part standard for the whole college. Such an outcome would of course satisfy one of the objectives of honors programs as envisioned by the ICSS: that they serve as foci for experimentation, the results of which would then be helpful for all.

Honors for freshmen

One of the most important functions of honors programs is to make sure that the interest of able students is not stifled because of lack of challenge. A principal criticism of the traditional pattern of honors in the small college—"junior-senior departmental, independent study, senior thesis"—is that honors work begins so late that some able students lose interest before they are exposed to a special program and therefore never achieve their full potential. The problem of challenging students as they enter the college has become so important that it is worthwhile to glance separately at what efforts the colleges are making at this level.

Not everyone agrees that a problem exists. To the extent that freshman work is repetitive of high school work, unimaginative, or too easy, criticism is justified. But is all freshman work so poor? At the first CCOS conference, one point on which there was wide difference of opinion was that "our freshman programs as they have been conducted in the recent past are not challenging the ablest freshmen." Although many agreed, a minority strongly dissented; some delegates felt that there were colleges where even the ablest freshmen were adequately challenged by the courses regularly available to them.

Where student abilities are reasonably uniform and the best teachers handle freshman classes, boredom is seldom a problem, especially in subjects, like philosophy and economics, that almost no freshmen have studied before. In many colleges most if not all of the incoming freshmen find a real intellectual challenge in the courses normally open to them. But if the best teachers are assigned only to upper-class courses or to graduate teaching, leaving the instruction of the freshmen to the inexperienced or the inept, boredom can be a serious problem.

Where freshmen differ greatly in abilities, preparation, and interests, it may be difficult for even the best teachers to stimulate the top students without leaving the weaker ones behind. There are, however, solutions outside a formalized honors program. Placement tests can be used to locate in the proper course students who are continuing in college a language studied in high school. Students can be placed in special sections of freshman mathematics and English courses on the basis of examination scores, the record of previous training, and in some cases information obtained in personal interviews. Well-prepared freshmen can be encourged to omit some freshman courses altogether. These devices are all widely used.

The most widespread, and in many respects the simplest, device for improving the education of the best freshmen is to offer them the same courses but separate them from the other students. An example is an "enrichment program" initiated in the fall of 1958 at Baldwin-Wallace College.[4] Single sections in required English, in history, and in religion are set aside for a group of twenty-two of the best freshmen, who thus take a large proportion of their first-year work together. Since the faculty teaching these special sections are "given complete freedom to develop their own techniques," there is no uniformity in the way these sections differ from the regular ones except that, all participants being much above average in ability, a higher standard of discussion prevails.

Honors programs open to freshmen are not numerous in the small colleges, but they do exist. At several colleges honors freshmen are admitted to a colloquium in which important intellectual issues are examined; a large proportion of such colloquia carry only one or two hours of credit, and so occupy only a small portion of the freshman's time and attention.

Other honors offerings for freshmen take the form of special courses, open only to selected students and designed to stimulate and challenge them in some special way. Very often these courses—and this characteristic is by no means limited to honors courses available to freshmen—have a strong interdepartmental or interdisciplinary flavor, by way of reaction against what many feel is a dangerous tendency toward overspecialization. An example is the Introduction to Knowledge course offered to "certain freshmen students" at St. Joseph's College, Rensselaer, Indiana. Participants are selected

---

[4] See *The Superior Student,* Nov., 1959.

on the basis of previous record; the course "is offered as an incentive and a directive to qualified students."

Finally, a few colleges—Beloit and Franklin and Marshall, which are described in detail above, are examples—offer established honors programs beginning in the freshman year (at Franklin and Marshall, during the second semester). These programs are similar to some of the best developed in the universities.

Intercollegiate cooperation

For many able students the greater diversity of offerings in the university gives it a real advantage over the college; it is difficult for a small college to offer work in all the areas in which bright students, even as undergraduates, might legitimately be interested.

By pooling resources and providing for the exchange of students, neighboring institutions can achieve together a richness in offerings impossible to one of them alone. When a university is included in the group, still greater diversity, including some work at the graduate level, can be made available to good students in the college who can profit from it.

Examples of such associations are those formed by the group of colleges at Claremont, California; the three "Quaker Colleges" near Philadelphia; and the Connecticut Valley group, which includes the University of Massachusetts in addition to three colleges, Amherst, Mt. Holyoke, and Smith.

With two or three exceptions, the institutions belonging to the Associated Colleges of the Midwest and the Great Lakes Colleges Association are geographically too remote from each other for daily exchange of students, but they benefit from association in other ways. One feature of such association, especially relevant to a discussion of honors since it is of special interest to some of the best students, is the Argonne Semester Program of the ACM. Each year three faculty members are selected from the ACM colleges to spend from ten to fifteen months at the Argonne National Laboratory, where they pursue a program of research and study; they are joined there by about twenty-five selected students from these colleges for periods of ten to sixteen weeks. At Argonne, these students "participate in seminars in their major fields and in an interdisciplinary seminar" under the direction of the faculty members from the ACM, and do research under the supervision of members of the Argonne staff. Thus this program gives them the experience of working with top scientists in superbly equipped laboratories.

Clearly, this is a program of the honors type. It directly benefits the students and faculty who participate, and it indirectly benefits those who remain at home, as the participants return to their campuses, talk about their experiences, and reflect them in their subsequent work.

One final example: A group called the Tri-College Cooperative Program for Gifted Students brings together the resources of three small neighboring colleges so that faculty members and gifted students from each can share in an intercollege honors program.[5] The program takes the form of a seminar on great issues; two of the early topics were "Problems of Free Men" and "East Meets West—Understanding Asia." Here is an illustration of the way in which a group of colleges together can do something that they would have difficulty doing separately.

[5] The colleges are St. Cloud State College, St. John's University, and the College of St. Benedict, all in Minnesota. See *The Superior Student*, Oct., 1958; April, 1959; Oct. 1960.

Acceleration or enrichment?

In addition to being offered honors programs during some or all of their college years, some bright students have encountered two other forms of special treatment: advanced placement and early admission. The Advanced Placement Program, discussed in more detail in Chapter 10, grew out of a deep concern for the future of the liberal arts college during a difficult period: in the midst of the Korean War and just after the tremendous dislocations of World War II. At the beginning it was largely an enterprise of the secondary schools and small colleges. The original idea was to give the superior student college-level work while he was in high school so that he would have to spend less time in college. Obviously, acceleration was the goal. What was eventually to become the program's most important consequence—encouragement of the schools to do a better job—came later.

Some colleges do not grant college credit for work done under this program; other colleges attract very few, if any, students who have participated in it. But there are also those where students who have taken advanced placement courses make up a third or more of the entering class. Very few colleges or universities have many students with enough advanced placement credits to entitle them to sophomore standing when they enter; most of the colleges of the type discussed here give entering students advanced placements credits in one or two courses at most. Thus use of these credits to help a student finish college early is not very common.

Another device aimed at accelerating the student's progress is early admission—allowing a student to enter college before he has completed twelfth grade. Few colleges have institutionalized the practice of early admission; however, many will, when it seems wise, allow an occasional student to enter the freshman class without completing high school. However important it may be to the occasional individual who profits by it, early admission does not appreciably affect the average age of graduation from college.

Some question the wisdom of a widespread policy of early admission because of the depressing effect on the secondary schools of removing their best students before the senior year. Improving the courses in the school, if it is possible, is generally considered preferable to removing good students from the school.

A discussion of advanced placement and early admission raises the question whether superior students should be pushed ahead faster so that they may graduate early, or should be encouraged to do harder work, or more work, or work of a different kind from that done by others. That is, should the emphasis be on *acceleration* or on *enrichment?*

It is common experience that few students see many advantages in acceleration, except as it can ease the very considerable financial burden. Their elders talk a lot about the length of the educational process, but unless financially pressed, most students seem to be in no hurry. The more able the student, very often the less interest he has in cutting short the process of his education. Even among advanced placement students granted sophomore standing on admission there are those who remain at college the full four years; some of them take the quite reasonable view that since it was something of a triumph to be admitted to *this* college in the first place, they might as well get out of it all to which they are entitled.

One idea is to establish a flexible time span as "normal" for granting the degree, allowing some students to graduate in three years without necessarily accumulating the number of credits usually required of those who graduate in four, and allowing others to remain, with no stigma attached to their doing so, for a fifth year at the college before receiving the degree. Since some students are more capable of self-education than others, and there are other sound and creative students who learn more slowly than their fellows, permitting variation in pace may make good educational sense.

Reed College, for example, states in its catalogue that:

> The requirements for the degree of Bachelor of Arts ... may be completed regularly in a period of time ranging from three to five years. As an ordinary minimum, the quantity requirement for graduation is the successful completion of thirty full units. It is expected that most students will accumulate between thirty and thirty-two units before graduation. However, students of exceptional preparation and ability may be recommended for graduation by the faculty at the end of three years and upon the completion of a minimum of twenty-seven units.

Such flexibility is difficult to administer, as is any system that depends on subjective judgments about individuals rather than the application of rules. The small college has an advantage here, since the possibility of permitting such flexibility is likely to diminish in proportion to the number of students to be considered.

Acceleration, of course, has its benefits. If appreciable numbers of incoming students, through use of such devices as advanced placement, independent study, credit by examination, year-long study, or carrying an overload, can finish in three years instead of four, the total output of a college can be increased—a net quantitative gain to society. Furthermore, there is an economic gain for the students involved; not only do they save a year's expense at college (less whatever extra it costs to carry an overload or go to summer school), but, other things being equal, they will have a longer productive life —if that is the proper term—before retirement.

But has society really gained very much? There are other ways in which the output of colleges can be increased. The *percentage* increase in "productive life" is small—one year gained in a productive life of forty years is only 2½ percent—and the same gain can be achieved by putting off retirement another year. Should the gain rather be qualitative? Does society want its adult members earlier or better educated? Instead of adding a particular person to the mainstream of adult life a year or two earlier, would not society gain by encouraging him to become better educated, and so better prepared to contribute creatively to society? For many students, *enrichment* might well be preferable to *acceleration*.

At one meeting of the CCOS, Dr. Carl M. Stevens of Reed College talked about "the acquisition of a certain set of properties which we may call 'B.A.-ness.'" If the object of an undergraduate education is to acquire these properties (whatever they may be), the time spent in college might be very small for some students; if this is the meaning of the degree, some able students should accelerate. But if the significance of the degree lies rather in "the fruitful employment of a certain period of time," the concept of enrichment is more appropriate for the outstanding student.

Further, if the bachelor's degree is regarded as implying a certain agreed-upon level of intellectual achievement, it is reasonable to ask whether that level is constant for all time. Suppose that an improvement in secondary education were so widespread and so general that the great majority of students could reach that level in three years of college work. Would it be to society's advantage if students generally were granted the degree then, or would society benefit more if colleges required four years of all, thus developing better-qualified citizens rather than graduating earlier persons of the same qualifications as before?

The honors approach has enrichment as its goal, whether achieved through special honors programs or through individualized treatment of students who can profit from it. With few exceptions the colleges, even those that offer no organized honors programs for their best students, seem to want to encourage enrichment rather than acceleration. The necessity for making a choice is growing, as improvements in secondary education and student motivation and other factors are vastly increasing the ability level of student bodies. Among the "other factors" are programs such as the National Science Foundation Summer Institutes and the increase in numbers of applicants, which has enabled selective colleges, without changing their admissions policies, to admit students of a higher caliber.

Pressures on the colleges

With few dissents, there seems to be a consensus that the preparation and, especially, the motivation of American college students have been significantly improved in recent years, and that this process can be expected to continue. Related to these improvements—partly cause, partly effect—are a number of developments that liberal arts colleges feel as pressures. The four-year liberal arts college, which has served society so well for many years, feels its integrity threatened as a result of these pressures.

Out of the deliberations of the College Committee on Outstanding Students came a statement of some of these issues, prepared by Dean Parker Lichtenstein:

> Certain facts make it appear almost certain that during the next few years there will be a decided improvement in the quality

of the student body at most private liberal arts colleges. The college-age population is increasing rapidly, and expansion of facilities in the private colleges has been, and probably will continue to be, slight. As selectivity increases, the problems of the outstanding student will assume a new significance.

If the private colleges pursue their present path of increasing selectivity, it may well be that their average students of the future will be able to carry programs equivalent to existing honors programs. In other words, by today's criteria most, if not all, of their students might be considered "outstanding." This condition in itself could give rise to serious consequences. Even now some outstanding students are accelerating, graduating in three or three and a half years. If their kind of performance becomes the norm, we may need to consider a three-year liberal arts program for those who come to us having essentially completed the first year of college work at the secondary level. Such an approach would have the advantage of moving students along as soon as they have demonstrated the level of achievement deemed necessary for a bachelor's degree. Bachelor's degree requirements would be stated, then, in terms of levels of achievement.

One danger in acceleration is that it tends to impair the integrity of the four-year liberal arts program. Not only is acceleration a problem, but other programs often taken by better students, such as Washington Semester, Junior Year abroad, etc., also serve to destroy the unity of the four-year curriculum. As an alternative to acceleration, then, it may be that the liberal arts colleges, enrolling high ability students with strong secondary preparation, may wish to develop a strengthened four-year program which would be required of all students. Many arguments could be advanced for such a plan. The four-year college experience permits maturation along many lines, not simply the intellectual. Young men and women need time and opportunity for social development, and for this reason early entrance into a graduate program may be premature and unwise. Furthermore, if four years are required of all students, the college can concentrate on a program of studies geared to the students' level of ability and achievement. The result would be maintenance of the liberal arts ideal, or to put it another way, the college would stand for something quite distinct in aim and purpose from either the secondary school or the graduate school. In an era of overspecialization the preservation of the liberal arts ideal may be most desirable.

Of course it is true that no matter how selective the liberal arts colleges become, some students will be more outstanding than others. The education of the top 5 or 10 per cent may always be a special problem. We feel, however, that the problem of an outstanding student body as against the problem of the outstanding student is deserving of very careful attention. . . . The question may be put in this way: how can the liberal arts college, in these times of rapid change and improvement in the quality of students, make the greatest contribution to the educational system, and more specifically, how can the college be of greatest value in furthering the educational aims of the student?

Much is said and written about the decreasing importance of the role of the small private college, most of it based on little more than impressions. An important task for the near future is to acquire reliable information so that the important problems can be clearly identified.

It seems certain that students will continue to improve. Even if in the future private colleges receive a smaller proportion of the best students than they have in the past, there will be more than enough good ones to justify efforts to ensure that the education they receive is worthy of their talents and their needs.

Chapter ten / Honors programs in the

secondary schools / Edwin Fenton,

Carnegie Institute of Technology

HONORS IN THE SECONDARY SCHOOLS defy precise definition. A bewildering variety of diverse programs and projects claim to belong under the honors label. At one end of the spectrum is the project initiated by the distinguished, dedicated teacher who gathers a few students in his home periodically for discussions, supplying refreshments from his meager salary. At the other end are entire schools, both public and private, dedicated to the cultivation of excellence and fully equipped with master teachers, well-stocked libraries, and modern laboratories surpassing the facilities of many a small liberal arts college. So we may seriously ask: What is a high school honors program?

High school honors programs defined

Knowing what a high school honors program is *not* should help to clarify the issue. Acceleration alone is not honors. Most authorities call at least three practices acceleration: admitting bright youngsters to the first grade at five or even four years of age; skipping grades —the third or the seventh, for example—when an able student demonstrates that he can handle the work at the next highest level; and allowing the student to complete high school in fewer than four years by taking extra courses and attending summer school.

Although these procedures have acknowledged educational value, none should be called honors. Students who enter school early, skip grades, or finish high school in three years often take exactly the same program as all other students enrolled in their school. They should graduate with approximately the same level of insight and attainment as they would if they had not been accelerated. An honors student, instead, should emerge from school with superior attainments, as the word "honors" itself implies. When not combined with grouping and a differentiated program, acceleration cannot properly be called honors.

Nor should we label as honors the practice of enriching the program of a student in a heterogeneously grouped class. Enrichment usually requires additional work of the more able students enrolled in a class, but often this additional work is only more of the same—ten extra problems or another of Shakespeare's plays. Sometimes it consists of assignments that differ from the work done by the remainder of the class—an original piece of research in history or a special experiment in science. But enrichment efforts do not usually involve the characteristics of a true honors program as spelled out below.

Finally, ability grouping by itself is not honors either. Many schools grouping by ability give all classes approximately the same course. All students use the same basic text and rely on the same library collection or laboratory equipment. Usually the more able students turn in extra reading reports or give some other evidence of an enriched educational experience. Use of the same basic materials usually means that what happens in the "honors" classroom will approximate what happens in other classes, particularly since the teacher who uses this material probably has a mind set about method and subject from teaching average students. To break this mind set, special materials must usually be combined with a fresh approach to teaching.

Honors programs in the schools must have several characteristics.[1] Students must be grouped by ability in special classes for a period of several years. The honors group must be restricted to no more than 20 percent of the student body in a typical school. Thus, the minimum IQ score for honors would fall no lower than a range between 115 and 120. The honors program must have different goals than those provided by standard academic fare. Among other objectives, it should aim for a firmer grasp of the method of a discipline, a greater reliance upon independent study, and a more conscientious attempt to see relationships and structure rather than to learn facts for themselves. These goals imply a carefully constructed set of courses spanning several years of education.

Also, the pace of an honors class should be different. This does not mean attempting to cover a greater chronological period in a history course or to read more authors in a literature course—quite the contrary. Most good honors courses cover a smaller number of subjects in greater depth. It does mean, however, that the class time usually devoted to determining whether students have mastered the essentials of reading material goes into examining the implications of that material and its connections with other topics. This practice results in a different pace; average students cannot take the intellectual hurdles of a good honors course at the same speed as their more able contemporaries.

[1] For comparison see the Sixteen Major Features of a Full Honors Program in the Appendix to Chap. 3 of this volume.

Finally, the materials used in an honors course should be different. The sciences should give greater emphasis to creative laboratory experiences; history courses should use more source materials; fewer but more sophisticated books should be read in literature and in advanced courses in foreign languages. One of the new math sequences should be adopted. Creditable honors courses cannot grow out of a standard high school text designed for average students at the same grade level. Material for good honors programs must be planned for sequential and cumulative learning experiences.

All of these characteristics—continuity, ability grouping, goals, pace, and materials—call for somewhat different teaching methods than those that typical teachers in typical secondary school classes employ. In discussions, honors teachers should ask different kinds of questions, questions designed to reveal the structure of a discipline or to disclose the relationships of one reading to another done several weeks previously. Students should be thrust on their own to make the sort of discoveries that delight professional scholars and attract creative men and women to teaching and research. Book reviews should replace book reports; creative experiments should replace the cookbook exercises that have so long made laboratory courses a series of dull classes illustrating generalizations that can be found in any textbook or laboratory manual. Without conscientious attention to methods of instruction, honors courses are not worthy of the name.

Organizing high school honors

Legitimate honors programs in the schools are organized more diversely than similar programs in colleges and universities. The two educational levels face somewhat different problems. While the schools must educate all of the children of all of the people, colleges can be more selective and admit only the able, as each institution defines the term. In some large cities, such as New York, thousands of students have IQ scores above 130. In such a city a few secondary schools can be more selective than most colleges or universities would dare to be. At the other extreme, more than half the high schools in the United States graduate fewer than 100 students a year. In most of these schools the number of potential honors candidates is small, and the difficulties in the path of an outstanding honors program loom ominously. Finally, many secondary schools do not have so many able instructors as typical colleges do. The relative scarcity of outstanding instructors helps to shape honors programs in the schools; a full-scale honors program will fail without distinguished teachers. Out of all these conditions, four patterns of organization have emerged.

THE DISCRETE COURSE

Thousands of high schools have organized one or two honors courses, particularly at the senior level.[2] The impetus for these courses often comes from students who request the school to offer another biology course or a seminar in Shakespeare. Sometimes a particularly gifted teacher supplies the incentive; sometimes it comes from a counselor or a principal or a parent. In some schools the program disappears once the original enthusiasm for it is dissipated; in others individual honors courses have lasted through several generations of students and a series of faculty leaders.

No one can generalize accurately about these efforts. When

[2] Such courses and their shortcomings are discussed in Frank O. Copley, *The American High School and the Talented Student,* Ann Arbor, Mich.: The University of Michigan Press, 1961, chap. 1.

students are poorly chosen and programs poorly conceived, ill-supplied with funds, and led by an unqualified teacher, these courses can have pernicious results. Honors seminars organized around discussions of "critical thinking" with no firm foundation in the structure of a discipline frequently result in nothing more than pooled ignorance; their existence implies that educated people condone undisciplined thinking. On the other hand, many honors classes have given students their first real insight into the world of learning and have been steppingstones to a whole new universe of knowledge.

Individual honors classes are usually too small to have much impact on other teachers, on the school's intellectual climate, or on the entire school curriculum. Nor do they usually affect the style of teaching of the individual in charge since no in-service work accompanies them. They are not true honors programs at all.

COOPERATIVE VENTURES

Schools with too few able students to support even one honors course sometimes work out cooperative schemes with neighboring institutions.[3] The courses offered are often extracurricular; they frequently meet in the evenings, on Saturday, or during the summer. Many of them grant no formal academic credit toward the high school degree. They are honors courses in the finest sense: taken for the honor of it and the intellectual stimulation they provide.

Perhaps an example will make the nature of these programs clear.[4] For the past seven years the Catskill Area School Study

[3] A number of these programs have been described in *The Superior Student,* Feb., 1960 and Nov.–Dec., 1963.

[4] For descriptions of this program see *The Superior Student,* Nov.–Dec., 1963 and Feb., 1960; and R. M. Porter, "Saturday Seminars Stimulate Students," *New York State Education,* January, 1962, pp. 21–23.

Council and the State University College at Oneonta, New York, have sponsored the Saturday Seminar Program for able students. Beginning with 57 students from 20 schools in the fall of 1957, the program grew to include 225 students from 32 schools in three counties by 1963. The typical school from which these students come enrolls about one hundred students in its combined junior and senior classes and sends about 5 percent of them to the Saturday Seminar Program. Local school boards or parents pay tuition of $35 per semester. Classes meet for twenty Saturdays during the fall and winter at the college. College professors serve as instructors and offer seven courses: two in humanities, two in the social sciences, and one each in mathematics, psychology, and science. The program has been so rewarding that a Summer Seminar, organized in July, 1963, attracted twenty-seven students from six schools to study modern Japan and the fine arts. Through these programs a number of school districts cooperating with a local college or university have given their best students an opportunity to pursue real honors work. Many schools, of course, have developed similar programs without the assistance of an institution of higher education.

How effective are these programs? No one has been able to assess them scientifically. Students testify to the stimulation they receive, and this stimulation is reason enough for the effort and funds they require. The programs do not, however, affect teachers in the high schools from which the students are drawn because most of the instruction is done by college personnel. Nor do they affect the intellectual climate of a school unless the desire to qualify spurs a student to additional work. Because they do not affect a significant number of teachers, these programs bring about little change in teaching methods, in the regular curriculum that students take during the school year, or in academic courses that precede the honors classes. Commendable as they are, these programs cannot become a full substitute for a comprehensive honors program which can have an impact on virtually every aspect of an entire school system.

HONORS SCHOOLS

In a few large cities entire schools have been set aside for honors work.[5] In many ways these schools resemble private preparatory academies which enroll only students of above-average abilities and offer a special curriculum for them. Indeed, admission standards of schools such as the Bronx High School of Science and the Hunter College High School are higher than those of any private school in the land. Other strictly academic high schools—Walnut Hills in Cincinnati, Benjamin Franklin in New Orleans, Central High School in Philadelphia, and a few more—are only somewhat less selective. In these few hundred schools, most of them private, almost all students take only honors courses. In many of them students enrolled in the regular courses take advanced placement examinations each year with conspicuous success. In other words, the standard courses in these secondary schools are of college caliber.

The New York City selective public schools like Bronx High and Hunter High admit students from all over the city on the basis of competitive examinations. Hunter admits about 300 students a year, none with an IQ score under 130. Bronx High admits almost 1,000. In both schools the student body as a whole ranks in the 99th percentile on standardized tests such as the Iowa series. Few drop out

[5] References to these schools are scattered throughout the issues of *The Superior Student*. See particularly, Jan.–Feb., 1963, pp. 48, 52–53, 55–56; also see *The Bronx High School of Science: 25th Jubilee,* Bronx High School of Science, New York, 1963 (mimeographed); and A. Taffel, "Bronx High School of Science," *Yearbook of Education,* Teachers College, Columbia University, New York, 1961, pp. 452–460.

after they are admitted, and few crack up under the pressure of the schools' strict standards. Almost every member of the graduating class from both institutions goes to college.

The curriculum in each school is geared to the needs of this special student body. Although the course titles are similar, the content in selective schools bears little relationship to the curriculum offered in comprehensive high schools. Bronx High requires four years of English, four years of social studies, four years of science, three years of one foreign language, three years of mathematics, one year of mechanical drawing, one-half year of science techniques laboratory, and courses in music, art, and health education. A number of special nonscientific courses are also offered in addition to a distinguished array of electives in science and mathematics. These courses are taught at an honors level by a distinguished faculty about half of whom hold doctorates.

Careful selection of students and specially designed courses have brought spectacular results. Eighty-five percent of Bronx High graduates win New York State Regents scholarships; these students also capture a host of other scholarships on both a local and national level. Seventy-three percent of the 1963 senior class at Hunter won letters of commendation in the National Merit examination. Other similar schools have established records only slightly less sensational. If the objective is academic excellence as measured by competitive examinations, no one can deny that special academic schools, both public and private, enrolling selected students and offering an honors curriculum, offer great promise.

But they also present drawbacks. Most parents cannot afford selective private schools and therefore most able students cannot attend them. The majority of cities and all towns and rural areas have too few pupils to fill a specialized high school. For these reasons alone the specialized academic school cannot solve the problem of honors work.

Many critics have pointed to additional drawbacks. The best teachers—at least the brightest and those with the most formal training—often prefer to teach in the selective schools. If a school system permits the able students to draw the cream of its teaching talent into one or two buildings, it undermines the education of the rest of the student body by removing from the schools they attend a disproportionate number of the sort of teachers who spark curriculum reform and inspire their colleagues. Honors programs segregated into special schools have minimal effect on teaching, on curriculum, and on the intellectual climate of other schools in the system.

THE TRUE HONORS PROGRAM

By far the most widespread and effective form of honors work in the secondary school is an honors program within a comprehensive high school. An honors program differs from a single course because it is permanent and it is organized centrally, usually at several grade levels and in a number of disciplines. It differs from extracurricular work on Saturdays, in the evening, or during the summer because it replaces rather than supplements the regular course offering or goes a step further by offering more advanced work, often at a college level. It differs from specialized high schools because it exists within the walls and the administrative structure of a comprehensive high school; thus it can affect students, curricula, and teachers far beyond those it itself involves. It usually takes the form either of an entire curriculum or track for honors students or of a special set of honors courses within an academic track.

Two examples chosen from among many can make the organizational patterns clear. Cherry Creek School District in Arapahoe County near Denver, Colorado, has organized an honors program in five academic areas.[6] The program has been carefully planned by the administration of the school. During the first years of their high school careers, all academic students enroll in the same courses. Then students who have shown outstanding ability can select honors work at advanced levels in mathematics, science, chemistry, the humanities, or English. Each course is restricted to selected students of proven ability. Each has been specially designed with new materials, a fresh approach to teaching, and a distinguished teacher. Students do an exceptional amount of independent work in the laboratory or library. Much of the material studied can be found in the freshman courses in good colleges; indeed, many students from the program have been exempted from college courses by placement tests.

The Pittsburgh public schools have been organizing a more far-reaching project called the Pittsburgh Scholars' Program.[7] Of the 5,000 eighth-grade students in the Pittsburgh public schools, about 1,000 have IQ scores of 115 or over, but they are scattered over the face of the city. In some schools only two or three able students are enrolled at one grade level. They cannot be given a comprehensive

[6] See *The Superior Student,* Nov.–Dec., 1963.

[7] The original plans for the Pittsburgh Scholars' Program were the work of Dean Alan Blackmer of Phillips Academy, Andover, Massachusetts, who spent a full year in Pittsburgh as a consultant to the schools on programs for able students. His *Work Papers,* Pittsburgh, 1961 (multilithed), contain his suggestions. Although a number of notices about the program have appeared in the daily press, the only extensive published account is Edwin Fenton, "Experiment in Excellence," *The Wooster Alumni Bulletin,* vol. 78, no. 7, April, 1964, pp. 4–7. Four accounts of the cooperative spirit between high school and college on which this program was built appeared in *The Superior Student,* Feb., 1960, pp. 21–22, 33–34; and Nov.–Dec., 1963, pp. 10–12, 13–16.

honors program under these conditions. In other schools a large percentage of the students are both able and ambitious—fallow ground for honors.

In order to cluster students effectively, school administrators selected thirteen elementary and junior high schools and six high schools as centers for the honors programs called the Pittsburgh Scholars' Program. Able students in other schools are transferred to these selected schools at the beginning of the eighth grade and placed in classes of standard size. Each school continues to serve all the children from its neighborhood so that it remains comprehensive. Within each school, a new five-year honors curriculum has been organized in each of six subject areas: mathematics, social studies, English, foreign languages, science, and the fine arts. The Scholars' curriculum is distinct from the courses taught in the regular academic track; it constitutes a true honors program.

During the last five years, each sequence of courses has been carefully planned. More than a million dollars in foundation grants has supported the development of new courses and the training of teachers for this program. Five major cooperative projects with the Carnegie Institute of Technology have resulted in entire new sequences of courses in five areas: the social studies, English, the natural sciences, mathematics, and the fine arts. In addition to working on some of the mathematics courses, the University of Pittsburgh has contributed funds and personnel to the three new five-year sequences of language courses in French, German, and Spanish.

A number of elements in this program define it as a true secondary school honors program. Students are actively recruited by two full-time counselors. They use both scores on standardized tests and the subjective judgments of teachers, principals, and counselors in the selection process. Every effort is made to persuade able students from disadvantaged homes to enroll in the program; counselors even call on parents who seem reluctant to enroll their students. In a democratic society, honors programs should include all able students, not only those from advantaged homes in good neighborhoods.

All of the courses have been designed as much as possible for inductive teaching in sequential and cumulative order. What a student learns in eighth grade is reinforced, used, and extended in succeeding years. Most of the material for the courses has been written by teams of university professors and high school teachers, who have combined the latest scholarly research and the latest knowledge of cognitive processes with practical experience in constructing new, imaginative courses. The pace of the classes surprises observers not accustomed to seeing eighth and ninth graders make the intuitive leaps that characterize so much creative thought. Because many classes meet only four days a week, there is time for independent work and for reading outside of course requirements. Through such flexibility the program attempts to combine the rigor of a carefully designed course with the freedom that encourages creativity.

Students are required to take five years of English and the fine arts (the latter taught twice weekly) and a minimum of four years of social studies, three of mathematics, three of science, and three of one modern language. Since the five-year sequences begin in eighth grade, plenty of time for electives remains. For example, all of the math, language, and science requirements can be fulfilled by the end of the tenth grade. Students who drop a sequence at this level are required to take a once-a-week, no-credit sustainer course in the discipline in order to maintain skills for college.

A full set of advanced placement courses tops the Scholars'

curriculum. Students may choose American history or biology in eleventh grade and English, modern languages, chemistry, physics, European history, and calculus in twelfth. The history, English, modern language, and mathematics courses replace the work that would ordinarily be done at the appropriate grade level in the subject. All of the advanced placement science courses, however, are second-year courses built upon the basic work done in the honors curriculum.

Teachers in the Pittsburgh Scholars' Program receive special in-service training. In the projects at Carnegie Tech, all of the teachers who are going to try out a new course in the fall help to write it during special summer work sessions. Additional teachers attend one-week workshops late in August each year designed to help them learn to teach the material in their course. Close supervision and periodic meetings throughout the academic year help to keep the faculty aware of the newer methods essential for maximum success with the Scholars' program. Since no teacher in the program is permitted to teach more than two classes, the entire faculty of the program spends most of its time instructing average or below-average students. In this way the in-service education designed for the honors programs benefits students enrolled in other tracks because their teachers have had an opportunity to learn new techniques. A surprising amount of material designed for the Scholars' Program has already worked its way into other courses of study. A successful honors program ought to have this secondary effect on the school.

Planning for the Pittsburgh Scholars' Program has been under way for four years. Preliminary work on many of the courses was done two or three years ago; courses have since been revised and perfected. The formal announcement of the beginning of the program was delayed until the spring of 1964 so that school officials would have time to plan everything carefully. The first eighth-grade class began the five-year sequence in September, 1964. After the first year, every course in which these students enroll will have been tried at least once by a number of teachers in preceding years. This degree of careful planning and experimentation is unusual in the schools. Excellent honors programs require it.

Hundreds of schools and school systems across the country have organized honors programs only a little less comprehensive than the Pittsburgh Scholars' Program. Many begin at the ninth- or tenth-grade level; a few start as early as the fourth. Most attempt to offer courses that suit the ambitions and needs of a variety of students interested in all the academic areas. Sequences of courses built one atop the other are common. So are special provisions for training teachers and for developing course content. The initiative for these programs has largely come from a variety of sources, most of which have developed significantly since World War II.

Stimulating honors: national programs

Three different types of efforts of national scope have affected the development of honors programs in the schools. They are the Project on the Academically Talented Student sponsored by the National Education Association, the Advanced Placement Program supported in recent years by the College Entrance Examination Board, and the major curriculum revision programs diversely supported by the government and by private foundations. Each of these efforts has had a somewhat different impact on honors programs.

PROJECT ON THE ACADEMICALLY TALENTED STUDENT

The Project on the Academically Talented Student began in the fall of 1957. It was designed to focus the attention of educational leaders on the problem of identifying and educating talented students in the secondary schools. A large number of committees led by distinguished educators sponsored conferences and published a number of pamphlets summarizing current practices in the education of the talented and recommending programs and appropriate literature.[8]

The essential purpose of the NEA project was to stimulate the effort of its members. And it succeeded. Copies of the NEA pamphlets have found their way into the libraries of almost every school administrator genuinely interested in honors programs. But beyond stimulation and a guide to appropriate literature, the NEA project could not provide material suited for honors programs or train the teachers to use it. Two other programs filled this vital gap.

ADVANCED PLACEMENT

The Advanced Placement Program was begun in 1953 to encourage the practice of teaching college-level courses in the secondary schools.[9] The program began as a joint effort of President Gordon

[8] This project has published thirteen pamphlets. The first, *The Identification and Education of the Academically Talented Student in the American Secondary School* (Washington, 1958) is a report on the original conference sponsored by the project. The remaining twelve are devoted to administration, guidance, research, bibliography, elementary education, music, science, English, art, mathematics, business and economic education, and modern foreign languages. Costing between 60 cents and $1.25 for single copies, these pamphlets are available from the National Education Association, Publication Sales Section, 1201 Sixteenth Street, N.W., Washington 6, D.C. The Association also offers consultative services in these areas.

[9] The history and achievements of the Advanced Placement Program are best summarized in Frank O. Copley, *op. cit.*, chap. 2. Copies of *Advanced Placement Program: Course Descriptions* ($1.50) and sets of sample examinations ($1) can be obtained from College Entrance Examination Board, Box 592, Princeton, N.J. Mr. Jack Arbolino, Director, The Advanced Placement Program, 475 Riverside Drive, New York 27, N.Y., will forward announcements of test dates and conferences and provide valuable assistance to schools that are beginning advanced placement programs. *The Superior Student* contains numerous accounts of advanced placement courses taught in the schools.

Chalmers of Kenyon College and Dr. William Cornog, then principal of Philadelphia's Central High School and now superintendent of New Trier High School in Winnetka, Illinois. At first financed by the Fund for the Advancement of Education, the program is now administered and supported financially by the College Entrance Examination Board.

This program has always had a dual purpose: to provide a deeper educational experience for the able student in the secondary school, and to enable exceptional students to earn college credit for courses taken in high school. Although the second of these two objectives receives the most publicity, the first has been more important to American education.

The College Entrance Examination Board writes and administers examinations in eleven subjects: English, mathematics, French, German, Spanish, Latin, American history, European history, biology, chemistry, and physics. Although the committees of college and secondary-school teachers who write the examinations describe recommended courses of study in general terms, they do not outline specific courses. Instead, they invite each school to make up its own syllabus from whatever materials and methods of study seem appropriate. Annual conferences held each June provide additional guidance for beginning teachers. There is no organization to join, no dues to pay, and no specific standards to meet.

Any student who applies may take a three-hour Advanced Placement Examination, which is given in the schools each May, and submit it with a request for credit to the college of his choice. The college receives a copy of the examination, the student's paper, the grade given to the paper by graders from school and college who have marked it from 1 (lowest) to 5 (highest), a description of the course the student took, and the recommendation of the student's teacher and/or counselor. On the basis of this information, the college can grant credit and place the student out of the equivalent course, or grant placement into an advanced course with no credit, or require the student to take the equivalent course over again. On the whole, the colleges most experienced with the program grant credit most liberally. Harvard, which gets far more advanced placement candidates than any other college in the nation, offers sophomore standing to any of its students who have passed three advanced placement examinations with marks of 3 or better. About half of each freshman class at Harvard gets credit for at least one advanced placement course; more than a hundred students each year receive sophomore standing.

Advanced placement has spread rapidly. During the first year, 532 students from 18 schools took 959 examinations and went to 94 colleges. In 1964, 28,857 students from 2,098 schools took 37,802 examinations and enrolled in 851 colleges. Participation in advanced placement has become one of the hallmarks of excellence in American secondary education. But the program has hardly scratched the surface.

Of America's 25,000 high schools, 23,000 do not offer a single advanced placement course. Many of the courses that have been started have failed to produce students who can earn grades of 3 or better on the examinations. Yet despite its limited scope and its incomplete success, advanced placement has probably been the most influential force working for honors programs in our secondary schools during the past decade.

The way in which advanced placement courses are organized in a school reveals some of the reasons for their profound influence. Although each school sets its own standards, most follow patterns that are becoming commonly accepted. Students are admitted to advanced placement courses on the basis of a number of measures: scores on standardized tests, grades in previous courses, recommendations of teachers and counselors, and occasionally a requirement that they volunteer. This procedure assures the school that advanced placement courses enroll students who are both able and ambitious. Although some school systems use arbitrary cutoff points on standardized test scores in admitting students (one well-known school admits only students with IQ scores of 130 or above), most do not. Many students who have scored between 110 and 120 in standardized IQ tests have performed creditably in college-level courses and earned grades of 3, 4, and 5 on advanced placement examinations. Knowing that past performance and the recommendations of teachers influence admission to advanced placement classes sometimes encourages students to work harder in ninth, tenth, and eleventh grades.

The most important variable in the program's success is the quality of the teacher, as most schools launching an advanced placement program begin in the subject for which they have the most distinguished teacher. The majority of successful advanced placement teachers have at least a master's degree in their subject; many have additional training. In the past ten years, a number of summer institutes have been set up to prepare advanced placement teachers. Several colleges run summer sessions especially designed to aid new advanced placement instructors. The institutes organized by the National Science Foundation have also helped to bring teachers up to date. No school should begin an advanced placement program without a distinguished teacher in each subject it undertakes.

Each school prepares its own course. Most beginning teachers attend the June Advanced Placement Conference in their subject field. The conference brings veterans in advanced placement teaching together with new teachers. The papers presented are often indispensable to the success of neophytes. In addition, most new instructors write to experienced advanced placement teachers for copies of their syllabi. Several syllabi from schools with successful programs provide a useful guide to successful practices.

Most advanced placement classes restrict the number of students admitted. Twenty per class is a commonly accepted limit. Where a school has only a few able students, teachers sometimes tutor them privately or give them extra work in a heterogeneously grouped class to prepare them for the advanced placement test. The most successful programs limit the total teaching load of advanced placement teachers. In the Pittsburgh public schools, for example, advanced placement teachers meet only four classes a day instead of five, and the advanced placement class is limited to twenty. In addition, the sum of $30 has been appropriated to purchase books and supplies for each student in each advanced placement course; a student in the history or English class receives his own copy of each of a dozen or so books. Only with liberal appropriations for books and supplies can a school system hope to approximate the conditions prevailing in freshman courses in the best universities. With plenty of supplies and a reduced load, teachers have time to read, to plan carefully, and to grade the large number of papers essential to success in the advanced placement program.

Advanced placement courses usually have profound effects on the schools in which they are taught. These effects go well beyond the college-level courses themselves. They have their greatest impact, however, upon the students enrolled, many of whom are challenged to the limit of their abilities for the first time in their academic careers. This challenge and the new attitude it breeds affects the entire intellectual climate of a school. Advanced placement students are proud to belong to the academic varsity; younger students often emulate them. Advanced placement helps to make learning in an honors program thoroughly respectable.

Advanced placement also affects teachers. Through this program many teachers too are challenged for the first time to work to their intellectual capacities. The demands of teaching college courses send them scurrying to the library and to summer schools. Attending advanced placement conferences or one of the special summer sessions designed for advanced placement teachers helps them discover new teaching techniques and new materials. Within a short time, most advanced placement teachers try these new ideas on their regular classes with excellent results. If colleagues sit in on the advanced placement class, these new methods soon spread throughout a school. Advanced placement has deeply affected the teaching of students of all abilities.

The Advanced Placement Program has contributed to the development of honors programs in many schools. Most of the first schools to adopt advanced placement already had honors programs; advanced placement became the capstone. Increasingly, schools without well-articulated honors sequences have tried advanced placement. At first, many of their students did poorly on the examinations. School officials then concluded that a fully successful advanced placement program should be built on a carefully devised sequence of courses beginning, at the latest, in tenth grade. This decision led to the development of full honors sequences; for example, the entire Pittsburgh Scholars' Program grew up in this way. Experience now indicates that no advanced placement program can be fully successful unless it is built on a firm foundation of honors work extending throughout a student's high school career. Just as the Advanced Placement Program has challenged the colleges to develop more stimulating courses for the new crop of distinguished students they are getting, it has challenged the schools to develop sequences of courses that can prepare students to do superior college work while they are still in high school.

The Advanced Placement Program has two cutting edges. One slices down into the schools to spur the development of new honors sequences leading to advanced placement courses; the other slices upward into the colleges, stimulating them to develop honors programs which can challenge graduates of advanced placement classes.

Advanced placement conferences and the annual grading sessions bring hundreds of college and high school teachers together each year to consider their mutual problems. They learn to see that education is a continuum, that barriers at the end of the twelfth grade are artificial. Honors programs in the colleges and honors programs in the schools are now beginning to merge. Harvard University, which has benefited most from the Advanced Placement Program, has now developed seminars for freshmen. Although not specifically designed to do so, these in effect link honors on the two academic levels. In the future, more and more colleges will follow this path.

THE CURRICULUM-REFORM PROJECTS

In the past ten years more than fifty major curriculum reform projects have been started in the United States.[10] Without exception, the teams of writers working on curricula include both univer-

---

[10] Listing these projects would require several pages in this volume. Four good descriptions of recent curriculum development projects are now available: Dorothy M. Fraser, *Current Curriculum Studies in Academic Subjects,* Washington, D.C.: National Education Association, 1962; John I. Goodlad, *School Curriculum Reform in the United States,* New York: Fund for the Advancement of Education, 1964; Robert W. Heath (ed.), *New Curricula,*

sity professors and high school teachers who work cooperatively. Although research evidence seems to indicate that the new curricula are at least as effective with average as with able students, many schools have adopted them first for students of honors caliber. The implications for learning of these new projects are so great that no reputable honors sequence can afford to ignore them. Although generalization about them is risky, five trends stand out.

The new curricula emphasize inductive teaching, sometimes called the discovery method. Instead of demanding the maximum retention of great bodies of fact, these courses invite students to build generalizations from factual material or from laboratory exercises. The responsibility for developing and checking hypotheses is thrust upon the student; texts no longer describe, they analyze; facts now serve as tools rather than as goals. Good honors programs in schools rely more and more upon inductive teaching.

The new curricula emphasize the discipline's mode of inquiry. In addition to teaching students what scientists know about physics or biology, these courses also help them to discover the way in which scientists know what they know. Attention to the mode of inquiry also extends to history, English, and the social sciences. This increased emphasis taps the creative abilities of students and builds into courses a number of opportunities to show the student how to transfer knowledge from one learning situation to another. An honors course particularly should attempt to teach the mode of inquiry on which scholarly knowledge in a given field is based.

New York: Harper & Row, Publishers, Incorporated 1964; and *Using Current Curriculum Developments,* Washington, D.C.: Association for Supervision and Curriculum Development, 1963. These volumes list the names and addresses of directors of various projects. Thousands of articles about new curricular projects have been published in periodicals and can be found through the standard guides.

The new curricula are being written in sequential and cumulative order. The committees of scholars and teachers who write them have established priorities for learning and have arranged topics so that the easier ones are taught in the lower grades and the more difficult ones introduced as appropriate in the sequence. Moreover, they have tried to arrange materials to reinforce and build upon principles from one year to the next. The anarchy of the typical school curriculum, in which teachers at one level know next to nothing about what is taught at other levels, is becoming a thing of the past. Honors curricula offer particularly challenging opportunities to arrange cumulative and sequential learning experiences.

The new curricula rely more heavily than in the past on a multimedial approach to learning. Many projects are creating their own audio-visual aids and relating them to specific learning experiences in specific lessons. The Physical Sciences Study Committee physics course is particularly noted for this approach. An honors curriculum should make use of a number of media so that it taps the student's full perceptual potential.

Finally, the new curricula provide maximum teacher aids. Many have produced day-to-day lesson plans or elaborate teachers' manuals with innumerable suggestions about imaginative teaching techniques. Committees have also provided full sets of examinations. In a number of disciplines, summer institutes have been organized to introduce teachers to new materials. Teachers in honors programs should take advantage of all this work.

The efforts of the national curriculum committees have profoundly affected honors programs in the secondary schools. Simply making new materials available is a substantial contribution; vigorous teachers everywhere have adopted these materials eagerly. The new emphases in teaching that accompany these new materials have helped to shape entire programs. Because both college professors and high school teachers have contributed to the writing of the new materials, some firm bonds have been established between these two levels of the educational system. Many men who develop honors programs in the universities have worked with the schools. They know what progressive high schools are now doing; they can make learning continuous from honors programs in the schools to honors programs in colleges.

Although the curricular revolution has only just begun, its effect is already measurable; in the future this effect will be even more marked. It will be marked upon the students. Accustomed in the schools to looking for reasons, to developing and testing hypotheses, to reading source materials, and to carrying out creative laboratory exercises, they will never be satisfied by dull college lecture courses. Honors in the schools will create even greater demands for honors in colleges. It will be marked upon teachers. Once they have taught the new curricula, most teachers are anxious to abandon textbook courses and the repetition of meaningless fact. It will have an effect on the intellectual climate of the school. Students may begin to turn their attention from television and sports to the pages of their new books. Finally, it will have the greatest impact of all on the curriculum itself. What is now used in honors programs for the able may soon become standard fare. If it does, the schools will be forced to develop even more stimulating honors programs, and the colleges will again be challenged to renewed efforts.

Stimulating honors: regional and state programs

In addition to the three programs of national scope discussed above, a number of regional and state efforts have stimulated the development of honors programs in the secondary schools. Of the regional efforts three have been particularly important: the Superior and Talented Research Project of the North Central Association of Colleges and Secondary Schools, the Southern Regional Project for the Education of the Gifted, and the Regional Commission on Educational Coordination sponsored by the University of Pittsburgh. Although similar in some ways, each of these efforts has had a somewhat different impact on the development of honors programs.

In 1958 a committee representing the Commission on Research and Service of the North Central Association of Colleges and Secondary Schools chose 100 high schools to be part of its Superior and Talented Student Project.[11] These schools each had a number of talented students, and school officials thought they were not being challenged sufficiently. Each school studied its own needs and, with the help of the North Central Association, worked out a program of action aimed at attacking the problems of guiding able students to develop their special talents. The project is now interregional; its principles have been adopted and its practices imitated in other parts of the country. Whether or not member schools developed a true honors program through this effort has depended on local conditions. The Commission did not attempt to set standards, prescribe programs, develop integrated series of courses, or train honors teachers. Although this project has relied more heavily on consulting services and on group study than the NEA project, its basic philosophy is similar.

The Southern Regional Project for the Education of the Gifted worked through officials of the Department of Public Instruction in

[11] See *Building a Program for Superior and Talented High School Students,* obtainable from the STS Project Office, South Shore Drive, Chicago 15, Ill.

nine Southern states.[12] Through a number of instructional seminars, observation tours, and planning sessions over a two-year period beginning in May, 1960, each responsible official designed a program for his state. A number of distinguished educators formed an advisory council to lend perspective to the project. The end results were the availability of a highly trained expert on the education of the gifted in each state and a new awareness of the problems of educating able students throughout the nine-state region. Again, however, whether or not true honors programs developed in a specific school because of this program has depended upon local initiative.

The Regional Commission on Coordinated Education at the University of Pittsburgh has tried to develop courses for college-bound students in the schools of western Pennsylvania, eastern Ohio, and northern West Viginia.[13] Leading educators from schools in the Ohio Valley met in a series of conferences to recommend guidelines for the development of continuous curricular programs from elementary school through college. Pitt then set up a Curriculum Continuity Demonstration at Frick Elementary School and Schenley High School in Pittsburgh. Cumulative and sequential series of courses, partly adapted from the work of national curriculum committees and partly written at the CCD headquarters, were installed in these two schools, tried out, revised, and disseminated to other schools in the project. The full kindergarten-to-college con-

---

[12] See *The Gifted Student: A Manual for Program Improvement,* 1962, available from the Southern Regional Educational Board, 130 Sixth Street N.W., Atlanta 13, Ga.

[13] See *The Superior Student,* Feb., 1960 and Nov.–Dec., 1963, and *Pittsburgh Curriculum Continuity Demonstration: Annual Report 1963,* available from the Learning Research and Development Center, University of Pittsburgh, Pittsburgh 13, Pa.

tinuum in five academic subjects is scheduled to be operative and ready for dissemination this year. In the spring of 1964, Pitt formed the Learning Research and Development Center to continue and expand the curricular work already completed. Whether or not this project results in an honors program in an individual high school depends upon the initiative of local officials. Pitt has provided courses of study suitable for honors and helped to prepare a number of teachers ready to instruct in honors sequences.

A number of single states too have mounted programs of their own that have stimulated honors.[14] Some of these have been associated with the Advanced Placement Program; others have not. Some have consisted mainly of attempts to prepare one expert on the state level as a consultant to schools; others have involved full statewide programs. None of them results in the establishment of true honors programs unless responsible school officials on the local level utilize the help made available.

A dozen states and Puerto Rico have established directorships of programs for the gifted within their state departments of education. An additional twenty-two states have assigned responsibility for this area to personnel who devote part of their time to able students. They organize in-service programs for teachers, serve as consultants, conduct demonstration classes, disseminate research findings, and work to institute college–high school cooperative projects. Since March, 1963, they have been organized into the Council of State Directors of Programs for the Gifted. Illinois, California, North Carolina, Oregon, and Ohio have begun particularly interesting programs. These state programs are developing a group of tal-

[14] See a summary of these programs in *The Superior Student,* Nov.–Dec., 1963, pp. 3–9. The same issue, pp. 32–71, contains short accounts of many statewide programs.

ented school administrators who can give indispensable help to school systems inaugurating honors.

Stimulating honors: college–high school cooperative projects

Until the end of World War II, the secondary schools and the colleges were two different worlds. In Charles R. Keller's phrase, a sheepskin curtain had rung down between them. Since the end of the war, and increasingly in the last decade, this curtain has been riddled by shots from all directions. Today the schools and the colleges are working together more closely than at any other period during the century. This new cooperative spirit bodes well for secondary-school honors programs in the future.[15]

Some of the cooperative ventures between school and college have already been mentioned. Almost every curriculum-development project enlists the efforts of both high school teachers and university scholars. The Advanced Placement Program similarly brings people from the two levels together. A number of colleges have been encouraging high school students to enroll in college classes while they are still in high school—either to prepare for the advanced placement examination or to earn college credit directly. Many others have organized special summer sessions for able high school students. Three or four universities have launched projects for the discovery and development of talent among secondary-school stu-

[15] *The Superior Student* contains a number of accounts of cooperative projects. The first issues in 1960 and 1963 were devoted wholly to this topic. Other accounts can be located through the Index. The volumes mentioned under the Advanced Placement Program and the programs for national curriculum development contain additional references and the addresses of people knowledgeable about these projects. Information about the John Hay Fellows Program can be obtained from its director, Charles R. Keller, The John Hay Fellows Program, 9 Rockefeller Plaza, New York 20, N.Y.

dents. Others have worked closely with local school systems to survey curricula and suggest changes in the courses given able students. The summer institutes sponsored by the National Science Foundation have brought thousands of high school teachers back to college campuses and involved hundreds of university scholars in the problems of the schools. The John Hay Fellows Program, which annually offers a full year's study in the humanities to eighty teachers and sponsors four summer institutes each year for high school teachers and administrators, has helped to bring professors and teachers in close contact with each other. Finally, the Inter-University Committee on the Superior Student, by stressing the development of honors programs in both school and college, has drawn attention to the common problems facing education on these two levels.

High school–college cooperative efforts defy generalization. They are as diverse as American education itself. We have had enough experience, however, to generalize about the conditions under which cooperative efforts are likely to succeed. Since the schools and colleges seem certain to launch further joint efforts in the future, a few guidelines may be helpful.

Cooperative efforts are most likely to flourish when they are genuine partnerships of school and college. The partnership should extend to all phases of a program: planning, direction, implementation, and evaluation. Many of the curriculum projects pair college and high school teachers; some even have codirectors from the two levels. In a number of instances college professors have left the campus to try out new materials in the schools; in one or two, faculty members from the schools have replaced professors in college. Involving both groups in the planning process assures each that its own best interests will be served.

Cooperative projects will have maximum effects on schools if certain optimal conditions obtain. They should take place in the school itself and not on a college campus. College courses or summer sessions for high school students help the individuals involved, but they do not help to reshape the schools or to improve teaching. They should involve the entire educational process, not just one part of it. Selecting students, preparing course content, developing teaching methods, training faculty, and evaluating the program are all integral parts of the most successful programs. Projects should involve a number of subjects—not just one—so that staff members in the school can become part of a significant endeavor and contribute to the development of an entire program with a common philosophy. Finally, they should continue over a number of years so that the original impact will not die out quickly. Crash programs lasting a year will probably not have much effect. It takes a year to break down barriers and to learn new tasks. Short-term projects are little more than academic stunts.

Honors programs make particularly good candidates for high school–college cooperative projects. College professors know most about the sort of education they want college freshmen to have. Teachers of honors courses are most likely to know the subject well and to get along with their counterparts from the universities. During the past decade we have built up a storehouse of experience in cooperative subjects through the Advanced Placement Program. All of these factors should contribute to the development of sound cooperative endeavors as the colleges and the secondary schools turn their attention to devising continuous honors sequences to span the gap that has so long separated one level of American education from the other.

Honors programs for teachers

In the last three or four years a number of college programs leading to honors in teaching have been launched in various universities in the country.[16] The content and philosophy of these programs do not fall within the scope of this chapter, but the effect these programs for teachers can have does. As the curriculum-reform projects have been developing new material suitable for high school honors, the new honors programs for teachers are starting to turn out men and women specifically trained to teach it. Without this new crop of excellent instructors, the development of high school honors programs would certainly be curtailed.

The various new honors programs for teaching have a number of elements in common. Each involves a vigorous attempt to recruit excellent students. Almost all require work toward an advanced degree, usually a Master of Arts in teaching or a Master of Arts in subject. Most place equal emphasis on subject matter and on teaching techniques. Extensive practice teaching or intern experience is usually an integral part of the program. Many are financed by foundations; the Ford Foundation has been particularly generous.

The long-run effect of these programs upon honors in the schools is not yet clear. Most are only a few years old and have graduated a mere trickle of students. But the trickle will soon approach flood proportions. Whether or not these promising young teachers will be used to staff honors programs in the schools will depend primarily upon the imagination and flexibility of school administrators. If personnel officers follow the traditional pattern of

[16] *The Superior Student* contains numerous references to these programs. See particularly May–June, 1962. Also see "Talent and Tomorrow's Teachers," *New Dimensions*, no. 11, 1963.

forcing beginning teachers to start at the bottom of the ladder teaching slow students in the lower grades, the effect of these programs will be minimized. If these teachers are placed directly into honors classes, they could contribute substantially to the education of able students.

Honors in the schools: present and future

Genuine honors programs in the schools are only beginning. Few school systems have set up first-rate programs involving the careful selection of students, the preparation of special curricula in all subject areas, the in-service training of teachers, the recruitment of new teachers with special preparation for honors work, and provisions for periodic careful evaluation. In most schools, honors still means only a course or two, usually at the senior level.

But good honors programs do exist and more can develop, particularly in schools that have been experimenting with advanced placement courses or with one or two honors classes. In smaller schools that cannot support a full honors program, special arrangements with nearby universities, cooperative interschool honors seminars, and special summer programs can supply some of the benefits of a full-scale honors program.

How rapidly honors programs develop now depends primarily upon local initiative in individual school systems. The Advanced Placement Program and the national curriculum committees are providing suitable materials. The new honors courses for teachers are turning out instructors. State departments of education and the Federal government are combining to train specialists in each state who can serve as consultants to school systems seeking advice. Literature is abundant; the NEA pamphlets alone provide excellent guidelines. A few excellent programs can serve as models for others. The universities seem ready to contribute whatever they can.

But unless school boards, principals, superintendents, counselors, teachers, and interested laymen cooperate to develop honors programs in the schools, all these resources will be wasted. Most decisions in American education are still made locally. No one can force a school system to begin an honors program unless the local board of education sanctions the idea. Most boards, in turn, rely on the recommendations of school administrators. Administrators respond to teachers and to professional organizations. In the long run, the layman as taxpayer must pay the bill. Honors programs grow out of the context of an entire community. The ingredients are at hand; each community must now decide whether or not to combine them.

Chapter eleven / Evaluating honors
programs: history, problems, and
prospects / Paul Heist, Center for
the Study of Higher Education,
University of California, and
Lois Langland, Scripps and Pitzer Colleges

Traditional ideas are never static. They are either fading into meaningless formulae, or are gaining power by the new lights thrown by a more delicate apprehension. They are transformed by the urge of critical reason, by the vivid evidence of emotional experience, and by the cold certainties of scientific perception. One fact is certain, you cannot keep them still.[1]

Traditional ideas concerning honors work, already transformed in part by the urge of critical reason and the vivid evidence of emotional experience, are now being examined and possibly transformed by the cold certainties of scientific perception. But we are just beginning to explore the contribution that scientific evaluation can make to that "more delicate apprehension."

Behavioral scientists have not until recently been very interested in lending their acumen to the study of honors programs or even education in general. At the same time, many directors of honors

[1] Alfred North Whitehead, *Science and the Modern World,* New York: The Macmillan Company, 1929, pp. 268–269.

programs, drawn for the most part from the humanities, have been wary of evaluative efforts that might appraise programs solely on the basis of the kinds of data to which conventional statistical procedures can be applied. Also, the humanities have been strongly emphasized in honors curricula, with less frequent inclusion of those disciplines that use a numerical language and that organize knowledge, at least in the undergraduate years, in a mandatory developmental sequence. Probably because these disciplines were less prominent in honors programs their methods were not often applied to evaluation of these programs.

Earlier evaluation efforts

The first evaluations of programs for students of superior ability rarely extended beyond assignment of grades for performance or, at best, a generalized qualitative assessment of the effect of program experiences. Some years after the first honors programs were initiated, a few staffs began to survey the opinions and reactions of students and faculty. In 1941, for example, the recent graduates of the honors program at the University of Colorado were surveyed by questionnaire to determine the value of honors to their academic and intellectual future. But no experimental attempts to determine objectively how attainments and achievements of honors participants compared with those of nonhonors students are recorded. Over-all, experimental or systematic evaluation of honors programs received very little attention until the present decade.

PIONEERING STUDIES AND EVALUATIONS OF EDUCATIONAL PROGRAMS

There are some exceptions to this pattern of limited evaluation; a noteworthy one is found in the honors program that was begun at

Swarthmore College in 1923 (see Chapter 2). Along with other modifications of current practices, the Swarthmore staff instituted a European-style single assessment of the honors student's performance at the completion of his college work, effected through a written and oral final examination. To attain greater objectivity, each student was examined by a panel of authorities brought in from outside the institution. In addition, in the mid-forties a number of Swarthmore faculty reported the results of a subjective appraisal of the honors seminars.[2] However, the knowledge and attainments of the honors students were never compared with those of students in the regular program.

Another noteworthy exception was the Experimental College at the University of Wisconsin. Before this short-lived program ended, a special faculty committee was appointed to plan an evaluation of the experiment's success from the standpoint of the impact on students and faculty. The Bureau of Guidance and Records was given the task of studying a variety of information and test data to determine the influence and effects of participation in the college. Alexander Meiklejohn's book on the program[3] serves as a general evaluation of the total program.

A few early investigations of the more general effects of college education might have served as models for the evaluation of honors experiences in which criteria other than course grades or grade point averages were used. For example, the Learned and Wood study of Pennsylvania colleges in the thirties was a comprehensive investigation that had some direct implications for both the selection of students for honors and the evaluation of performance in honors.

---

[2] Swarthmore College Faculty, *An Adventure in Education: Swarthmore College under Frank Aydelotte,* New York: The Macmillan Company, 1941.

[3] *The Experimental College,* New York: Harper & Row, Publishers, Incorporated, 1932.

A major conclusion of this study was that the amount of time spent or number of courses taken by a student had only a limited relation to a body of ideas retained and understood as the result of learning.[4]

Two other studies, both in the late thirties, were important for their possible contribution to evaluation of honors experiences. E. N. P. Nelson reported findings on changes in attitudes, presumably related to learning experiences, for students in a variety of colleges and universities.[5] And a study made by Theodore Newcomb [6] set a predominant pattern for later research on students; it dealt in part with the assessment of changes in attitudes and in basic values, and represents the first comprehensive evaluation conducted of educational influence over four college years. These three studies were less noteworthy for presenting conclusive results than for giving new emphasis to the complicated problem of understanding the relationship between ability, motivation, and attitudes and the process of learning.

The most extensive study in recent decades, and undoubtedly the most illuminating, designed to discover the components of more effective education through evaluation, was reported by P. L. Dressel and L. B. Mayhew.[7] In an eleven-year investigation of general education, a committee of the American Council on Education closely examined whether a number of institutional programs were accomplishing certain major learning objectives for participating

[4] W. S. Learned and B. D. Wood, *The Student and His Knowledge,* New York: The Carnegie Foundation for the Advancement of Teaching, 1938.

[5] E. N. P. Nelson, "Radicalism-Conservatism in Student Attitudes," *Psychological Monographs,* 1938.

[6] Theodore M. Newcomb, *Personality and Social Change,* New York: The Dryden Press, Inc., 1943.

[7] P. L. Dressel and L. B. Mayhew, *General Education: Explorations in Evaluation,* Washington, D.C.: American Council on Education, 1954.

students. Dressel and Mayhew showed that these programs increased the students' ability to think critically, but that the amount of gain varied considerably with the institution. Analysis strongly suggested that course organization and the teacher involved were important factors.

The *methods* of evaluation of growth and change used in the Dressel and Mayhew studies are still suited to evaluating honors; two of the special tests devised to examine the type and quality of a student's thinking—the Inventory of Critical Thinking and the Inventory of Belief—are particularly relevant. It is not known to what extent these tests have been used in studies of honors; however, judging by the evaluative studies that we have examined, the type of assessment facilitated by the use of inventories like these has not been attempted to any appreciable degree.

INFORMAL STUDENT EVALUATION ON ONE CAMPUS

As we indicated above, evaluation of honors programs has for the most part been subjective and nonscientific. A particularly good example of this type of evaluation is the work done at the University of Colorado.[8] The honors system at Colorado, initiated in the fall of 1930, was to become a prototype for the planning and development of honors work in numerous other public institutions. The early leaders built one evaluative aspect into the program from the beginning in that they attempted to eliminate grades as a sole criterion of success or of the effect of honors work.

The matter of general qualitative evaluation of the honors program was brought rather forcibly to the university's attention about nine years after the program began. Growing student dissatis-

[8] Walter D. Weir, *History of Honors at the University of Colorado*, vol. III, *Evaluation of the Honors Program*. (Mimeographed.)

faction had led to the appointment of a special student government committee, and this group issued a report, filled mostly with criticism and protest, which was based on a sampling of the opinions of honors students. Perhaps the earliest evaluation of a formal honors program, this report started a pattern of collecting student and faculty reactions at Colorado and resulted in a series of developments that continued over several years.

A joint review by students and the Honors Council in the spring of 1940 resulted in several major decisions about the program's future. It also led to a statement that summarized the first ten years of honors work, voiced the need "to evaluate the success of the ten-year experiment," and listed reasons for appointing a director to the program.

In the fall of 1940, the newly appointed director of honors, E. F. D'Arms, issued the first comprehensive report on the honors system at the University of Colorado. Though chiefly a description of how the system was to be reorganized, this report included a general evaluative review of the program to date, drawn from reactions expressed by students and faculty. In it D'Arms stated that "The Honors System . . . at its worst . . . is an educational experiment worthy of objective, scientific attention." To implement evaluation he strongly encouraged interviewing present students and graduates for their opinions about the program. He also spoke of the possibility of appointing an expert on testing, of making follow-up surveys of the accomplishments of honor students, and of eventually comparing honors students and nonhonors students in the College of Arts and Sciences.

It is especially interesting that concern for the quality of this program came originally from the students, and it was largely they who pressured for change and improvement. In this case general reactions and subjective evaluations, unsolicited and springing up independently of objective measurement, provided sufficient impetus for constructive change.

THE ICSS PROGRAM AND RENEWED ATTENTION

Although the major concern of the Inter-University Committee for the Superior Student, established in 1956, was the development of new honors programs, some attention was soon given to evaluating existing programs. That the Committee's Advisory Board gradually began to give time to evaluation and research at its meetings during the first three years can be credited to the special concern of several board members, particularly Robert Macleod, a well-known social scientist. This changing orientation of the board, together with the concern developed over two decades by the ICSS director, Joseph Cohen, came to visible fruition in Cohen's thinking and activities in 1959 and 1960. In those years Cohen personally carried a message regarding the need for evaluation to the Carnegie Foundation, the sponsors of the ICSS, and to existing agencies conducting research on superior students. Two such agencies contacted on several occasions were the National Merit Scholarship Corporation (Evanston, Illinois) and the Center for the Study of Higher Education (Berkeley, California). Neither organization was ready to study honors programs as such, but their staffs were responsive to the request for assistance.

Members of the research team at the Berkeley Center for the Study of Higher Education had become increasingly interested in the problems of adequately educating superior students. In two articles, perhaps more specifically relevant than several others to honors work, Paul Heist and Harold Webster called particular attention to the significant diversity among high-ability students on measured values, attitudes, and interests.[9] They argued that these differences in nonintellective traits and characteristics merited serious attention, especially in educating the gifted or mentally superior, and, thus, in selecting students for honors and conducting and evaluating honors programs. They also discussed the "climates and subcultures" resulting from the affiliation and subgrouping of certain types of students on some campuses, implying that segregation of bright students into special programs should be viewed as a factor contributing to the general learning situation and as a possible research variable to be brought into analyses. Along these lines, Theodore Newcomb has been chiefly responsible in recent years for examining the grouping of students, peer-group influences, and the idea of "structured" subcultures.[10]

In 1960 Joseph Cohen contacted the Committee on Personality Development in Youth of the Social Science Research Council; this committee, under the chairmanship of Ralph Tyler, had been serving as a coordinating agency for a variety of research projects developed since 1955 and aimed at increasing knowledge about college students, their educational attainments and general psychological growth, and development of the postadolescent. During 1960–1961 a small group representing this SSRC committee met with and served as consultants to the ICSS staff. This association culminated

[9] Paul Heist and Harold Webster, "Differential Characteristics of Student Bodies: Implications for Selection and Study of Undergraduates," *Selection and Differential Education,* Berkeley, Calif.: Field Service Center and Center for the Study of Higher Education, 1960, pp. 91–106; and "A Research Orientation to Selection, Admission and Differential Education," in Sprague and Hall (eds.), *Research on College Students,* Boulder, Colo.: Western Interstate Commission for Higher Education, 1960, pp. 21–40.

[10] See Theodore M. Newcomb, "Exploiting Student Resources," in Sprague and Hall (eds.), *ibid.,* pp. 3–20.

in a research conference at the University of Illinois directed and
supervised by several members of the Committee on Personality Development in Youth and devoted to several topics seen as fundamental in planning and organizing evaluation projects: major
considerations underlying the establishment of sound evaluative
research, the pertinent characteristics of superior students, identification and selection of students, the institutional and social setting for
honors programs, pertinent problems of measurement, and research
design and method. Directors of programs in participating institutions were asked to send social scientists interested in conducting
research in an educational setting. The conference opened the door
to communication among institutions on such matters as cooperative evaluation projects.

RECENT RELATED STUDIES AND EVALUATIONS

The first broad analysis of the effect of participation in honors involving students in numerous colleges was a study of National
Merit Scholars reported by Donald Thistlethwaite.[11] He found that
honors students were influenced by their honors experiences and
tended to raise their educational aspirations more often than those
not in honors.

In a more specialized investigation of honors work, Lloyd
Urdal and Robert Ballantyne reported on an exploratory examination of selection criteria.[12] However, these analyses were limited by

[11] Donald L. Thistlethwaite, "Fields of Study and Development of Motivation to Seek Advanced Training," *Journal of Educational Psychology,*
April, 1962, pp. 53–64.

[12] Lloyd B. Urdal and Robert H. Ballantyne, "An Analysis of Certain
Selection Criteria for College Honors Students," paper presented at annual
meeting of American Educational Research Association, February, 1962.

use of an inadequate performance criterion: grades. Another example of a rather specialized evaluative effort is a survey of instructors in honors courses and honors sections of large classes made by Phyllis Pilisuk at the University of Michigan.[13] Although the faculty manifested some critical concerns about the special program for superior students, most instructors liked to teach in the program; however, they strongly emphasized the necessity of sharpening procedures for selecting program participants.

E. Jackson Baur and his associates at the University of Kansas, another institution with an honors program of long duration, have recently undertaken a comprehensive study (as yet unpublished) of the effects of the honors program on the student's self-conception and how in turn his definition of his role affects his academic achievement. In an early comparative analysis between honors and nonhonors students they found that honors students held more positions of leadership, were more deeply involved with ideas, placed value on scholarly attributes, worked harder on their studies, tended more to broaden their scholarly interests in the undergraduate years, and more often planned to enter graduate or professional school than nonhonors students.

In recent years Harvard College has initiated a variety of small-enrollment seminars in numerous topical areas for first-year students. Though not conceived of as an honors program, most aspects of this seminar approach typify the desirable characteristics of honors. From the beginning the seminars were described as an experiment, and the program incorporated some form of evaluation even during the first year.

During the program's fourth year, and after a total of 130 semi-

[13] Phyllis E. Pilisuk, "Faculty Evaluation of Honors Classes at the University of Michigan, Fall, 1959," *The Superior Student*, 2, 6 (1959).

nars, the sophomores, juniors, and seniors who had been members of one or more freshman groups, as well as the faculty, participated in a postexperience evaluation.[14] The variables of assessment centered chiefly in the opinions and reactions of the student and faculty, but to provide an objective basis for analyzing background, achievement, and persistence data, a matching sample of nonseminar students was used as a control group. On the whole the results were very favorable, especially from the standpoint of expressed satisfaction and perceived gains. The comparative data showed either no differences, or minimal differences consistently in favor of those who had taken advantage of the seminar experiences.

Current evaluation efforts

The best source of information about the kinds of evaluation of honors programs carried out in very recent years and prevalent now is the ICSS newsletter, *The Superior Student* (published from 1958 to 1965). Especially valuable is the report by Raymond Cuzzort,[15] which contains findings of a survey of current evaluative efforts by honors program staffs. Other issues have contained commentaries on evaluating honors and descriptions of several evaluation systems currently in use. Some of the information presented by Cuzzort and in other issues of *The Superior Student* is summarized below, along with a review of what appear to be the most comprehensive evaluation studies or evaluative programs in honors today.

[14] Byron Stookey, "The Freshman Seminar Program," *A Report to the Faculty of Arts and Sciences,* Harvard University, Cambridge, Mass., February, 1963.

[15] Raymond P. Cuzzort, "Evaluating Honors Programs," *The Superior Student,* 6, 2 (1964).

EVALUATION IN TRANSITION

Among current approaches and methods reviewed in *The Superior Student,* informal surveys of student and faculty reactions continue to be the most common. The appraisals based on these reactions are usually laudatory, providing encouragement for the continuation of programs and occasionally suggesting some basis for improvement.

More recently, honors program staffs have increasingly surveyed student and faculty opinions and attitudes by questionnaire. Some of these questionnaires have been designed to generate quantitative as well as qualitative data, and when this is the case the same or a similar questionnaire has sometimes been used in more than one institution to broaden the data and provide opportunities for comparing results.

A few studies of the criteria for selecting participants for honors programs have been made in an attempt to discover what measurements besides grade point average and aptitude test scores might be used. The reasoning behind these studies is that selection criteria may have an important relationship to the success with which a given honors program achieves its goals, and analysis may reveal ways in which selection methods can be improved.

Judging from information in *The Superior Student,* the attitudes, values, interests, and basic personality characteristics of students and faculty remain largely unexplored. Obviously, knowledge of these and how they change is very relevent to program content and methods. As was indicated earlier, researchers have noted the differences in nonintellective characteristics of college students and have stressed the theoretical importance of taking these differences into account, especially in educating the gifted or mentally superior and in conducting special programs. This view has more recently been reemphasized by George Yonge [16] and Lois Langland,[17] again as it applies particularly to superior students in honors programs. But there is room for a great deal more study in these areas.

The report on the findings of a survey of evaluation of honors programs in the issue of *The Superior Student* cited above highlights the fact that formal comprehensive appraisals of honors programs are still rare. Of the 113 directors of honors programs in colleges and universities who replied to the survey questionnaire, more than 80 percent said that in their institution occasional verbal comments on the honors program are solicited from honors students and faculty and some attempt is made to determine whether selection criteria are valid. Fifty-six percent said that simple statistical examinations of the number of dropouts from their programs have been made. But a committee of honors students is asked to prepare an evaluative report on the honors program in less than 10 percent of these institutions. And only between 10 and 20 percent schedule regular meetings between students and instructors in honors to evaluate and revise the program, conduct followup studies of honors students regardless of whether they continue in graduate school, make followup studies of honors and nonhonors students on standardized comprehensive examinations in specific fields, and distribute formal evaluative questionnaires to students and/or faculty in honors. Almost half of all directors reported that their staffs had conducted or begun *formal* evaluations (i.e., studies leading to a written report or

[16] George Yonge, "The Diversity of Attitudes Within Selected High Ability Groups: Implications for Honors," paper presented at annual meeting of the American Psychological Association, Philadelphia, 1963.

[17] Lois Langland, "Some Characteristics of Gifted College Students: Implications for Honors," paper presented at annual meeting of the American Psychological Association, Philadelphia, 1963.

at least a collection of some kind of empirical data) at some time within the past five years, but only 21 percent had any copies of evaluation reports available. And no respondent reported an investigation based on an experimental design, using some form of control group for comparative purposes.

This, then, is the general state of attempts to evaluate honors programs today. What quality control is incorporated into existing programs is obtained primarily by one mode of "knowing": the subjective. More adequate tools of objective appraisal and more defensible methods of assessment are just beginning to come into play.

However, the fact that even such a small minority of honors programs have some of the features mentioned above indicates a trend toward more interest in evaluation. Now that higher education has become much more a part of the public domain and can no longer be classed as a luxury in our society, appraisal of education efforts is becoming more and more urgent. To help meet this need a variety of methods of obtaining essential information should be widely used in studying and assessing honors programs. A brief look at the work in several public universities can give us an idea of what some of these methods are.

THREE COMPREHENSIVE EVALUATION PROGRAMS

The Universities of Michigan, Oregon, and Illinois have initiated investigations of their honors programs from several vantage points. These investigations have been or are being carried out by staff members assigned to them and with the assistance of grants or special funds (which suggests that thorough evaluation of honors programs requires qualified personnel and adequate time and funds). These examples indicate that ongoing evaluation by competent personnel can be budgeted and built into honors programs when directors and staff realize the importance of evaluation in efforts to improve the honors programs.

The results of one major attempt to appraise the effectiveness of an honors program was reported by Phyllis Pilisuk.[18] This study at the University of Michigan included four groups of students identified as (1) "continuous honors"—successful honors students who remain in the program over a period of time; (2) "controls" —the top 7 percent of the 1956 class at Michigan, which entered the university before honors was instituted; (3) "new honors"— students of high ability just beginning honors in their junior year, a second control group; and (4) "drops"—students who were not successful in maintaining a 3.0 average and were asked to discontinue honors work. She also surveyed a sample of nonhonors sophomores ("average students") about their perceptions of honors students and the program and about various academic values.

The study was conducted primarily through questionnaires and interviews, but included the examination of achievement data. The purposes of this evaluation were to obtain information about four areas of concern: Did the Michigan honors program provide the educational advantages it aimed to provide? To what extent did it allow opportunity for other than academic development? To what extent did it contribute to the development of learned, independent scholars with a bent toward creative work? Did honors students form a respected community of scholars within the larger university, a community that permitted the interchange of ideas and set an example for the rest of the student body?

Findings indicated that the program was providing the hoped-

[18] Phyllis E. Pilisuk, *The Effectiveness of the Honors Program in the College of Literature, Science and the Arts,* mimeographed report, Honors Council, University of Michigan, Ann Arbor, Mich., November, 1960.

for educational advantages, but that some students felt there was too much "busy work" and that continuous honors students took part in fewer self-initiated intellectual activities than did new honors students. Further, although honors students did perform better on the area tests of the graduate record examinations, they preferred clear organization to self-direction in the classroom, thus suggesting they were not essentially independent scholars, at least not by choice.

Finally, the answer to the question whether honors students formed a respected and exemplary community of scholars within the larger university was a qualified "yes." The extent of friendships in the program was found to be at a level much greater than chance; the major point of difference noted between themselves and other students centered on their academic seriousness and interest in learning. Findings indicated that honors students were beginning to develop the characteristics of a community, and that they were neither particularly respected nor particularly resented by the college sophomore group used to represent "average" students.

Data on the "drop" students suggested that these people were not disillusioned, independent intellectuals. However, the "drops" did say that they particularly disliked forced requirements, dull courses, and "busy work." How prevalent these criticisms were and whether they were valid or not is not known.

The Pilisuk study was conducted at the level where most evaluative studies will probably have to begin, with cross-sectional, descriptive data. However, it did lay some groundwork for longitudinal studies, and it included a control group. Also, attention was given to the effects honors might have on the sociology of campus life at a large university. Most of the findings have implications for planning the content and conduct of future honors programs and for further development of evaluative procedures.

The program in honors at the University of Oregon was set up as a separate entity, "a college of select and self-motivated students within the larger University"; the special course work leads to the degree of Bachelor of Arts (Honors College).

Plans for evaluation were built into the program at its inception. Robert Ellis and Lucian Marquis conducted an initial evaluation study which asked three questions: What type of students enter the honors college? Does the honors college have a distinct impact on the students enrolled in it? What effect does it have on the other undergraduates not participating in the program?[19] The study was also designed to gain preliminary information on the social, psychological, and intellectual characteristics that may differentiate students who participate successfully in the honors-college program from those who do not. Three samples of students were identified in the freshman class entering the University of Oregon in the fall of 1961: (1) all freshmen in the honors college; (2) a control sample of freshmen drawn to match the males in the honors college on intelligence, high school records, and selected social-demographic characteristics; and (3) a 20 percent probability sample of the freshman class. The first sample was augmented by additional samples of honors-college matriculants in 1962 and 1963.

The study also considered a good deal of other relevant information. Evaulations by counselors residing in freshman dormitories provided cross-validating information gained from the students themselves and a means for determining how other persons in the students' environment reacted to them. On some measurements interuniversity comparisons were also brought into the design; students in the honors college were compared with a sample of undergraduates at Stanford University involved in a similar study.

A few significant findings of this early investigation are that

[19] Robert A. Ellis and Lucian Marquis, "Evaluation of the University of Oregon's Honors College," *The Superior Student,* Jan.–Feb., 1964.

students in the honors college are more likely than other students to have had a long-standing commitment to go to college and to hold values conducive to gaining intellectual benefits from their college experience, and less likely to place major importance on the instrumental purposes of an education. They are also more likely to emphasize the importance of gaining a sense of self-fulfillment from their occupation and to deemphasize the importance of such rewards as money, prestige, and security.

The academic performance of these honors students is at the same level as that of students in the matched sample, at least in terms of freshman-year grades. The data also indicate that the honors-college program has succeeded in gaining widespread acceptance on the campus. This is substantiated in a report by Robert Ellis and J. Spencer Carlson noting that both honors-college freshmen and freshmen in general tended to feel that students generally were impressed with the honors college.[20] Eighty-five percent of honors college participants said that if they had it to do over again they would enter the honors college. Approximately half of the freshmen not enrolled in the honors college indicated they would like to avail themselves of this opportunity, even though it would mean harder work and more intensive preparation for long-range academic goals.

The Oregon evaluation project was carefully planned, it used a variety of approaches to data acquisition, and it gained added perspective from interuniversity comparisons. The project was designed with both practical and theoretical questions in mind, and cross-sectional data were collected in such a way as to provide a basis for longitudinal research.

[20] Robert A. Ellis and J. Spencer Carlson, "Reaction to the University of Oregon Honors College Program," *The Superior Student,* March–April, 1963.

The honors program at the University of Illinois represents a third example of a program committed to evaluation in its earliest stages; research on various facets of the program has been flourishing since the introduction of honors activities in the fall of 1959. The 1962–1963 Annual Report submitted by Director Robert E. Johnson attests to the vigor of the program and its researchers.[21] This report evaluates the program's general situation at the completion of a four-year experience by the first group of James Scholars, as honors students are called.

Over the program's first few years a variety of data and information have been used in deciding about applicants' probability of success in honors work, and selection criteria have been modified. The work on selection criteria resulted in the seemingly paradoxical finding that a better-qualified group of honors students (that is, chosen by "improved" selection procedures) had a higher attrition rate than an earlier, less-superior group. Other findings suggest the need for continuing appraisal of selection procedures and point up the breadth of considerations made by the Illinois staff. A few examples will illustrate: Students not admitted to the program when they entered the university but later invited to participate on the basis of performance are the most successful Scholars, as judged by long-term academic success and continuation in the program and in the university.[22] Unsuccessful Scholars tend to be those who had not had an academically challenging program of high school work. Study of high school teachers' recommendations showed that having taken some work identified as "honors" in high school appears

[21] Robert E. Johnson, *Annual Report, 1962–1963,* University Honors Programs, University of Illinois, Urbana, Ill. (Offset.)

[22] Dora E. Damrin, *College Honors Courses: Privilege or Penalty? A Comparative Study of Academic Grades,* University of Illinois, Research Report no. 5, Urbana, Ill., February, 1962. (Mimeographed.)

to have no significant relationship to college success; this finding has led to revisions in the form aimed at assessing preliminary promise. Student values and other personality characteristics have also come under consideration as factors related to attrition; recent participants (1963) have been interviewed regarding their values and long-range goals, while several widely known personality tests were administered to all members of the previous honors group.

From the standpoint of program effectiveness, analyses of the number of on-campus and off-campus awards won by the first class of James Scholars in June of 1963 indicate that the proportion of honors won by Scholars far exceeds the proportion won by non-Scholars. Of this group, approximately twice as high a percentage of both sexes plan to continue their schooling as compared with non-Scholars students. And of all students entering graduate school, more than twice as many honors students as nonhonors students received financial assistance for advanced academic work.

Dora Damrin also investigated two aspects of the Illinois program (advanced placement and academic grades) that have immediate relevance for future policy and procedure. In her studies of advanced placement,[23] she found an appalling variability in amounts of credit accorded test papers with the same grades; the reasons seemed to be changes in standards within a department and the effects of departmental review. Analyzing grades made by James Scholars in honors and nonhonors courses, she found that Scholars consistently did less well in their nonhonors than in their honors work.

In three separate reports Dora Damrin also analyzed the opin-

[23] Dora E. Damrin, *An Evaluation of the Advanced Placement Program at the University of Illinois,* University of Illinois, Research Report no. 7, Urbana, Ill., August, 1962. (Offset.)

ions and reactions of University of Illinois students. The first [24] examined the Scholars' views of the program, which were drawn from a brief questionnaire mailed to all Scholars of a single semester. The primary finding is that over three-fourths of the Scholars regarded their appointment as an advantage, the remainder viewing it with mixed feelings. The more extrinsic advantages of the program (prestige, possible later occupational benefits) were mentioned hardly at all, while better academic opportunities were stressed. But the disadvantages of the program, too, were perceived largely as academic (too difficult, too much work, and so on).

In a report on student attitudes toward the James Scholar, Damrin analyzed the data from a questionnaire filled out by a large percentage of on-campus students (N = more than 4,700).[25] Nearly three-fourths of the respondents knew enough about the program to have formed opinions regarding its worth, and well over half of these reported having a friendly, personal relationship with one or more of the Scholars. The data, Damrin notes, "argue that intellectually, personally, and morally the typical Scholar is not only accepted by his peers but also is held in rather high regard by them." About half of all students, regardless of sex or class year, considered the appointment as a James Scholar to be an advantage.

The third report dealt with the James Scholars' opinions on an honors residence hall.[26] This study illustrates a possible means of

[24] Dora E. Damrin, *The University Honors Program as Viewed by the Edmund J. James Scholar,* University of Illinois, Research Report no. 4, Urbana, Ill., January, 1962. (Offset.)

[25] Dora E. Damrin, *Student Attitudes Toward the Edmund J. James Scholar at the University of Illinois,* University of Illinois, Urbana, Ill., October, 1961. (Offset.)

[26] Dora E. Damrin, *James Scholars' Opinions Regarding the Creation of an Honors Residence Hall,* University of Illinois, Research Report no. 6, Urbana, Ill., July, 1962. (Mimeographed.)

checking hypotheses that the administration and faculty might have about directions an honors program could take. Scholars were asked to evaluate a faculty proposal that certain residence halls be designated as cultural-intellectual living centers in which honors students would be given first choice of rooms. In all three class years (freshman, sophomore, and junior) more students were against the proposal than favored it. Members of fraternities and sororities were most heavily opposed; of those in university-controlled houses, a slight preponderance were also opposed. The study results were interpreted as a good indication that student opinion should be sampled before proposals like this one are acted upon.

Obviously, the evaluative studies built into the honors programs at Michigan, Oregon, and Illinois have something to offer in providing bases for ongoing decisions required to operate and maintain any program. And the results are significant to an examination of whether such programs are reaching the kind of students for which they are designed and whether the students are benefiting from participating in honors programs.

Important considerations in evaluation

Much evidence presented in this volume and elsewhere indicates that there are numerous good honors programs—from the standpoints of curricula, faculty, and students—now in operation. However, almost all of the programs seem considerably better in their structure and organization and in the educational experiences they provide than in the methods and means used to appraise them. The evaluative research conducted on honors programs to date has not provided a very adequate basis for ascertaining the real values, as well as the weaknesses, of special programs for the superior or gifted student. Exactly how much is being accomplished, what causes variations in attainment, and how appropriately these programs are selecting participants are some of the questions still almost completely unanswered.

Designing a sound evaluation project that incorporates the necessary basic procedures is not terribly difficult; the staffs in a few institutions have recently given attention to the design requirements of defensible evaluation and initiated research projects that should bring us closer to long-sought information on the impact of experiences in honors. The real problem, however, lies in devising and carrying through the kind of comprehensive, long-range project that theoretically examines the "whole" truth and that meets both the demands of the humanities faculty and the requirements of the social scientists. In this connection it is encouraging that in two or three recent investigations collaboration between disciplines has been structured into rather complex projects. True, time and money, as well as faculty skepticism, pose deterrents to the execution of extended investigations. However, with the psychological instruments now available and with almost unlimited facilities for data analysis by electronic computers, other reasons will have to be given if the dearth of evaluative programs in honors continues.

This chapter concludes with illustrative but cursory reviews of two levels of approaches to evaluating honors programs. These illustrations are limited to an examination of what happens to the program participants. Clearly, a complete evaluation of any program would include many other aspects of the program that could be viewed and measured as important variables—for example, the faculty, the course content and its presentation, the program's physical and social context, cost (the extent to which objectives are attained as compared with expense involved). But space does not allow discussion of such a complete project here.

The two levels of approaches considered below are (1) postexperience assessment—testing of students at the end of their honors experience (as we have seen, this is the most common practice), and (2) pre- and postexperience assessment—testing of students at both the beginning and the end of a program or thereafter. The levels are in part distinguished by the type of questions asked. Although most researchers would not see much merit in working at the first of these levels, perhaps even submitting that it would not represent true evaluation, it is safe to predict that most evaluation will continue to be of this elementary type, and therefore it deserves our attention. Concern with good design and the use of control groups is desirable in conducting research at both levels, but no matter how thorough, it cannot counteract the limitations and weaknesses inherent in evaluation confined to postexperience assessment.

Finally, we should note that the objectives or purposes of a program must constitute the chief guide to the type of information an evaluation study should obtain, the methods it should use, and the interpretation of its results. If, for example, an honors program's major purposes are a gain in knowledge and the acquisition of general intellectual appreciation and skills in critical thinking, the questions or hypotheses underlying evaluation can be explicitly stated and the means of collecting essential information will be more readily available at one level than at another.

POSTEXPERIENCE ASSESSMENT

Postexperience assessment involves administering tests and questionnaires *after* a course or program has been completed, or some time thereafter. It is thus not much different from the type of evaluation applied to most college work that serves as a basis for assigning grades. In interpreting the results of the test or questionnaire the investigator generally assumes that the knowledge or manifested attitudes being measured are the product of or have been influenced by the particular course or program. The key concern is whether the effects of the honors experiences are equivalent to or greater than what the effects and accomplishments of regular course work would have been.

Although it may not be at all legitimate to speak of *increase* in knowledge, since there is no base point with which to compare the results, it is certainly defensible and valuable to obtain reactions to and appraisals of a course and the instruction, and to inquire about the degree of satisfaction and change the participant feels he has experienced. This subjective information can be employed to help understand what happened to a student by determining what he himself thinks he experienced or gained.

A minor refinement in analytic procedures at this level involves categorizing the students according to some characteristics and comparing the responses and measurements among the different categories. For example, the honors participants might be subdivided by sex, major, measured ability, the amount of previous relevant course work, or measured values or attitudes. Comparisons make it possible to study the relationship of attitudes and background variables to achievement and reactions to the course, and findings may have implications for recruitment and selection.

The use of a control group is one additional means of partially circumventing the limitations of this method of evaluation. The students in the control group may be drawn at random from all those enrolled in the regular course work or they may be matched with honors students on one or more criteria. Much of the testing administered to the honors students would also be given to the control group. Use of such a group can provide reference data against which to compare both the subjective reactions (opinions, feelings of satisfaction, etc.) and the objective test results (for example, on selected standardized achievement tests) of program participants.

Only a pre- and postexperience testing scheme can completely fulfill the major purpose of an evaluation project—to determine the effects of and gains resulting from specific learning experiences. Students entering any new or advanced level of education are products of their previous learning experiences—that is, they already possess a certain amount of knowledge and a certain orientation toward learning. To assess gain or change, especially that resulting from any particular program, this base point of existing knowledge or skills must first be established.

A second, absolutely essential complement to a defensible assessment procedure is the element of control. Thus, preexperience and postexperience tests should be administered to a group of students who are *not* in the honors program as well as to the honors students being tested. The concern here is with any differences between the honors group and the control group in the amount and quality of change evident between the first and second testing.

These two principles—the importance of assessment at the beginning of a program and the use of control groups—are the foundations of what we call "experimental design." The attention given to the planning (design) of an evaluation study represents an attempt to eliminate or control the influence of irrelevant factors (at least in the statistical analysis) and also to discover the key reasons for any changes observed or measured. Thus, similar (or matched) groups are given different treatments (honors versus nonhonors courses), permitting an investigator to "control" or lessen the influence of sex, intelligence, socioeconomic background, value orientations, and so on. When feasible, more than one control group may be used, thus strengthening the design and possibly improving the precision of study results.

Figure 1 is a graphic outline of an experimental design. The approach of most evaluative work to date in honors, as well as the schema for postexperience assessment presented above, is represented by the limits of the area identified as *d*. Relegating research to what is encompassed by *d* alone illustrates the incompleteness of a design that lacks a preexperience testing stage and an effort to institute controls. Any evaluation program attempting to assess the effectiveness of honors experiences for particular students must, we feel, include the rudiments of the design shown in Figure 1.

The recruitment and selection process, noted at the extreme left in the diagram, need not always be included in the study design. Data collection can begin at the point of preexperience testing (i.e., after selection of students), *or* the selection criteria may be included and serve as independent or predictive variables. The second alternative makes it possible to identify several "types" of students (subgroups) entering honors who may be influenced differentially by the curriculum and experiences because of their backgrounds or orientations.

How inclusive the preexperience testing phase is—how many tests and questionnaires it involves and how complex they are—will depend somewhat on how much information is obtained during the selection phase. For example, academic aptitude scores and background information may already be available, along with previous academic records. What data are collected at this stage may also depend on whether a control group or groups are used. The matching of students in Group B (see Figure 1) to those in Group A

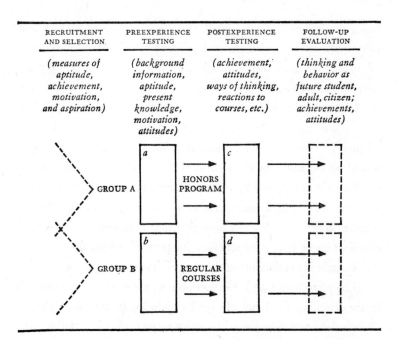

RECRUITMENT AND SELECTION	PREEXPERIENCE TESTING	POSTEXPERIENCE TESTING	FOLLOW-UP EVALUATION
(measures of aptitude, achievement, motivation, and aspiration)	(background information, aptitude, present knowledge, motivation, attitudes)	(achievement, attitudes, ways of thinking, reactions to courses, etc.)	(thinking and behavior as future student, adult, citizen; achievements, attitudes)

HONORS PROGRAMS: COHEN

Figure 1. Diagrammatic presentation of the elements of a research design for longitudinal evaluation of the students in honors programs.

would usually be accomplished through aptitude scores and biographical or social background information.

As we have already stated, the major determinant of what to include in the preexperience (and postexperience) testing should be the objectives of the honors program. To accommodate some of the demands of pre- and postexperience testing, a variety of standardized tests are available (e.g., the Graduate Record Examination Area Tests and various inventories measuring attitudes and values); local researchers must construct other tests and means of assessment to meet the requirements of specific program objectives.

Postexperience testing will not, of course, be limited to materials and instruments that were used for preexperience testing. Some of the information required is obviously obtainable only at the end of the program—for example, information on the courses, the faculty, the participant's peers. And some questions asked of the honors students have no application to the control group or groups.

The value of surveys at postgraduate stages, referred to previously, seems quite obvious. An essential characteristic of important educational objectives is that they can truly be measured only in terms of long-range performance. The best testimony for the real success—or failure—of any honors experience would undoubtedly be found in the thinking and behavior of an adult citizen. If it cannot be shown that education in general or honors work leads to more constructive, productive, or meaningful lives, then the system and the programs need reexamination.

Index

Abbott, Charles D., 23
Ability grouping, freshmen at
    Haverford, 205
  secondary schools, 220
Academically talented student,
    identifying of, 233
  project on, 233–234
  (*See also* Gifted student; Hon-
    ors students; Superior stu-
    dent)
Acceleration, in high schools,
    219
  in small colleges, 212–215
    dangers of, 217
  (*See also* Advanced placement;
    Early admission)
Adams, Henry, 20, 108

Advanced placement, 234–240, 246,
    247, 249, 251
  challenge to colleges, 239–240
  contribution to honors, 239
  description of, 235–236
  effect, on school, 238
    on teachers, 237, 239
  at Harvard, 15
  at Haverford, 204–205
  and IQ, 237
  in limited scope of, 236
  in Pittsburgh schools, 231–232,
    238
  size of classes in, 238
  in small colleges, 212–214
  specialization fostered by, 15
  studied at Illinois, 272

Grades, and honors, 21, 85–86
   in colloquia, Colorado, 23
   ICSS attitude toward, 30
   of honors students in nonhonors
     courses, 272
   inadequacy as performance cri-
     terion, 262
   skepticism of honors students
     about, 58

Hamline University, 36
Handlin, Oscar, 81
Hantz, Harold, 83
Harding, Harold F., 26n., 28
Harvard freshman seminars, 7, 15–
   16, 171
   and advanced placement, 240
   evaluation of, 263
   extended to sophomores, 16
   and grades, 86
   has honors characteristics, 262
   and seminar-colloquium ap-
     proach, 81
   Stookey report on, 16
   survey of sciences in, 184–185
Harvard University, 12, 19, 24, 262
   and advanced placement, 15,
     236, 240
   elective system, 13–14
   freshman seminar, 8, 15–16, 81,
     86, 171, 184–185, 263
   type of science honors, 177

Harvard University, type of science
   honors, for nonscience majors,
   171, 184–185
Haverford College, xviii
   honors program, 204–205
Hawaii, University of, 111, 117n.
Hays, Samuel P., 28
Heath, Robert W., 240n.
Heist, Paul, xviii, 259–260
Holton, G., 173
Honors, definition of, 1
   examinations, 87
   general, at Colorado, viii
     faculty support, viii
   major conferences on, listed, 48–
     49
   means of institutional change,
     vii–viii
   philosophical aspects of, v–viii,
     xv–xvi, 1–8, 11, 96–102
   student-sponsored honors activi-
     ties, 73–74
Honors approach, viii, 6–8, 197,
   216
   in sciences, 172–175
Honors awards, viii–ix, 21, 86–87,
   153, 195–197
   examinations for, 87
   grade standard for, abandoned,
     Colorado, 21
Honors classes, secondary schools,
   discrete, 223–224
   materials used in, 222, 229, 231